BEGINNING GAME PROGRAMMING

SECOND EDITION

JONATHAN S. HARBOUR

THOMSON

COURSE TECHNOLOGY

Professional ■ Technical ■ Reference

ISBN-10: 1-59863-288-4
ISBN-13: 978-1-59863-288-0
Library of Congress Catalog Card Number: 2006904402
Printed in the United States of America
07 08 09 10 11 PH 10 9 8 7 6 5 4 3 2 1

THOMSON
COURSE TECHNOLOGY
Professional ■ Technical ■ Reference

Thomson Course Technology PTR,
a division of Thomson Learning Inc.
25 Thomson Place
Boston, MA 02210
http://www.courseptr.com

**Publisher and General Manager,
Thomson Course Technology PTR:**
Stacy L. Hiquet

Associate Director of Marketing:
Sarah O'Donnell

Manager of Editorial Services:
Heather Talbot

Marketing Manager:
Heather Hurley

Senior Acquisitions Editor:
Emi Smith

Marketing Coordinator:
Adena Flitt

Project Editor:
Jenny Davidson

Technical Reviewer:
Joshua R. Smith

PTR Editorial Services Coordinator:
Erin Johnson

Interior Layout Tech:
ICC Macmillan Inc.

Cover Designer:
Mike Tanamachi

CD-ROM Producer:
Brandon Penticuff

Indexer:
Kelly D. Henthorne

For My Mother,
Vicki Myrlene Harbour

FOREWORD

"I want to be a game designer, how do I get a job?" This is a question I field very often when I do interviews or talk to students. I've even been accosted by the parents of an apparently gifted teenager as I left the stage with my band. My usual answer is, "so what have you designed?" The vast majority of the time, I am given a long explanation about how the person has lots of great ideas, but is in need of a team to make them a reality. My response to this is to try to explain how everyone I work with has great ideas, but only a small percentage of them are designers.

I don't mean to be harsh, but the reality is that there are no successful companies out there that will give someone off the street a development team for 18+ months and a multimillion dollar budget without some sort of proof of concept. What sets someone like Sid Meier (legendary game designer with whom I'm honored to work at Firaxis Games) apart is his ability to take an idea and make something fun out of it. Of course, Sid now gets large teams to do his projects, but he always starts the same way—a team of one cranking out prototypes cobbled together with whatever art and sound he can either dig up or create himself. It's these rough proofs of concept that allow people uninvolved with the creation process to immediately see the fun in a given idea, and that's what gets you a budget and a team. Every budding designer should take note and ask, "What would Sid do?"

That's when a book like this is invaluable. I became acquainted with Jonathan a couple of years ago when I picked up the original version of this book at the bookstore at the Game Developer's Conference. A programmer buddy of mine helped me pick it out from among numerous similar books. He thought it was very well written and thought the emphasis on DirectX would be very applicable to what we do at Firaxis. Another buddy mentioned that he had read Jonathan's work on programming the Game Boy Advance and was very impressed. In my opinion, they gave me great advice and I enjoyed myself immensely while working through the book. While reading, I noticed that Jonathan was a big fan of our game, *Sid Meier's Civilization III*. I contacted him because I have worked on numerous *Civ* titles and we have kept in contact ever since.

The beauty of a book like this is that it takes away all of the excuses. It provides an excellent introduction to game programming. It takes you by the hand and walks you through the seemingly complex process of writing C code making use of DirectX. Before you know it, you'll have a fully usable framework for bringing your ideas to life. You are even provided with tools to create your own art and sound to help dress up the game. In other words, you will have all the tools you need to start making prototypes and prove that you are much more than just someone with great ideas. Believe me; taking this crucial next step will put you at the top of the heap of people looking for jobs in the industry. You will have the ability to stand out and that's vital when so many people are clamoring for work in game development.

So, what would Sid do? Well, when he was prototyping *Sid Meier's Railroads!* last year, he wrote the entire prototype in C. He didn't have an artist (they were all busy on another title at the time), so he grabbed a 3D art program, made his own art, and threw it in the game—often using text labels to make sure players knew what things were in the game. He used audio files from previous Firaxis games and the Internet, and sprinkled them around to enhance the player's experience. He created something—in a fairly short amount of time—that showed our publisher and others just how much fun the game was going to be. And he did it on his own . . . just like the "old days" when he worked from his garage.

So what should you do? Well, if you want to get a job in the industry as a game designer or even if you just want to make a cool game to teach math to your daughter, you should buy this book. Jump in and work through the exercises and develop the beginnings of your own game library—Sid has some code he's used since the Commodore 64 days. Let your imagination run wild and then find ways to translate your ideas into something people can actually play. Whatever you do, just do *something*. It's the one true way to learn and develop as a designer and it is your ticket to finding game designer fulfillment and maybe even a job. And if Sid wasn't Sid, and didn't already have all of those tools at his disposal, it just might be what he would do too.

Barry E. Caudill
Executive Producer
Firaxis Games
2K Games
Take 2 Interactive

ACKNOWLEDGMENTS

I am grateful to my wife, Jennifer, for giving me the time and space to write while also working full time, which takes away most of my free time. Thank you for being so supportive. I love you. It's hard to believe, but since the first edition of this book was published, we've added two more members to our family. Jeremiah and Kayleigh have welcomed Kaitlyn and Kourtney to our home in the past two years. I thank God for all of these blessings.

I am indebted to the hard working editors, artists, and layout specialists at Thomson Course Technology PTR and to all of the freelancers for doing such a fine job. Many thanks especially to Jenny Davidson, Brandon Penticuff, Mitzi Koontz, and Emi Smith. Thanks go to Joshua Smith for his technical review, which was invaluable. I believe you will find this a true gem of a game programming book due to all of their efforts.

About the Author

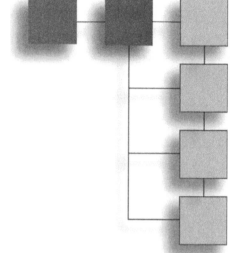

Jonathan S. Harbour is a senior instructor of game development at the University of Advancing Technology (www.uat.edu) in Tempe, Arizona, where he teaches a variety of game programming courses. When not teaching others about games, writing about games, or playing games, he enjoys audio/video editing, wrenching on old Fords (and going to local car shows), and watching movies. His favorite game development tools are DarkBASIC, Allegro, and DirectX. Jonathan is the author of these recent books: *Game Programming All in One, Third Edition; DarkBASIC Pro Game Programming, Second Edition* (with Joshua Smith); *Beginning Java 5 Game Programming;* and *The Gadget Geek's Guide to Your Xbox 360.* Jonathan founded a small, independent game studio, Primeval Games, as a creative outlet for producing humorous casual games, and is working on several unique, new games, including a space shooter. He lives in Arizona with his wife, Jennifer, and four children: Jeremiah, Kayleigh, Kaitlyn, and newcomer Kourtney. He can be reached at www.jharbour.com.

CONTENTS

INTRODUCTION

This book will teach you the fundamentals of how to write games in the C++ language, using the powerful but intimidating DirectX 9 SDK. Game programming is a challenging subject that is not just difficult to master; it is difficult just to get started. This book takes away the mystery of game programming using the tools of the trade: C++ and DirectX. You will learn how to harness the power of Windows and DirectX to write both 2D and 3D games, with an especially strong emphasis on some of the more advanced topics in 3D programming for a beginning book.

You will learn how to write a simple Windows program. From there, you will learn about the key DirectX components: Direct3D, DirectSound, and Direct-Input. You will learn how to make use of these key DirectX components while writing simple code that is easy to understand, at a pace that will not leave you behind. Along the way, you will put all of the new information gleaned from each chapter into a framework, or game library, that will be readily available to you in future chapters (as well as your own future game projects). After you have learned all that you need to know to write a simple game, you will do just that. And it is not just the usual sprite-based game either; it's a complete, fully functional 3D game, using collision detection, with real 3D models. A complete chapter will teach you just how to create your own models using the popular and free Anim8or modeling program (included on the CD-ROM).

Where to Begin?

My philosophy for game development is neither limited nor out of reach for the average programmer. I want to really get down to business early on and not have to explain every function call in the standard C++ library. So you will want to begin learning C++ right now if you are not familiar with the language. There are certainly a lot of great products you can use that are as powerful (or more so) as the language used in this book. There are products like Blitz Basic (see *Game Programming for Teens* by Maneesh Sethi) and DarkBASIC (see *DarkBASIC Pro Game Programming, 2nd Edition* by Jonathan Harbour and Joshua Smith). These are two examples of game development tools that provide you with a complete package: compiler, editor, game library/engine, and the ability to produce a standalone Windows/DirectX game without the need for a runtime library of any kind. If you are fairly new to the C++ language or have no experience with it at all, I strongly suggest that you read a C primer first (such as *C Programming for the Absolute Beginner* by Michael Vine). I often use the terms "C" and "C++" interchangeably to avoid confusion, but most of the code in this book is actually just basic C rather than C++.

Why am I recommending so many books? Well, the books on BASIC are just mentioned in passing (as a subject that you may wish to pursue), while I do recommend that you read a C primer before continuing with this book. Game programming as a subject is not something that you just pick up after reading a single book. Although this book has everything you need to write simple 2D and 3D games (and granted it does cover a lot of useful information in that regard), no single volume can claim to cover everything because game development is a complex subject. I am confident that you will manage to follow along and grasp the concepts in this book just fine without one, but a C primer will give you a very good advantage before getting into Windows and DirectX programming. This book spends no time at all discussing the C language; it jumps right into Windows and DirectX code fairly quickly, followed by a new subject in each chapter!

This book was written in a progressive style that is meant to challenge you at every step, and relies on repetition rather than memorization. I don't cover a difficult subject just once and expect you to know it from that point on. Instead, I just present similar code sections in each program so you'll get the hang of it over time. The learning curve here is modeled after driving a car: once you have learned to use the accelerator and brake pedals, the actual process of learning to drive comes from practice. You wouldn't dare attempt to compete in a NASCAR race after simply reading a driving book, would you? Of course not! But after many hours behind the wheel, you would at least be qualified to drive around the track.

I would rather you learn to draw a Bresenham line on your own than to copy someone else's texture-wrapped polygon code. There are a lot of things we will have to just take for granted in this book, because the goal is to teach the basics and prepare you for further study. But at the same time, I don't want to give you the impression that you can get by just by copying and pasting code to accomplish what you need for a particular game. On the contrary, the up-front learning curve is a challenge, and can be frustrating at times, but you have to get started somewhere, so my goal is to help you develop a love of learning and foster that love for video games that prompted you to pick up this book.

So, where to begin? If this book is going to teach you the basics of DirectX, so that you can write your own games, then we need to start with the basics of a Windows program.

What Will You Learn in This Book?

This book will teach you how to write a Windows program, and from there, the sky's the limit! You will learn about DirectX; you will dive into Direct3D head-first and learn all about surfaces, textures, meshes, 3D models, and that is just the beginning!

You will learn how to interface with your computer's hardware using DirectX components, and use those hardware devices in your games!

Since this book is dedicated to teaching the basics of game programming, it will cover a lot of subjects very quickly, so you'll need to be on your toes! I use a casual writing style to make the subjects easy to understand and use repetition rather than memorization to nail the points home. You will learn by doing and you will not struggle with any one subject, because you will practice each topic several times throughout the book. Each chapter builds on the one before, but may be considered independent, so if there is any one subject that you are very interested in at the start, then feel free to skip around. However, the game framework built in this book does refer back to previous chapters, so I recommend reading it one chapter at a time.

This book spends a lot of time on 3D programming, but in order to get to the 3D material, there is a lot of information that must be covered first. Those topics are covered quickly so you will be learning some of the advanced topics in 3D programming in no time. In order to load a 3D model, for instance, you will need to learn how to *create* a 3D model first, right? Well, you will learn just how to do that in this book!

Anim8or is a powerful 3D modeling program that is free and included on the CD-ROM that accompanies this book. You will learn how to use Anim8or in Chapter 13 to create a complete model of a car.

After you have learned the ropes of 3D modeling, you will also need to learn how to convert your 3D models to a format that Direct3D will understand. Chapter 14 explains how to convert the models exported from Anim8or to the Direct3D format.

What Compiler Should You Use?

This book uses the C++ language and all examples are compiled with Microsoft Visual C++ 2003. You should be able to compile and run the programs using another Windows compiler such as Borland C++Builder or with another version of Visual C++ (6.0 and later should work fine). You may also use the free Visual C++ 2005 Express Edition, available for download from Microsoft's Web site.

What About the Programming Language?

This book focuses on the C++ language. This book is not a primer on the C++ language, but rather makes use of this very powerful, low-level language to write games. The examples and source code are mostly C, except for the use of some specific C++ here and there. You will get by just fine with a basic understanding of the C language. Just know that I do not teach the language in this book—we get down to business writing games very quickly and do not have time for a tutorial on C/C++ programming.

As such, you *do* need to know C in advance (preferably, C++). If this is your first experience with the C language, and you have not used it before, I'll be honest with you, you will have a very hard time with the source code in this book. If you feel that you are up to the challenge, then you *might* be able to wade through the C code and make some sense out of it. But I want to warn you in advance: I don't spend even a single paragraph trying to teach you anything about the C language! This book is about game programming, and it assumes that you already know C. I recommend that you acquire a C primer to read before delving into this book, or to keep handy for those parts that may confuse you.

What About a Complete Game?

Beginning Game Programming, Second Edition is not a tutorial on how to program in C, and not a DirectX reference. This book is all about game programming. You will learn the skills to write a complete 3D game in C and DirectX 9 called *Bash*. *Bash* demonstrates wireframe and solid rendering with materials and textures using Direct3D, and uses real 3D models created with Anim8or.

Creating this game is not just a matter of typing in some source code and compiling it, then away you go. On the contrary, you need to create your own 3D models for this game. I encourage this throughout the book, because if you want to master game programming, you need to become proficient with a modeling package like Anim8or (which is almost as feature rich as 3ds max and Maya, for our purposes here). You will actually see how the artwork for *Bash* is created. Since you learn how to create your own models in Chapter 13, you will be able to enhance and modify *Bash* to suit your own tastes by modifying the 3D models in Anim8or. How would you like to add your own photos to be used as textures in the game? No problem, you will learn how to do things like that in this book.

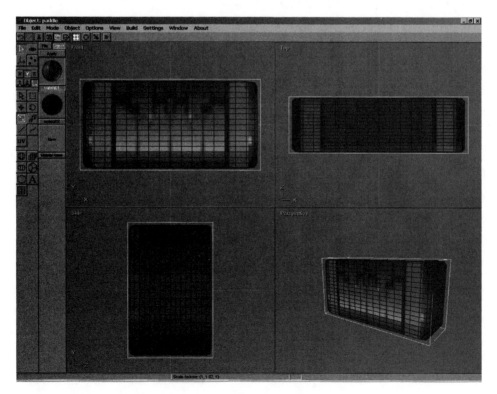

You will learn how the models for *Bash* were created.

Conventions Used in This Book

The following styles are used in this book to highlight portions of text that are important. You will find note, tip, and caution boxes here and there throughout the book.

Note

This is what a note looks like. Notes are additional information related to the text.

Tip

This is what a tip looks like. Tips give you pointers in the current tutorial being covered.

Caution

This is what a caution looks like. Cautions provide you with guidance and what to do or not do in a given situation.

Book Summary

This book is divided into three parts:

- **Part I: Windows Programming.** This first section provides all the information you will need to get started writing Windows code. By the time you have completed the first four chapters, you will have a solid grasp of how a Windows program works.

- **Part II: DirectX Programming.** This section is the meat and potatoes of the book, providing solid tutorials on the most important components of DirectX, including functions for loading images, manipulating sprites, double-buffering, keyboard and mouse input, sound effects, and other core features of any game.

- **Part III: 3D Programming.** This section provides four chapters dedicated to creating 3D models, loading them with DirectX 9 code, and creating a 3D game.

PART I

WINDOWS PROGRAMMING

The first part of the book provides an introduction to Windows programming, which is a foundation that you'll need before getting into DirectX programming. The four chapters in Part I will give you an overview of how Windows works, explain how to write a simple Windows program, discuss the Windows messaging system, and go over real-time programming by showing you how to create a non-interrupting game loop.

CHAPTER 1

GETTING STARTED WITH WINDOWS AND DIRECTX

Game programming is one of the most complicated forms of computer programming you will ever have the pleasure of endeavoring to master. Games are as much works of art as they are grand technical achievements. Many technically fantastic games go unnoticed and unappreciated, while less technically savvy games go on to widespread fame and bring fortune to their makers. Regardless of your ultimate goals as a game programmer, this is one of the most enjoyable hobbies that you could ever take up, and the results will both frustrate and exhilarate you at the same time—I hope you're ready for the adventure that is about to begin! This chapter provides the crucial information necessary to get started writing Windows games; it leads into the next three chapters, which provide an overview of the mechanics of a Windows program.

Here is what you will learn in this chapter:

- How to put game programming into perspective.

- How to choose the best compiler for your needs.

- How to determine your skill level and realize what you need to learn.

- How to get started learning about Windows programming.

Welcome to the Adventure!

Welcome to the adventure that is game programming! I have enjoyed playing and programming games for many years, and probably share the same enthusiasm for this once-esoteric subject that you do. Games, and by that I mean PC games, were once found within the realm of Geek Land, where hardy adventurers would explore vast imaginary worlds and then struggle to create similar worlds on their own; meanwhile, out in the real world, people were living normal lives: hanging out with friends, flirting with girls (or guys), going to the movies, cruising downtown.

Why did we choose to miss out on all that fun? Because we thought it was more fun to stare at pixels on the screen? Precisely!

But one man's pixel is another man's fantasy world or outer-space adventure. And the earliest games in "gaming" were little more than globs of pixels being shuffled around on the screen. Our imaginations filled in more details than we often realized when we played the primitive games of the past.

So, what's your passion? Or rather, what's your favorite type of game? Is it a classic arcade shoot-em-up, a fantasy adventure, a real-time strategy game, a role-playing game, a sports-related game? I'd like to challenge you to design a game *in your mind* while reading this book, and imagine how you might go about creating that game as you delve into each chapter. This book was not written to give you a "warm fuzzy" feeling about game development, with a few patchy code listings and directions on where to go next. I really take the subject quite seriously and prefer to give you a sense of completion upon finishing the last chapter. This is a self-contained book to a certain degree, in that what you will learn is applicable toward your own early game projects. What you will learn here will allow you to write a complete game with enough quality that you may feel confident to share it with others. What I will *not* do is give you a game engine or a sample game (per se) and tell you to "go for it."

Let's Talk About Compilers

The programs in this book were written mainly for Microsoft Visual C++. Although there are many Windows compilers on the market (some no longer available at retail), very few of them will compile the programs in this book due to the DirectX SDK, which was written with and for Visual C++.

Figure 1.1 shows Visual C++ 6.0, which was a very popular and solid version of MSVC for many years and used to develop hundreds (if not thousands) of retail games. There is a freeware compiler called Dev-C++ 5.0, available for free from Bloodshed Software, which is fully capable of compiling Windows code. Unfortunately, the DirectX SDK is not available for this compiler. The same may

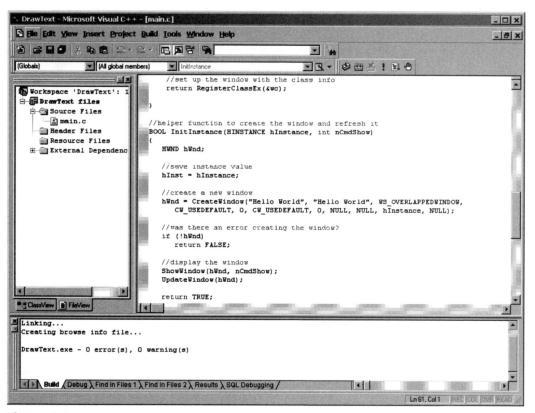

Figure 1.1
Microsoft Visual C++ 6.0

be true of the once-popular Borland C++ and C++Builder products, which once supported DirectX, but that is no longer certain. Since we're focusing on the June 2006 version of DirectX, the code probably will not compile with Dev-C++ or Borland or most other compilers.

As is the case with most Windows compilers, more recent versions should work fine with the source code in this book. For example, Visual Studio .NET 2002, 2003, and 2005 Express Edition will all compile the code without complaint. The free version of Visual C++ 2005, called the Express Edition, is available for download from Microsoft at http://msdn.microsoft.com/vstudio/express/visualc/. This compiler is not limited in any way, even though it's free! It's an unprecedented move on the part of the world's largest software maker. You can compile the code in this book using 2005 Express Edition, and the configuration is similar to MSVC 2003, which is shown in Figure 1.2.

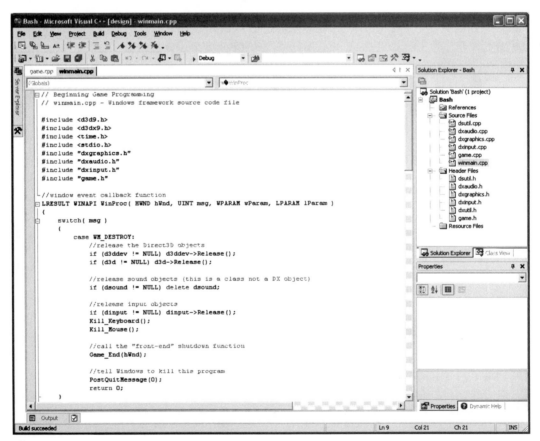

Figure 1.2
Visual C++ 7.1 (2003)

Tip

I recommend using Visual C++ 2005 for DirectX programming, because it is the latest and greatest compiler, and is certain to support every feature of DirectX for the foreseeable future. In fact, the free version of XNA Game Studio uses Visual C++ 2005 Express Edition, and this tool supports Xbox 360 development—without requiring the official (and expensive) dev kit.

Although I am very fond of Dev-C++ and C++Builder, I focus on Visual C++ exclusively here because it is guaranteed to work with DirectX without a hitch. If you're unhappy with that statement, here's what I've got to say—stop reading, because you aren't a beginner! If you want a good, solid tutorial on using Dev-C++ and other open-source game programming tools, see my book *Game Programming All In One, Third Edition*. In that book, I do not cover DirectX, but focus on an open-source, cross-platform game library called Allegro. How lucky you are in this day and age! Years ago, it was quite a struggle for a student or hobby programmer to even *find* a good retail compiler when computer stores were few and far between. Today, not only do all the major computer stores carry every compiler imaginable, but you even have free compilers! My, how times have changed.

What's Your Skill Level?

This chapter moves along at a brisk pace, so if you already have some experience writing Windows code, it shouldn't bore you. On the other hand, if you have never written a Windows program before, this may be a bit of a challenge for you because I'm going to assume that you already have some familiarity with the C language. I just want you to be prepared! If you picked up this book thinking that it would teach you absolutely everything you need to know to write a computer game using the C language, and all you'll need to know about Windows and DirectX to boot, well, you may be in for a surprise, because we only have time to cover the key topics in order to build two games in such a short amount of time and space! I'm going to assume that you have already studied the basics of the C language at least. If you have trouble with the `main` function, then I encourage you to pick up a primer first. We have *so* much information to cover in this book—if I don't move along at a pretty good pace, we'll never get into the good stuff, like loading and drawing 3D models!

As I've said, the journey to becoming a master game developer is a long and arduous one, and you may be taking the first tentative steps here. I want to encourage you to invest in good C and Windows references, as well as in additional game programming books (on whatever game genre interests you). I have a feeling—if you share some of the same interests that I do—that this book will whet your appetite and you'll be clamoring for more by the time you're done with the last chapter! You are certain to find a book about any subject you want to learn about by visiting www.courseptr.com.

Do you want to get up to speed quickly and produce something *good* right away? Learn the art of focusing your entire being on a single goal and then eat, drink, sleep, and breathe programming. Early on, if you are a normal person, other aspects of your life may suffer while you are working on your "zen." You will learn in time to juggle the basic responsibilities of life, friends, and family while also having focus. In the martial arts, you learn to focus all of your energy into a strike to deal a powerful blow to an opponent. Learn to use this kind of focus and energy with everything you do in life, including game programming or any other endeavor. The idea is to get past the "beginner" stage so that you are able to study, understand, and discuss the more advanced topics on your own. By focusing on mastering a subject early on, you can get the gist of it fairly quickly.

I remember how, when I was just getting started, I had assumed that so much of the work involved in a computer program is done automatically (or rather, was handled by the O/S). It's quite a shock when you realize that *nothing* is given to you—that *you* must write all the code to get anything at all to come up on the screen. Now, it isn't as bad as it was in the early years of the PC, when MS-DOS was the most common O/S (up until the mid-1990s). Back then, you really did have to screw with the video card registers and literally program it using very low-level assembly language.

Note

I have a huge book on that subject by Michael Abrash called *Graphics Programming Black Book* (no longer in print). Michael developed his graphics coding wizardry *before* he was hired as a graphics consultant by studios such as Valve, id Software, and Croteam, and he was the ultimate graphics programming guru! To read some of Michael's commentary about programming *Quake*, visit http://www.bluesnews.com/abrash/.

I found this much easier than assembling a program and linking to it (the last stage of compiling your program). Figure 1.3 shows the compilation process.

As compilers became more powerful, standard O/S libraries that abstracted the computer system hardware and raised it up a notch became available. No longer did programmers have to write all the interface code to the hardware (if you have

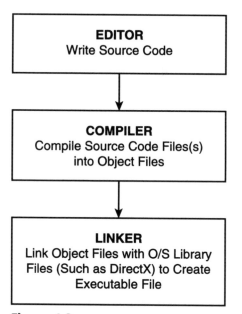

Figure 1.3
The compilation process takes a source code file, compiles it, and then links it into an executable.

been playing games for a long time, you may remember how convoluted some of the older MS-DOS game installs used to be). Back in the MS-DOS days, game programmers had to write their own video card and sound card drivers! Imagine that! If you want some classic examples, look up *Dungeon Keeper* and *Jedi Knight*. Instead, Windows, the device drivers, and DirectX provide a layer of abstraction over the hardware. You can focus on the design and programming of your game rather than spending so much time writing hardware interface code (which was the subject of all game programming books in the early days, when game design was unheard-of). I suspect that these limitations in the operating system are what limited game development to the real ultra-guru and prevented many aspiring game designers from getting into the business in the '80s and early '90s. You simply had to be technical, as well as creative, to succeed at that time. But when Microsoft released DirectX for Windows 95, and then continued to improve it over the next ten years, it took all of that complexity and simplified it down to a common game API—application programming interface. The new features added to each new version of DirectX (a result of all the advances in 3D graphics technology) greatly enhanced the original version of DirectX, which was designed to bring gaming to Windows in a big way. However, during the

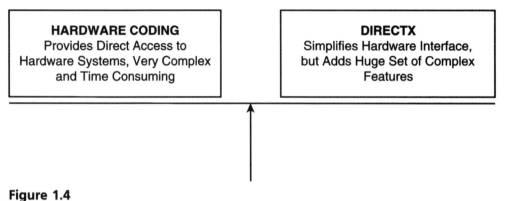

Figure 1.4
What DirectX does to simplify the hardware interface is countered by an extremely large and complex set of features.

intervening years, DirectX has grown to become immensely large and complicated, and again we are faced with barriers to entry once again (see Figure 1.4).

Of course, it is better to have DirectX (on the right side of the teeter-totter) because you don't have to use or even look into all the advanced features if you don't need them for your game. That's the good news, really; if you want the power, it's available, but you can learn the basics and start seeing progress with simple games very quickly.

An Overview of Windows Programming

If you are new to Windows programming, then you're in for a treat, because Windows is a fun operating system to use for writing games. First of all, there are so many great compilers and languages available for Windows. Second, it's the most popular operating system in the world, so any game you write for Windows has the potential to become quite popular. The third great thing about Windows is that you have the amazing DirectX library at our disposal. Not only is DirectX the most widely used game programming library in *existence*, it is also easy to learn. Now, don't misunderstand my meaning—DirectX is easy to learn, but *mastering* it is another matter. I will teach you how to use it—and wield it, so to speak—to create your own games. Mastering it will require a lot more work and knowledge than this single book provides.

Before you can start writing DirectX code, you will need to learn how to write a simple Windows application and learn how Windows handles messages. So let's start at the beginning. What *is* Windows? Windows is a multi-tasking, multi-threaded operating system. What this means is that Windows can run many programs at the same time, and each of those programs can have one or more threads running as well. As you might imagine, this operating system architecture lends itself well to multi-processor systems, such as the Pentium D and Intel Core Duo chips, as well as multi-processor motherboard systems.

"Getting" Windows

Few operating systems will scale as well as Windows from one version to the next. The numerous versions of Windows that are in use—from Windows Vista to Windows XP Home to Windows 2000 Professional—are all so similar that programs can be written for one version of Windows that will run almost without change on other versions of Windows. For instance, a program that you developed with Microsoft Visual C++ 6.0 back in 1998 under Windows NT 4.0 or Windows 98 will still run on the latest Windows XP Professional or Windows Vista. You may even have a few games in your game library that came out in the late 1990s that supported an early version of DirectX (for instance, DirectX 6.0); don't be surprised if such games will still run on a new PC running Windows XP.

So we have established that Windows programs have a lot of longevity (also known as "shelf life" in the software industry). What can Windows really do?

Note

Whenever I refer to "Windows" in this book, I'm including every recent version of Windows that is relevant to the topic at hand—that is, PCs and game programming. This should include all previous, current, and future versions of Windows that are compatible. For all practical purposes, this really is limited just to 32-bit programs. You may assume any reference to "Windows" from here on includes all such versions. At the very least, this will include Windows 2000, XP, 2003, and Vista.

Windows programming can be simple or complex, depending on the type of program you are writing. If you have a development background with experience writing applications, then you probably have a good understanding of how complex a graphical user interface (GUI) can become. All it takes is a few menus, a few forms, and you will find yourself inundated with dozens (if not hundreds) of controls with which you must contend. Windows is very good as a multi-tasking operating system because it is message-driven. Object-oriented programming proponents would argue that Windows is an object-oriented operating system. In fact, it isn't. The latest version of Windows today functions almost exactly the same way that early versions of Windows (such as the old

Windows 286, Windows 3.0, and so on) functioned, in that *messages* drive the operating system, not objects. The operating system is similar to the human nervous system, although not nearly as intricate or complicated. But if you simplify the human nervous system in an abstract way, you'll see impulses moving through the neurons in the human body from the senses to the brain, and from the brain to the muscles.

Understanding Windows Messaging

Let's talk about a common scenario to help with the analogy of comparing an operating system to the human nervous system. Suppose that some *event* is detected by nerves on your skin. This event might be a change of temperature or something may have touched you. If you touch your left arm with a finger of your right hand, what happens? You "feel" the touch. Why? When you touch your arm, it is not your arm that is feeling the touch, but rather, your brain. The sense of "touch" is not felt by your arm, per se, but rather, your brain localizes the event so that you recognize the source of the touch. It is almost as if the neurons in your central nervous system are queried as to whether they participated in that "touch event." Your brain "sees" the neurons in the chain that relayed the touch message, so it is able to determine where the touch occurred on your arm. Now touch your arm, and move your finger back and forth on your arm. What do you sense is happening? It is not a constant "analog" measurement, because there are a discrete number of touch-sensitive neurons in your skin. The sense of motion is, in fact, digitally relayed to your brain. Now you might refute my claim here by saying that the sense of pressure is analog. We are getting into some abstract ideas at this point, but I would pose that the sense of pressure is relayed to your brain in discrete increments, not as a capacitive analog signal.

How is this subject related to Windows programming? The sense of touch is very similar to the way in which Windows messaging works. An external event, like a mouse click, causes a small electrical signal to pass from the mouse to the USB port into the system bus, which might be thought of as the nervous system of the computer. From there, the signal is picked up by the operating system (Windows) and a message is generated and passed to applications that are running (like your game). Your program, then, is like a conscious mind that reacts to that "sense of touch." The subconscious mind of the computer (the operating system that handles all of the logistics of processing events) "presented" this event to your program's awareness.

It seems that over time, our advanced information systems start to mimic the natural world, and when we have finally built the ultimate supercomputer, it may just resemble a human mind.

There is yet another issue at hand. We humans have two brains, after all. Remember my comment about technology mimicking biological brains? Well, most processor builders today are heading in the direction of incorporating multiple processor cores into a single silicon chip. Within a few years, multi-processor systems will be the norm, because they will be available right inside a standard processor chip.

Multi-Tasking

First and foremost, Windows is a *preemptive* multi-tasking operating system. This means that your PC can run many programs at the same time. Windows accomplishes this feat by running each program for a very short amount of time, counted in milliseconds, or thousandths of a second. This jumping from one program to another very quickly is called *time slicing,* and Windows handles time slicing by creating a virtual address space (a small "simulated" computer) for each program in memory. Each time Windows jumps to the next program, the state of the current program is stored so that it can be brought back again when it is that program's turn to receive some processor time. This includes processor register values and any data that might be overwritten by the next process. Then, when the program comes around again in the time-slicing scheme, these values are restored into the processor registers and program execution continues where it left off.

Note

If this sounds like a wasteful use of processor cycles, you should be aware that during those few microseconds, the processor is able to run a few hundred thousand instructions at the very least—modern processors that approach the gigaflop rating will run several million instructions in a short "time slice."

The Windows operating system might be thought of as having a central nervous system of its own—based on events. When you press a key, a message is created for that *keypress* event and circulated through the system until a program picks it up and uses it. I should clarify a point here, as I have brought up "circulation." Windows 3.0, 3.1, and 3.11 were *non-pre-emptive* operating systems that technically were just very advanced programs sitting on top of 16-bit MS-DOS. These early versions of Windows were more like MS-DOS shells than true operating systems, and, thus, were not able to truly "own" the entire computer system. You could write a program for Windows 3.x and have it completely take over the system, without freeing up any processor cycles for other programs. You could even lock up the entire operating system if you wanted to. Early Windows programs had to release control of the computer's resources in order to be "Windows Logo" certified (which was an important marketing issue at the time). Windows 95 was the first 32-bit version of Windows and was a revolutionary step forward for this operating system family in that it was a *pre-emptive* operating system.

What this means is that the operating system has a very low-level core that manages the computer system, and no single program can take over the system, which was the case under Windows 3.x. *Pre-emptive* means that the operating system can pre-empt the functioning of a program, causing it to pause, and the operating system can then allow the program to start running again later. When you have many programs and processes (each with one or more threads) begging for processor time, this is called a time-slicing system, which is how Windows works. As you might imagine, having a multi-processor system is a real advantage when you are using an operating system such as this. Ignoring all reviews and opinions to the contrary on this matter, a dual-processor Athlon 64, Opteron, Xeon, Itanium, Pentium D, or Core Duo system (if you can afford one!) is a great setup for a game programmer or any developer for that matter. For one thing, SMP (symmetric multiprocessing) processors usually have more internal cache memory because they are designed for servers. Another point is that, regardless of the raw benchmarks that may or may not shed a good light on such systems, we are talking about multi-tasking here, so the more processing power the better! While you may have had to turn off most applications while doing game development in the past, with these modern multi-core systems, you can leave other apps running in the background while working on a game and you will not notice any drag on the system. Of course, a ton of memory helps too! I recommend 2GB of RAM for game development—and make it the fastest memory chips your system can handle while you're at it! (My main PC is a little underpowered because I opted for a Micro ATX system in one of those tiny cases during my last system build! But it sure beats lugging a gigantic tower case to LAN parties.)

Figure 1.5 shows an overview of how non-preemptive multi-tasking works. Note how each program receives control over the processor and must then explicitly

Non-Preemptive Multi-Tasking

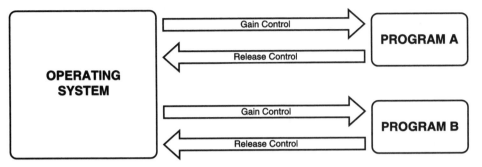

Figure 1.5
Non-preemptive multi-tasking requires the voluntary release of control by each program. The O/S is very limited in control over applications.

Preemptive Multi-Tasking

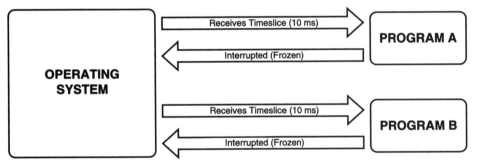

Figure 1.6
A preemptive multi-tasking O/S has full control over the system and allocates slices of time for each running process and thread.

release control in order for the computer system to function properly. Such programs must also be careful about using too much time; in essence, non-preemptive O/S programs must voluntarily share the processor.

The next illustration, Figure 1.6, shows how preemptive multi-tasking works. As you can see, the diagram is similar (so it is easy to compare), but the O/S now controls everything and need not wait for the programs to "play nicely" and share processor time. The O/S will simply suspend a program after an allotted number of milliseconds of timeslice and then give the program more processor time after looping through all processes and threads running in the system.

Multi-Threading

Multi-threading is the process of breaking up a program into multiple, independent parts that might work together to accomplish a task (or that might perform completely independent tasks). This is not the same as multi-tasking on the system level. Multi-threading is sort of like multi-multi-tasking, where each program has running parts of its own, and those small program fragments are oblivious of the time-slicing system performed by the operating system. As far as your main Windows program and all of its threads are concerned, they all have complete control over the system and have no "sense" that the operating system is slicing up the time allotted to each thread or process. Therefore, multi-threading means that each program is capable of delegating processes to its own mini-programs. For instance, a chess program might create a thread to think ahead while the player is working on his next move. The "thought" thread would continue to update moves and counter-moves while waiting for the player. While this might just as easily be accomplished with a program loop that thinks while waiting for user input, the ability to delegate the process out to a thread might have significant benefits for a program.

Just as an example, you can create two threads in a Windows program and give each thread its own loop. As far as each thread is concerned, its loop runs endlessly and it runs extremely fast, without interruption. But at the system level, each thread is given a slice of processor time. Depending on the speed of the processor and operating system, a thread may be interrupted 50, 100, or even 1000 times per second, but will be oblivious to the interruption. Figure 1.7 illustrates the relationship between program, processes, and threads.

Note

Multi-threading is a fascinating subject, and worth your time to learn about! I covered this subject in *Game Programming All In One, Third Edition,* and explained how to use the Pthread-Win32 library, which makes multi-threading a snap. That may be a good next step after you've finished this book. I've found that most beginners can learn the Allegro game library very quickly.

Multi-threading is very useful for game programming. The many tasks involved in a game loop might be delegated into separate threads that will execute independently, each one communicating with the main program. A thread might be set up to handle screen updates automatically. All the program would have to do then is make sure the double buffer gets updated at a specified time with all of the objects on the screen, and the thread will do the work on a regular

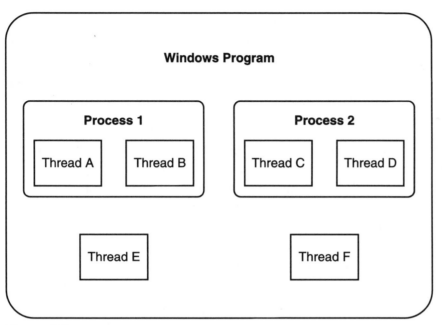

Figure 1.7
A multi-threaded program might feature multi-threaded processes and independent threads.

basis—perhaps even with timing built in so that the game will run at a uniform speed regardless of the processor. Most of the popular game engines are multi-threaded, meaning that they inherently support multiple processors. This is a boon for gamers who have forked over the additional cost for a dual-processor system! What is even more useful is when a standalone game server (which is often provided with popular online games so that players can run their own games) supports multiple processors, because it takes a lot of processing power to handle large games with many players. A dual-processor game server is even more capable of handling a large allotment of players.

Tip

A double buffer is sort of a bitmap image in memory that you can use to draw the graphics for your game, and this image is then copied to the screen resulting in a very smoothly rendered display.

Event Handling

At this point, you might be asking yourself, "How does Windows keep track of so many programs running at the same time?" Windows handles the problem, first of all, by requiring that programs be event-driven. Secondly, Windows uses system-wide messages to communicate. Windows messages are small packets of data sent by the operating system to each running program with three primary features—window handle, instance identifier, and message type—telling that program that some event has occurred. The events will normally involve user input, such as a mouse click or key press, but might be from a communications port or a TCP/IP socket.

Each Windows program must check every message that comes in through the message handler to determine whether the message applies to that program. Messages that are not identified are sent along to the default message handler, which puts them back into the Windows messaging stream, so to speak. Think of messages as fish—when you catch a fish that is too small or that you don't like, you throw it back. But you keep the fish that you want. It is similar in the Windows event-driven architecture; if your program recognizes a message that it wants to keep, that message is taken out of the message stream and no other program will see it.

Once you have experimented with Windows programming and have learned to handle some Windows messages, you will see how it was designed for applications, not games. The trick is learning to "tap into" the Windows messaging system and inject your own code, such as a Direct3D initialization routine or a function call to refresh the screen. All of the actions in a game are handled through the Windows messaging system; it is your job to intercept and deal with messages that are relevant to your game. You will learn how to write a Windows program in the next chapter, and will learn more about Windows messaging in the next couple of chapters.

A Quick Overview of DirectX

I've covered a lot of information in a short amount of time on Windows theory, just to get to this point—where I can finally introduce you to DirectX. You've probably heard a lot about DirectX, because it is a buzzword that many people use in the industry, but that few in the mainstream truly understand. DirectX provides an interface to the low-level hardware interface of a Windows PC, providing a consistent and reliable set of functions for games that does not rely on the Windows API or GDI (which means DirectX is much faster). See Figure 1.8.

DirectX is closely integrated into Windows and will not work with any other O/S, as it relies on the basic libraries in the Windows API to function, as shown in Figure 1.9.

```
DirectX 9 SDK

DirectX Graphics
        Direct3D

DirectX Audio
        DirectSound
        DirectSound3D
        DirectMusic

DirectInput

DirectPlay
```

Figure 1.8
The primary components of DirectX 9

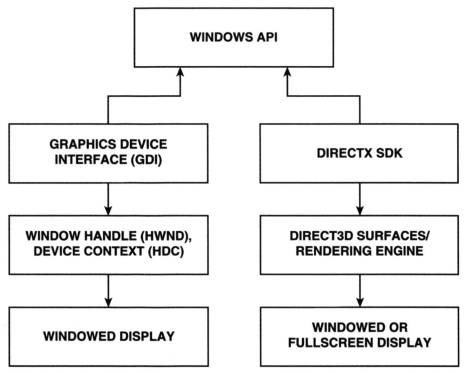

Figure 1.9
DirectX, an alternative to the slow GDI, still relies on the Windows API.

Here is a rundown of the DirectX components:

■ **DirectX Graphics.** This is the graphical system of DirectX that provides access to 3D accelerator cards and fast 2D graphics via a component called DirectDraw, suitable for arcade-style games as well as real-time strategy, role-playing, and other 2D games. 3D games have access to the latest video cards through the Direct3D interface. DirectX 9 still provides backward compatibility for DirectDraw games, but it is recommended that all new code take advantage of the improvements to Direct3D for both 2D and 3D coding.

■ **DirectX Audio.** This component includes interfaces for playing digital sound files, as well as digital and MIDI music, using a standard interface that supports all sound cards and formats on all PCs; this includes a built-in, real-time, multi-channel sound and music mixer. Basically, all of your sound and music needs are taken care of with DirectX Audio.

■ **DirectInput.** This component provides access to the peripherals on a Windows PC, such as the keyboard, mouse, and joystick, with support for unusual hardware such as flight sticks, steering wheels, pedals, and force-feedback devices (such as a gamepad with rumble feature).

■ **DirectPlay.** This component provides an interface for writing networked games with lobby support (a virtual "room" where players can interact and chat before a game starts). DirectPlay is highly optimized and efficient at handling a large number of players, but was designed for generally single-server games with up to 32 players; it is generally suitable for 99 percent of games. What DirectPlay does not provide is support for massively multi-player online games (although DirectPlay can be used to connect clients/players to game servers).

What Is Direct3D?

Direct3D is the technical term for DirectX Graphics, the graphical part of DirectX that does all the 2D and 3D rendering (and as such, is the most important part of DirectX). I'll teach you to use Direct3D 9 in an upcoming chapter. You will learn how to load bitmaps and draw them on the screen (in 2D mode), as well as use bitmaps to add textures to 3D models in future chapters.

I have to admit, I'm a huge fan of 2D games, especially turn-based strategy games like *Sid Meier's Civilization* series, and others, such as *Panzer General III* and most real-time strategy games (come on, how could you *not* have fun with *Command & Conquer* or *Starcraft*?). And to be honest, I have been such a proponent of 2D that it is what I write about most often. You can still develop an entire 2D game using Direct3D, or use 2D bitmaps and sprites to enhance a 3D game. You always have to display stats and other information on the screen that must be drawn as a 2D image, so learning how to draw and manipulate 2D graphics is a necessity. For the short term, a brief overview of 2D surfaces and sprites (using Direct3D) will help you to understand the whole DirectX Graphics system when I take you into 3D land later in the book.

Just to keep things on track, let me reiterate one of the goals of this book: to develop an understanding of 2D and 3D graphics and the knowledge needed to create games. My goal is not to make you an expert game programmer, just to give you enough information (and enthusiasm!) to take yourself to the next level and learn more about this subject. I will be getting into 3D models, texturing, lighting, and all the other subjects needed to write a simple 3D game. I'll even go over the basics of using popular 3D modeling programs in this book! What I'm getting at is that I want you to have *fun* with the material, and not get bogged down in the details! Because the details of 3D game programming are huge and complex, the average beginner's eyes tend to glaze over when hearing about vertex buffers and texture coordinates. I can relate, because it takes time to build up to details like that when you're just getting started! While I'm not exactly sheltering you from the complexity, by ignoring all the details and just focusing on what *works right now,* we can move forward onto subjects that are often left out of books on this material.

It is possible to just jump in and start writing Direct3D code at this point, but sooner or later you'll need to learn the basics of Windows programming and get some exposure to `WinMain` and the other Windows core functions, as this is at the very center of a DirectX program.

What You Have Learned

In this chapter, you have learned the basics of Windows programming in preparation for DirectX coding! Here are the key points:

- You learned what it takes to get into game programming and got a glimpse of the "bigger picture" and what may be in store for you in the near future.

- You learned all about compilers and whether your favorite compiler will work or not, and whether you might need to consider a free compiler like Dev-C++.

- You learned how to judge your own skills and what you'll need to focus on to raise your programming skill in order to write better, faster, more complex games.

- You learned the basics of what makes Windows tick and how you might tap into the Windows system with your own programs.

Review Questions

Here are some review questions that will help you to think outside the box and retain some of the information covered in this chapter.

1. What type of multi-tasking does Windows 2000 and XP use, preemptive or non-preemptive?

2. What compiler is primarily featured in this book (although the programs are compatible with any Windows compiler)?

3. What scheme does Windows use to notify programs that events have occurred?

4. What is the process called wherein a program uses multiple, independent parts that might work together to accomplish a task (or that might perform completely independent tasks)?

5. What is Direct3D?

CHAPTER 2

WINDOWS PROGRAMMING BASICS

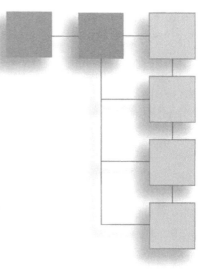

In this chapter, I am going to show you what a simple Windows program looks like. This is valuable information that you will need in the following two chapters, which build on this knowledge. These topics will come back to haunt you later on if you have not mastered them, as the chapters to follow will rely on your basic understanding of how Windows works. It will be very helpful if you have some experience writing Windows programs already, but I won't assume that you do. Instead, I'll just cover the basics of a Windows program—all that is necessary to start writing DirectX code.

Windows programming is fun, as I'm sure you'll find out in a few minutes. If you feel even a little bit overwhelmed by any subject in this chapter, don't worry too much because repetition in later chapters will nail the points home for you. Although I could have just explained WinMain and WinProc as I showed you how to write the DirectX programs, it's probably easier to understand these concepts when you're not trying to learn something else at the same time. So this chapter focuses on showing you how to write a simple Windows program, create the project, type in the code, and compile and run it.

Here is what you will learn in this chapter:

- How to create a Win32 Application project.
- How to write a simple Windows program.
- How to understand the WinMain function.
- How to understand the WinProc function.

The Basics of a Windows Program

Are you ready to get started writing Windows programs? Good! This chapter provides the "prerequisites" you'll need in future chapters to write DirectX code. Every Windows program includes a function called WinMain at minimum. Most Windows programs also include an event callback function called WinProc that receives messages so that you can write the code to deal with certain types of messages. If you were writing a full-blown Windows application (for instance, a commercial software product like 3ds max), then you would have a very large and complicated WinProc function in the program to handle the many program states and events. But in a DirectX program, you don't really have to mess with events because your main interest lies with the DirectX interfaces that provide their own functions for dealing with events. DirectX is also mostly a *polled* library, in that you must ask for data rather than having it thrown at you (which is the case with WinProc). For instance, when you start learning about DirectInput, you'll find that keyboard, mouse, and joystick input is mainly gathered by calling functions to see what values have changed.

Creating a Win32 Project

In this book, every project will be the same, so once you have learned to create a new project in Visual C++, then you'll be able to use the same strategy to create all the projects in the rest of the book.

What is a project, you may ask? Well, a project is a file, re
source code files in a program. All of the simple programs
single source code file (at least until we build the game fran
games have many source code files. You might have sou
Direct3D routines, DirectInput code, DirectSound code, a
also have the main code for the game itself. The project l
source code files, and is managed from within the IDE of yo
sake of simplicity, I'll just refer to Visual C++ (or the short
now on.

The usual project that you will want to set up in your compiler is a Win32 application, which is what I have selected in the Visual C++ project dialog in Figure 2.1. Name the new project "HelloWorld".

To do this, first start up Visual C++ 2003 or 2005, then open the File menu and select New. (Specifically, I am pulling screenshots for the figures from Visual C++ 2003, although 2005 is similar.) Select "Visual C++" from the Project Types list, and this is where you will find all the project types. Look for an item called "Win32 Project." That is the one you want. There are many types of Windows programs you can create with Visual C++, as you can see. Try not to get lost in the list of project templates; stick to the "Win32" types to avoid confusion.

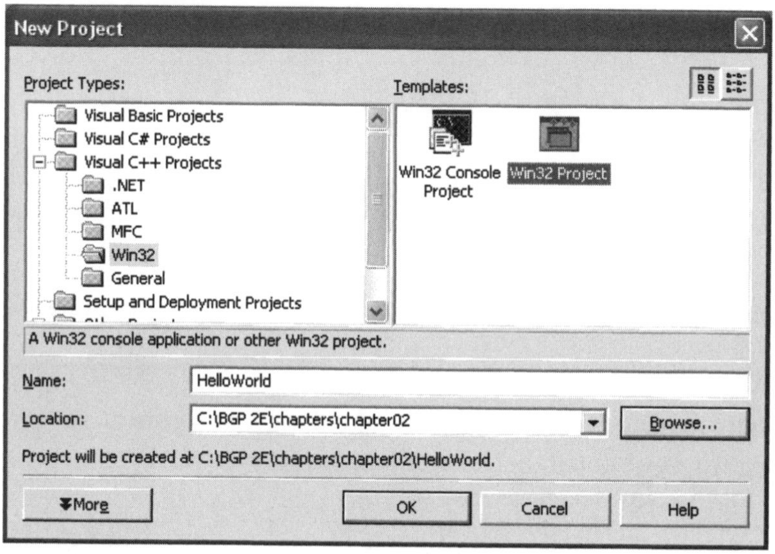

Figure 2.1
Creating a new Win32 application-type project

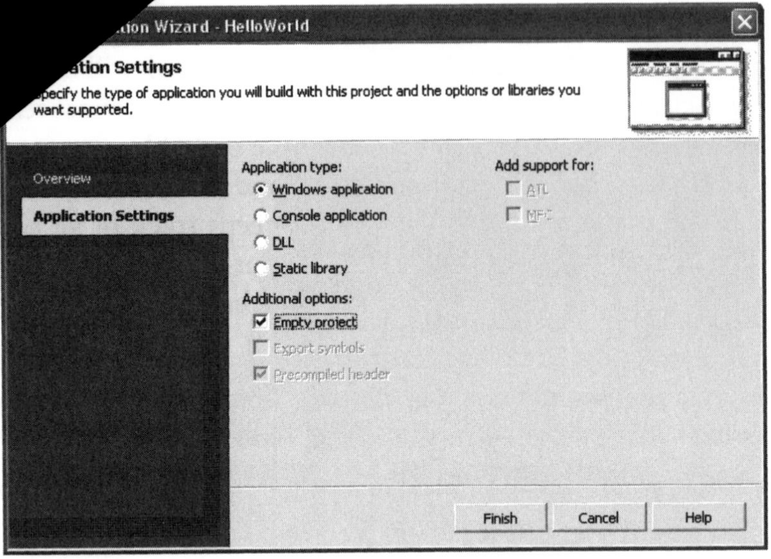

Figure 2.2
Creating a new Win32 project.

Most Windows compilers default to C++ files. Although we are writing mostly C code in this book, it doesn't make much difference in the filenames, so you will want to stick with source code files with an extension of .cpp. Always choose "empty project" so that you can add your own file to the project. This is the standard that I will use in this book.

Next up is the Application Settings dialog. Click the Application Settings tab on the left to bring up the dialog shown in Figure 2.2. Note that from the choices, I've selected "Windows application" and "Empty project".

Tip

Try not to let file extensions confuse you. All modern C++ compilers use the .cpp file extension, regardless of whether you are writing C or C++ code. For the sake of simplicity, I use the .cpp extension, although the trend in years past was to use the .c extension. Due to the way in which modern compilers work, it is just easier to use .cpp, because the .c extension causes some problems when compiling DirectX programs.

Now that you have a new project ready to go, let's take a look at a complete (but simple) Windows program, so you can better understand how it works. Since we haven't added a new file to the project yet, let's do that now. If you have a completely blank project (as expected), you'll need to add a source file to the project. You can do so by opening the File menu and selecting New to bring up the

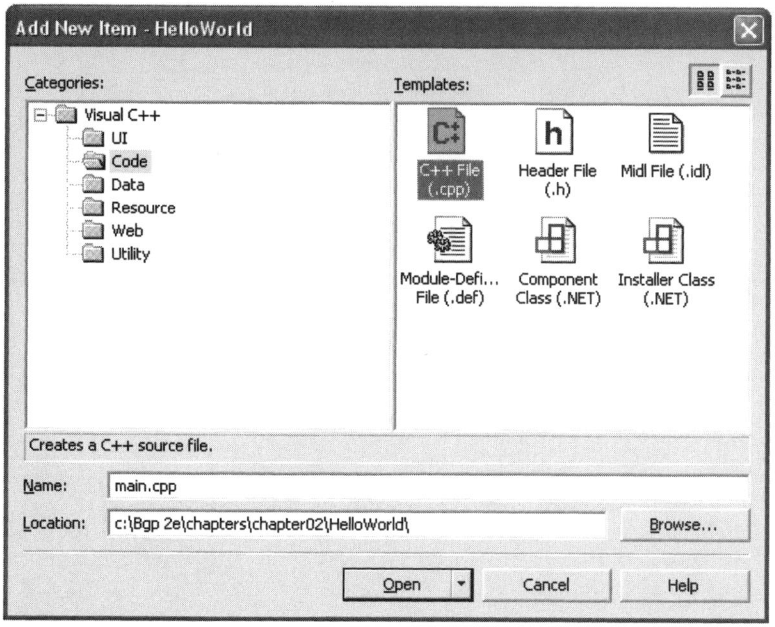

Figure 2.3
Adding a new file, main.cpp, to the empty project

New file dialog (the same dialog you used to create the new project). There are several other ways to add a new source file to the project as well. You can open the Project menu and select Add New Item, or you can right-click the project name in the Solution Explorer (the list of files on the right side of the Visual C++ IDE) and choose the same option from the context pop-up menu. Look for the C++ Source File item in the list and give the file a name (I recommend main.cpp), as shown in Figure 2.3.

After you have added the new source file, the project will look something like that in Figure 2.4.

Here is the source code for the HelloWorld program. This is a complete Windows program! You see, Windows programming doesn't really have to be all that difficult when you strip out all the app stuff, like menus, that aren't needed for writing games.

```
// Beginning Game Programming, 2nd Edition
// Chapter 2
// HelloWorld program
#include <windows.h>
```

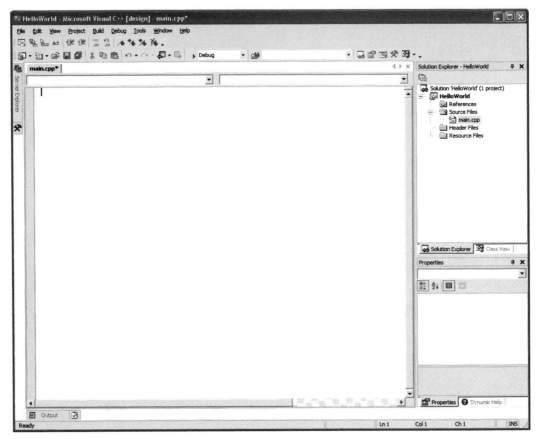

Figure 2.4
A new source file has been added to the project, ready for your source code.

```
int WINAPI WinMain(HINSTANCE hInstance, HINSTANCE hPrevInstance,
   LPSTR lpCmdLine, int nShowCmd)
{
   MessageBox(NULL, "Motoko Kusanagi has hacked your system!",
      "Public Security Section 9", MB_OK | MB_ICONEXCLAMATION);
}
```

This program simply displays a dialog box on the screen, as shown in Figure 2.5. What is the most important thing you should glean from this example? That WinMain does not *need* to be a big, ugly, complex hodge-podge of app code. When you compile a program with Visual C++, the executable file is located in a folder called Debug (inside your project's folder).

Figure 2.5
Output from the "Hello World" program

In the tradition of climbing the learning curve, I'll expand this little example a bit and show you how to create a standard program window and draw on it. This is the next step before you actually learn to initialize and use Direct3D.

Now that you've seen what a very simple Windows program looks like, let's delve a little further into the magical realm of Windows programming and learn to create a real window and draw stuff on it—using MessageBox is a bit of a cheat! What you really want is your very own window, which you'll create in the next chapter. Ironically, you won't need a main program window when you start writing DirectX code, because DirectX interfaces directly with the video card. The one exception would be if you were to write DirectX programs that run in a window. In my opinion, doing this defeats the purpose of DirectX, though, because a game shouldn't run in a window, it should *always* (without exception) run fullscreen. Do you want players focusing on your game or on instant messages and e-mail?

Understanding WinMain

As you have just learned, every Windows program has a function called WinMain. WinMain is the Windows equivalent of the main function in standard C programs, and is the initial entry point for a Windows program. The most important function in your program will be WinMain, but after you have set up the messaging calls you will probably not come back to WinMain while working on other parts of the program.

WinMain hasn't changed since 16-bit Windows 3.x, in order to retain backward compatibility. WinMain is the boss, the foreman, and handles the top-level part of the program. The job of WinMain is to set up the program, and then to set up the main message loop for the program. This loop processes all of the messages received by the program. Windows sends these messages to every running program. Most of the messages will not be used by your program, and so the O/S doesn't even send some messages to your program. Usually, WinMain will send

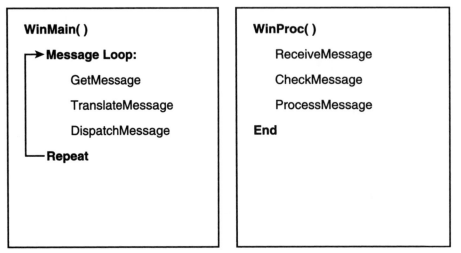

Figure 2.6
WinMain and WinProc work hand-in-hand to handle application events (such as painting the screen and responding to mouse clicks).

messages over to another function called WinProc, which works closely with WinMain to process user input and other messages. See Figure 2.6 for a comparison of WinMain and WinProc.

The WinMain Function Call

The function call for WinMain looks like this:

```
int WINAPI WinMain( HINSTANCE hInstance,
                    HINSTANCE hPrevInstance,
                    LPTSTR    lpCmdLine,
                    int       nCmdShow )
```

Let's go over these parameters:

- **HINSTANCE hInstance.** The first parameter identifies the instance of the program being called, as a program may be run several times. The Windows architecture is such that program code actually runs in a single memory space to conserve memory, while program data and variables are stored in individual memory spaces. The hInstance parameter tells the program which instance is trying to run. For the first instance, you will want to initialize the program (covered later). But if the program is run multiple times in Windows, the general practice is to just kill the new instance (also covered later).

- **HINSTANCE hPrevInstance.** The second parameter identifies the previous instance of the program and is related to the first parameter. If hPrevInstance is NULL, then this is the first instance of the program. You will want to check the value of hPrevInstance before initializing the current instance. This is absolutely critical to game programming! You will never want to have two instances of your game running at the same time.

- **LPTSTR lpCmdLine.** The third parameter is a string that contains the command-line parameters passed to the program. This could be used to tell the program to use certain options, such as "debug," which might be used to dump program execution to a text file. Usually a Windows program will use a settings (INI) file for program parameters used for runtime. But there are many cases where you would use program parameters; an image viewer, for instance, will often be passed the name of a picture file to display.

- **int nCmdShow.** The last parameter specifies how the program window is to be displayed.

You might have noticed that WinMain returns a value with the words int WINAPI in front of the function call. This is also standard practice and goes back to Windows 3.x. A return value of zero indicates that the program never made it to the main loop and was terminated prematurely. Any non-zero value indicates success.

The Complete WinMain

Listed below is more of a standard version of WinMain that you will often see in app code. I will explain each part of the function following the code listing presented here:

```
int WINAPI WinMain(HINSTANCE hInstance,
                   HINSTANCE hPrevInstance,
                   LPSTR     lpCmdLine,
                   int       nCmdShow)
{
  // declare variables
  MSG msg;
```

```
// register the class
MyRegisterClass(hInstance);

// initialize application
if (!InitInstance (hInstance, nCmdShow))
    return FALSE;

// main message loop
while (GetMessage(&msg, NULL, 0, 0))
{
    TranslateMessage(&msg);
    DispatchMessage(&msg);
}
return msg.wParam;
}
```

WinMain couldn't get much simpler than this, considering that the function processes the Windows messages for your program (I'll explain the new stuff shortly!). Even the simplest of graphics programs will need to process messages. Believe it or not, doing something as simple as printing "Hello World" on the screen requires that you wait for a message to come along for painting the screen. Infuriating, isn't it? Message handling does take some getting used to if you are used to just calling a function when you need something (like displaying text on the screen) done. Fortunately, we won't spend much time in the basics of Windows because soon I'll take you into the realm of DirectX. Once you have initialized Direct3D, there's no need to return to WinMain (patience, Grasshopper!).

Now let me explain what is going on inside WinMain in the following paragraphs. You are already familiar with the function call, so let's move along to the real code. The first section declares the variables that will be used within WinMain:

```
// declare variables
MSG msg;
```

The MSG variable is used by the GetMessage function later to retrieve the details of each Windows message. Next, the program is initialized with the following:

```
// register the class
MyRegisterClass(hInstance);
```

```
// initialize application
if (!InitInstance (hInstance, nCmdShow))
    return FALSE;
```

This code uses the hInstance variable passed to WinMain by Windows. The variable is then passed on to the InitInstance function. InitInstance is located further down in the program, and basically checks to see if the program is already running and then creates the main program window. I will go over the MyRegisterClass function shortly.

Finally, let's look at the main loop that handles all of the messages in the program:

```
// main message loop
while (GetMessage(&msg, NULL, 0, 0))
{
    TranslateMessage(&msg);
    DispatchMessage(&msg);
}
```

The while loop in this part of WinMain will continue to run forever unless a message to kill the program comes along. The GetMessage function call looks like this:

```
BOOL GetMessage(LPMSG lpMsg,
                HWND hWnd,
                UINT wMsgFilterMin,
                UINT wMsgFilterMax)
```

Let's decipher the parameters:

- **LPMSG lpMsg.** This parameter is a long pointer to a MSG structure which handles the message information.

- **HWND hWnd.** The second parameter is a handle to a specific window's messages. If NULL is passed, then GetMessage will return all of the messages for the current instance of the program.

- **UINT wMsgFilterMin** and **UINT wMsgFilterMax.** These parameters tell Get-Message to return messages in a certain range. The GetMessage call is the most crucial line of code in the entire Windows program! Without this single line in WinMain, your program will be sensory-deprived, unable to respond to the world.

The two core lines of code within the GetMessage loop work to process the message returned by GetMessage. The Windows API Reference states that the

`TranslateMessage` function is used to translate virtual-key messages into character messages, and then sent back through the Windows messaging system with `DispatchMessage`. These two functions will jointly set up the messages that you will expect to receive in `WinProc` (the window callback function) for your game window, such as `WM_CREATE` to create a window and `WM_PAINT` to draw the window. I will cover `WinProc` later in this chapter. If you feel confused about Windows messaging, don't worry about it, because this is just a precursor to working with DirectX; once you have written a Windows message loop, you will not need to deal with it again and can focus on your DirectX code.

What You Have Learned

In this chapter, you have learned how to write a simple Windows program and have explored the purposes of `WinMain` and `WinProc`. Here are the key points:

- You learned some basic Windows programming concepts.

- You learned about the importance of `WinMain`.

- You wrote a simple Windows program that displayed text in a message box.

- You learned about Windows messaging and the `WinProc` callback function.

Review Questions

Here are some review questions that will help you to think outside the box and retain some of the information covered in this chapter.

1. What does the hWnd variable represent?

2. What does the hDC variable represent?

3. What is the main function in a Windows program called?

4. What is the name of the window event callback function?

5. What function is used to display a message inside a program window?

On Your Own

These exercises will challenge you to learn more about the subjects presented in this chapter and will help you to push yourself to see what you are capable of doing on your own.

Exercise 1. The HelloWorld program displays a simple message in a text box with an exclamation point icon. Modify the program so that it will display a question mark icon instead.

Exercise 2. Now modify the HelloWorld program so that it will display your name in the message box.

CHAPTER 3

WINDOWS MESSAGING AND EVENT HANDLING

The last chapter provided you with an overview of WinMain and WinProc, and you wrote a simple Windows program. This chapter takes the ball and runs with it, going over a complete windowed program that displays something on the screen, thereby showing you how the window handle and device context work to produce output in a window. This will reinforce your grasp of the basic Windows programming model; it will also give you a glimpse of the Windows GDI (graphical device interface) and show you why it is better suited for applications rather than games (for which we have DirectX!). By dividing the tutorial on Windows programming into several chapters, my goal is to help you digest the information in a way that helps improve. Rather than going into detail and providing complete examples using the GDI (which is a waste of time), I'll go over the material quickly because I want to get into DirectX right away. If you feel that you have a solid understanding of Windows programming already, you may skip to the next chapter to learn how to write a real-time game loop. Otherwise, read on!

Here is what you will learn in this chapter:

- How to create a window.

- How to draw text on the window.

- How to draw pixels on the window.

- How the WM_PAINT event works in the WinProc callback function.

Writing a Full-Blown Windows Program

Okay, let's use the new information you learned in the last chapter to write a slightly more complicated program that actually creates a standard window and draws text and graphics on the window. Sounds pretty simple, right? Well, it is! There's a lot of startup code when you need to draw on a window, so let's learn by example.

Create another Win32 Application project (call it "WindowTest") using Visual C++ and add a new main.cpp file to the project. I want to give you a complete listing for a more fully functional Windows program, after which we will reverse-engineer the program and explain each line of code in detail. See if you can figure out what's going on as you type in the program. If you would prefer to not type in the program, you can open the project from the CD-ROM in \sources\ chapter03\WindowTest (and don't worry, I won't call you lazy).

After you have compiled and run the program, you should see output like that in Figure 3.1. Oops, not sure how to compile the program? No problem, let me show you. The easiest way is to press Ctrl+F5 to build and run the program (assuming there are no errors). If you want to just compile the code, press Ctrl+Shift+B (for build). You can also perform these actions from the Build menu (Build Solution) and the Debug menu (Start Without Debugging).

Figure 3.1
The WindowTest program

```
// Beginning Game Programming
// Chapter 3
// WindowTest program

//header files to include
#include <windows.h>
#include <stdlib.h>
#include <time.h>

//application title
#define APPTITLE "Hello World"

//function prototypes (forward declarations)
BOOL InitInstance(HINSTANCE,int);
ATOM MyRegisterClass(HINSTANCE);
LRESULT CALLBACK WinProc(HWND,UINT,WPARAM,LPARAM);

//the window event callback function
LRESULT CALLBACK WinProc(HWND hWnd, UINT message, WPARAM wParam, LPARAM lParam)
{
    PAINTSTRUCT ps;
    HDC hdc;
    char *szHello = "Hello World!";
    RECT rt;
    int x, y, n;
    COLORREF c;

    switch (message)
```

```
{
  case WM_PAINT:
      //get the dimensions of the window
      GetClientRect(hWnd, &rt);

      //start drawing on device context
      hdc = BeginPaint(hWnd, &ps);

      //draw some text
      DrawText(hdc, szHello, strlen(szHello), &rt, DT_CENTER);

      //draw 1000 random pixels
      for (n=0; n<3000; n++)
      {
          x = rand() % (rt.right - rt.left);
          y = rand() % (rt.bottom - rt.top);
          c = RGB(rand()%256, rand()%256, rand()%256);
          SetPixel(hdc, x, y, c);
      }
      //stop drawing
      EndPaint(hWnd, &ps);
      break;

  case WM_DESTROY:
      PostQuitMessage(0);
      break;
  }
  return DefWindowProc(hWnd, message, wParam, lParam);
}

//helper function to set up the window properties
ATOM MyRegisterClass(HINSTANCE hInstance)
{
  //create the window class structure
  WNDCLASSEX wc;
  wc.cbSize = sizeof(WNDCLASSEX);

  //fill the struct with info
  wc.style          = CS_HREDRAW | CS_VREDRAW;
  wc.lpfnWndProc    = (WNDPROC)WinProc;
  wc.cbClsExtra     = 0;
  wc.cbWndExtra     = 0;
  wc.hInstance      = hInstance;
```

```
   wc.hIcon              = NULL;
   wc.hCursor            = LoadCursor(NULL, IDC_ARROW);
   wc.hbrBackground      = (HBRUSH)GetStockObject(WHITE_BRUSH);
   wc.lpszMenuName       = NULL;
   wc.lpszClassName      = APPTITLE;
   wc.hIconSm            = NULL;

   //set up the window with the class info
   return RegisterClassEx(&wc);
}


//helper function to create the window and refresh it
BOOL InitInstance(HINSTANCE hInstance, int nCmdShow)
{
   HWND hWnd;

   //create a new window
   hWnd = CreateWindow(
        APPTITLE,               //window class
        APPTITLE,               //title bar
        WS_OVERLAPPEDWINDOW,    //window style
        CW_USEDEFAULT,          //x position of window
        CW_USEDEFAULT,          //y position of window
        500,                    //width of the window
        400,                    //height of the window
        NULL,                   //parent window
        NULL,                   //menu
        hInstance,              //application instance
        NULL);                  //window parameters

   //was there an error creating the window?
   if (!hWnd)
        return FALSE;

   //display the window
   ShowWindow(hWnd, nCmdShow);
   UpdateWindow(hWnd);

   return TRUE;
}


//entry point for a Windows program
int WINAPI WinMain(HINSTANCE hInstance,
```

```
                    HINSTANCE  hPrevInstance,
                    LPSTR      lpCmdLine,
                    int        nCmdShow)
{
  // declare variables
  MSG msg;

  // register the class
  MyRegisterClass(hInstance);

  // initialize application
  if (!InitInstance (hInstance, nCmdShow))
      return FALSE;

  //set random number seed
  srand(time(NULL));

  //main message loop
  while (GetMessage(&msg, NULL, 0, 0))
  {
     TranslateMessage(&msg);
     DispatchMessage(&msg);
  }
  return msg.wParam;
}
```

Okay, well that's the complete listing for the WindowText program, your first complete Windows program that features a standard program window. Now let's reverse-engineer it and see what makes a Windows program tick, shall we?

Understanding InitInstance

InitInstance is the first function called by WinMain to set up the program. InitInstance basically just creates the program window. This code could be just inserted into WinMain, but it is more convenient to have it in a separate function (this has something to do with dealing with multiple instances, when you run a program more than once). Note that InitInstance is not a primary Windows function like WinMain, but simply a "helper" function to which you could give a different name if you wished. The instance handle is a global variable used in the program to keep track of the main instance. I will show you what the function call looks like and what a typical InitInstance should do. You shouldn't treat this as the law, though, because it's just a standard practice, not a requirement.

The InitInstance Function Call

The function call for InitInstance looks like this:

```
BOOL InitInstance( HINSTANCE hInstance,
                   int       nCmdShow )
```

Let's go over the parameters here:

- **HINSTANCE hInstance.** The first parameter is passed by WinMain with the program instance that it receives from Windows. InitInstance will check this with the global instance to see if the new instance needs to be killed (the usual procedure in Windows). When this happens, the main instance of the program is set as the foreground window. To the user, it will seem as if running the program again just brought the original instance forward.

- **int nCmdShow.** The second parameter is passed to InitInstance by WinMain, which receives the parameter from Windows. The most common values for this parameter include SW_HIDE and SW_SHOW, and are often sent by Windows based on events in the operating system (such as a power down).

The InitInstance function returns a BOOL value, which is either TRUE or FALSE, and simply tells WinMain whether startup succeeded or failed. Note that WinMain does not send InitInstance any of the command-line parameters. If you want to process the lpCmdLine string, then you can either create a new function to handle it or just process the parameters inside WinMain, which is how it is usually done.

The Structure of InitInstance

Quite often in application programming it is recommended that you use a resource table for string handling. Resource strings are really a matter of preference (and I, for one, do not use them). There is the possibility that you will want to port the text in your games to another language, and this is where storing strings as resources will come in handy. In general practice, however, it's not commonly used. The code to display a simple message from a resource causes a program to look up every string used, which slows down the program and adds a lot of clutter to the code, especially from the point of view of a beginner.

The InitInstance function is pretty simple, as shown here. I will explain each section of the function after the code listing that follows:

```
BOOL InitInstance(HINSTANCE hInstance, int nCmdShow)
{
    HWND hWnd;

    //create a new window
    hWnd = CreateWindow(
        APPTITLE,                //window class
        APPTITLE,                //title bar
        WS_OVERLAPPEDWINDOW,     //window style
        CW_USEDEFAULT,           //x position of window
        CW_USEDEFAULT,           //y position of window
        500,                     //width of the window
        400,                     //height of the window
        NULL,                    //parent window
        NULL,                    //menu
        hInstance,               //application instance
        NULL);                   //window parameters

    //was there an error creating the window?
    if (!hWnd)
        return FALSE;

    //display the window
    ShowWindow(hWnd, nCmdShow);
    UpdateWindow(hWnd);

    return TRUE;
}
```

Note that until this section of code, there was actually no user interface for the program at all! The main window that is created with the CreateWindow function becomes the window used by your program. The whole point of InitInstance is to create the new window needed by this application and display it. The list of parameters for CreateWindow includes comments that describe what each parameter does. After the window has been created (and verified), the last few lines of code are used to actually display the newly created window:

```
ShowWindow(hWnd, nCmdShow);
UpdateWindow(hWnd);
```

The hWnd value is passed to these functions by the CreateWindow function. At the point of creation, the window existed in Windows but was not yet visible. UpdateWindow tells the new window to draw itself by sending a WM_PAINT message to the window handler. Oddly enough, the program talks to itself quite often in this manner; this is common in Windows programming. The final line in InitInstance returns a value of TRUE back to WinMain:

```
return TRUE;
```

If you recall, WinMain took this return value very seriously! If InitInstance doesn't like something that is going on, WinMain will end the program:

```
// initialize application
if (!InitInstance (hInstance, nCmdShow))
    return FALSE;
```

Returning a value from within WinMain, whether it is TRUE or FALSE, will terminate the program immediately. If InitInstance returns a value of TRUE, recall that WinMain will then go into the message handling while loop, and the program will start to run.

Understanding MyRegisterClass

MyRegisterClass is a very simple function that sets up the values for the main window class used by your program. The code in MyRegisterClass could have easily been placed inside WinMain, and MyRegisterClass could also have easily been put inside WinMain. In fact, all of this stuff could have been crammed into WinMain and Windows would not have complained. But it makes the program a whole lot easier to understand when the initialization code for a Windows program is segregated into recognizable (and standard) helper functions. WinMain calls InitInstance and sets up the program window by calling MyRegisterClass. This is another optional helper function that is not required (although you must insert the code *somewhere*, so why not just use it?). You may rename the function if you wish, also.

The MyRegisterClass Function Call

MyRegisterClass is passed two parameters by InitInstance so that it can set up the window class settings:

```
ATOM MyRegisterClass( HINSTANCE hInstance,

                      LPTSTR szWindowClass )
```

You are already familiar with both of these parameters. hInstance is the very same instance passed to InitInstance by WinMain. This variable gets around! As you recall, hInstance stores the current instance of the running program, and is copied into a global variable in InitInstance. The second parameter is easy enough to follow, as it was set up in InitInstance as a char * with an initial window class name (in this case, "Hello World"). Recall also that this can be a Unicode string.

It is also possible to use a LPTSTR or TCHAR and avoid the pointer symbol. Often a LPTSTR is more clear, but many C programmers are used to the common char *szVar format, which is why I used char * originally. There really is no standard, and it is primarily a matter of programmer preference (or perhaps part of a set of coding standards set forth by an employer). I tend to use whatever seems to make the most sense in a given situation. If char * seems easier to understand in a code listing, that is what I use (especially when communicating with a beginner on a sticky programming issue like initializing a Windows program).

The Structure of MyRegisterClass

The MyRegisterClass() function is listed below. I will explain the function in detail following the code listing:

```
ATOM MyRegisterClass(HINSTANCE hInstance)
{
    //create the window class structure
    WNDCLASSEX wc;
    wc.cbSize = sizeof(WNDCLASSEX);

    //fill the struct with info
    wc.style          = CS_HREDRAW | CS_VREDRAW;
    wc.lpfnWndProc    = (WNDPROC)WinProc;
    wc.cbClsExtra     = 0;
    wc.cbWndExtra     = 0;
    wc.hInstance      = hInstance;
    wc.hIcon          = NULL;
    wc.hCursor        = LoadCursor(NULL, IDC_ARROW);
    wc.hbrBackground  = (HBRUSH)GetStockObject(WHITE_BRUSH);
    wc.lpszMenuName   = NULL;
    wc.lpszClassName  = APPTITLE;
    wc.hIconSm        = NULL;
```

```
    //set up the window with the class info
    return RegisterClassEx(&wc);
}
```

First, MyRegisterClass defines a new variable, wc, of type WNDCLASS. Each member of the structure is defined in MyRegisterClass in order, so there is no need to list the struct.

The window style, wc.style, is set to CS_HREDRAW | CS_VREDRAW. The pipe symbol is a method for combining bits. The CS_HREDRAW value causes the program window to be completely redrawn if a movement or size adjustment changes the width. Likewise, CS_VREDRAW causes the window to be completely redrawn when the height is adjusted.

The variable, wc.lpfnWinProc, requires a little more explanation, as it is not simply a variable, but a long pointer to a callback function. This is of great importance, as without this value setting, messages will not be delivered to the program window (hWnd). The callback window procedure is automatically called when a Windows message comes along with that hWnd value. This applies to all messages, including user input and window repaint. Any button presses, screen updates, or other events will go through this callback procedure. You may give this function any name you like, such as BigBadGameWindowProc, as long as it has a return value of LRESULT CALLBACK and the appropriate parameters.

The struct variables wc.cbClsExtra and wc.cbWndExtra should be set to zero most of the time. These values just add extra bytes of memory to a window procedure, and you really do not need to use them.

wc.hInstance is set to the hInstance parameter passed to MyRegisterClass. The main window needs to know what instance it is using. If you really want to confuse your program, set each new instance to point to the same program window. Now that would be funny! This should never happen because new instances of your game should be killed rather than being allowed to run.

wc.hIcon and wc.hCursor are pretty self-explanatory. The LoadIcon function is normally used to load an icon image from a resource, and the MAKEINTRESOURCE macro returns a string value for the resource identifier. This macro is not something that is commonly used for a game (unless the game needs to run in a window).

wc.hbrBackground is set to the handle for a brush used for drawing the background of the program window. The stock object, WHITE_BRUSH, is used by default. This may be a bitmap image, a custom brush, or any other color.

`wc.lpszMenuName` is set to the name of the program menu, also a resource. I will not be using menus in the sample programs in this book.

`wc.lpszClassName` is set to the `szWindowClass` parameter passed to `MyRegisterClass`. This gives the window a specific class name and is used for message handling along with `hWnd`.

Finally, `MyRegisterClass` calls the `RegisterClassEx` function. This function is passed the `WNDCLASS` variable, `wc`, that was set up with the window details. A return value of zero indicates failure. If the window is successfully registered with Windows, the value will be passed back to `InitInstance`.

Whew—how about that to rack your brain?! I don't expect you to remember all of this information right now, but it is always a good idea as a game programmer to understand how everything works so you can get the most out of the hardware you're working on.

Understanding WinProc

`WinProc` is the window callback procedure that Windows uses to communicate events to your program. Recall that `MyRegisterClass` set up the `WNDCLASS` struct that was passed to `RegisterClassEx`. Once the class is registered, the window can then be created and displayed on the screen. One of the fields in the struct, `lpfnWinProc`, is set to the name of a window callback procedure, typically called `WinProc`. This function will handle all of the messages sent to the main program window. As a result, `WinProc` will typically be the longest function in the main program source code file. Figure 3.2 shows how `WinProc` handles event messages.

The WinProc Function Call

The window callback function looks like this:

```
LRESULT CALLBACK WinProc( HWND hWnd,
                          UINT message,
                          WPARAM wParam,
                          LPARAM lParam )
```

You will want to get to know this function, because it is the key to initializing Direct3D. The parameters are simple and straightforward, and represent the real "engine" of a windows program. Recall that this information was retrieved earlier by the `GetMessage` function in `WinMain`. Do not confuse `InitInstance` with `WinProc`, though. `InitInstance` is only run once to set up the window callback

Program Event Handler

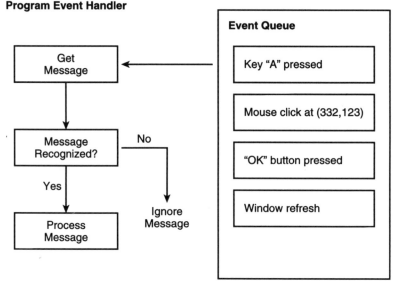

Figure 3.2
The WinProc callback function handles events related to the application.

procedure. After that, InitInstance is out of the picture and WinProc takes over, receiving and handling all messages.

Let's take a look at the parameters for WinProc:

- **HWND hWnd.** The first parameter is the window handle. Typically in a game, you will create a new handle to a device context, known as a hDC, using the hWnd as a parameter. Before DirectX came along, this was once crucial in the development of Windows games. Now, after you receive the window handle and pass it to DirectDraw/Direct3D, it is no longer needed.

- **UINT message.** The second parameter is the message that is being sent to the window callback procedure. The message could be anything, and you might not even need to use it. For this reason, there is a way to pass the message along to the default message handler (discussed in the next section).

- **WPARAM wParam and LPARAM lParam.** The last two parameters are the high and low bit value parameters passed along with certain command messages. I'll explain this in the next section.

The Structure of WinProc

The window callback procedure will get modified quite a bit during a game development project, but it is the goal of the game library developed later in the book to help you avoid mucking around inside WinProc. The game library will outsource, so to speak, the window messages to custom classes that will handle each message individually. There are really only a handful of messages related to game programming, and those are the only messages we want to see. The game library will make it easy to work with these messages.

Here is a simple version of a window callback procedure, with an explanation following:

```
LRESULT CALLBACK WinProc(HWND hWnd, UINT message, WPARAM wParam, LPARAM lParam)
{
    PAINTSTRUCT ps;
    HDC hdc;
    char *szHello = "Hello World!";
    RECT rt;
    int x, y, n;
    COLORREF c;

    switch (message)
    {
      case WM_PAINT:
        //get the dimensions of the window
        GetClientRect(hWnd, &rt);

        //start drawing on device context
        hdc = BeginPaint(hWnd, &ps);

        //draw some text
        DrawText(hdc, szHello, strlen(szHello), &rt, DT_CENTER);

        //draw 1000 random pixels
        for (n=0; n<3000; n++)
        {
          x = rand() % (rt.right - rt.left);
          y = rand() % (rt.bottom - rt.top);
          c = RGB(rand()%256, rand()%256, rand()%256);
          SetPixel(hdc, x, y, c);
        }

        //stop drawing
        EndPaint(hWnd, &ps);
        break;
```

```
        case WM_DESTROY:
            PostQuitMessage(0);
            break;
    }
    return DefWindowProc(hWnd, message, wParam, lParam);
}
```

As you are already familiar with the parameters, I'll get right down to business. This function can be broken down into two main parts, the declaration and the switch statement, which is like a large nested if statement. Within the switch statement, there are also two main parts, case statements for a command message and for regular messages. A command will use the last two parameters of WinProc, wParam and lParam, while regular messages usually do not need the parameters.

There are several variables declared at the top:

```
PAINTSTRUCT ps;
HDC hdc;
char *szHello = "Hello World!";
RECT rt;
int x, y, n;
COLORREF c;
```

The PAINTSTRUCT variable, ps, is used in the WM_PAINT message handler to start and stop a screen update, sort of like unlocking and then locking the device context while making updates (so the screen is not garbled in the process). The variable, hdc, is also used in the WM_PAINT message handler to retrieve the device context of the program's window. The other variables are used to display the message on the screen (szHello) and draw pixels on the window (x, y, n, and c).

Following the variable declarations is the switch (message) statement. This is basically an easy way to handle multiple messages, and is far better than using nested if statements. switch is far better able to handle a large number of conditional tests, which is why it is used in WinProc to check the messages.

Let me explain WM_DESTROY first. The WM_DESTROY message identifier tells the window that it is time to shut down; your program should gracefully close down by removing objects from memory and then call the PostQuitMessage function to end the program. When you take the next step and start writing Direct3D code, this will be the only message of concern, as WM_PAINT is not needed in a Direct3D program.

Okay, now back to the first message identifier, WM_PAINT. This is definitely the most interesting message for game programming because this is where the window updates are handled. Take a look at the code for WM_PAINT again:

```
//get the dimensions of the window
GetClientRect(hWnd, &rt);

//start drawing on device context
hdc = BeginPaint(hWnd, &ps);

//draw some text
DrawText(hdc, szHello, strlen(szHello), &rt, DT_CENTER);
//draw 1000 random pixels
for (n=0; n<3000; n++)
{
    x = rand() % (rt.right - rt.left);
    y = rand() % (rt.bottom - rt.top);
    c = RGB(rand()%256, rand()%256, rand()%256);
    SetPixel(hdc, x, y, c);
}

//stop drawing
EndPaint(hWnd, &ps);
break;
```

The first line calls BeginPaint to lock the device context for an update (using the window handle and PAINTSTRUCT variables). The next line calls GetClientRect to copy the program window's rectangular area into a temporary RECT variable. This is used by DrawText to center the message in the window. Note that BeginPaint returns the device context for the program window. This is necessary at every refresh because, although it is uncommon, the device context is not guaranteed to be constant while the program is running (for instance, imagine that memory runs low and your program is filed away into virtual memory and then retrieved again—such an event would almost certainly generate a new device context).

The only line that actually does something to the user interface is the third line, which calls DrawText. This function displays a message at the destination device context. The DT_CENTER parameter at the end tells DrawText to center the message at the top center of the passed rectangle. Of course, there is also the section of code that draws pixels on the screen. Did you know that if you resize the window, all the pixels will be redrawn? Go ahead and try it! Pretty cool, huh? That demonstrates WM_PAINT perfectly: it is called when the window needs to be redrawn. If you resize the window, multiple calls to WM_PAINT occur, each time with a different rectangle (returned by GetClientRect).

The last line of the paint message handler calls EndPaint to shut down the graphics system for that iteration of the message handler.

Note

WM_PAINT is not called continuously, as in a real-time loop, but only when the window must be redrawn. Therefore, WM_PAINT is not a suitable place to insert the screen refresh code for a game. Instead, as you will learn in the next chapter, you must modify the loop in WinMain to have code run in a real-time loop.

What You Have Learned

In this chapter, you have learned the basics of Windows programming in preparation for DirectX coding. Here are the key points:

- You learned even more Windows programming concepts.

- You wrote a simple program to display "Hello World."

- You learned how to draw pixels in a window.

- You dissected a complete Windows program and learned how it works.

Review Questions

Here are some review questions that will help you to think outside the box and retain some of the information covered in this chapter.

1. What does the WinMain function do?

2. What does the WinProc function do?

3. What is a program instance?

4. What function can you use to draw pixels in a window?

5. What function is used to draw text inside a program window?

On Your Own

These exercises will challenge you to learn more about the subjects presented in this chapter and will help you to push yourself to see what you are capable of doing on your own.

Exercise 1. The window in the WindowTest program has a white background (WHITE_BRUSH). Modify the program so that it uses a black background.

Exercise 2. The WindowTest program displays a text message at the top center of the program window. Modify the program so that it displays the text message at the upper left corner of the program window.

CHAPTER 4

THE REAL-TIME GAME LOOP

Chapter 3 was basically the final one to discuss the basics of Windows programming. This chapter moves on to explore real-time game loops—specifically, how to get a real-time loop out of WinMain, which doesn't seem to have any support for it! You will learn a few new tricks in this chapter that will get the real-time loop going in preparation for DirectX in the next chapter. By the time you have finished this chapter, you will have learned how to write a game loop that will drive the rest of the code in the book. So pay attention!

Here is what you will learn in this chapter:

- How to create a real-time game loop.

- How to call other game-related functions from `WinMain`.

- How to use the `PeekMessage` function.

- How to draw bitmaps using the GDI.

What Is a Game Loop?

There's a lot more to Windows and DirectX than I will cover in these few chapters. I want to focus on game creation rather than spending 200 pages discussing the logistics of the O/S or game library (DirectX, in this case). What I'd really like to do is get away from the Windows code and come up with just a simple, run-of-the-mill `main` function, which is standard in C ++ programs (but which is missing from Windows programs, which use `WinMain`).

One way to do this is to stick all of the basic Windows code (including `WinMain`) inside one source code file (such as winmain.cpp) and then use another source code file (such as game.cpp) just for the game. Then, it would be a simple matter to call some sort of `main` function from within `WinMain` and your "game code" will start running right after the program window is created and all the Windows overhead is handled. This is actually a standard practice on many systems and libraries, abstracting away the O/S and presenting the programmer with a standard interface. One such library is Allegro, a cross-platform game library available for Windows, Linux, Mac OS X, and Unix systems. If you write a program that uses Allegro, then your program can be compiled on any of these systems without modification! This brings "porting" down to a manageable level, because it requires little effort to re-compile a program for Linux after it has been developed for Windows (and vice versa). I don't really want to move in that direction here, but it is a good example of how beneficial it is to abstract your code as much as possible.

The Old WinMain

Here's the version of `WinMain` that you saw in the last few chapters:

```
int WINAPI WinMain(HINSTANCE hInstance,
                   HINSTANCE hPrevInstance,
                   LPSTR     lpCmdLine,
                   int       nCmdShow)
```

```
{
    MSG msg;
    MyRegisterClass(hInstance);
    if (!InitInstance (hInstance, nCmdShow))
        return FALSE;

    while (GetMessage(&msg, NULL, 0, 0))
    {
        TranslateMessage(&msg);
        DispatchMessage(&msg);
    }
    return msg.wParam;
}
```

There's just one problem with this version of `WinMain`; it doesn't have a continuous loop, just a limited loop that processes any pending messages and then exits.

The Need for Continuity

When you have sprites or 3D models animating on the screen, with enemy characters moving around and with guns and explosions and thermonuclear detonations in the background, you need things to keep moving regardless of Windows messages! In short, listed above is a stodgy, inanimate version of `WinMain` that is totally unsuitable for a game. You need something that keeps on running regardless of whether there are event messages coming in. The key to creating a real-time loop that keeps running all of the time regardless of what Windows is doing is modifying the `while` loop in `WinMain`.

First of all, the `while` loop is conditional upon a message being present, while a game should keep running through the loop regardless of whether there's a message or not. This definitely needs to be changed! See Figure 4.1 for an illustration of the current `WinMain`.

The Real-Time Terminator

Notice how the main loop terminates if there are no messages, but will keep on processing any messages that *are* present. What would happen if the main game loop were called from this version of `WinMain`? Well, once in a while the game loop would execute and things would be updated on the screen, but more often it would do nothing at all. Why is that? Because this is an event-driven `while` loop,

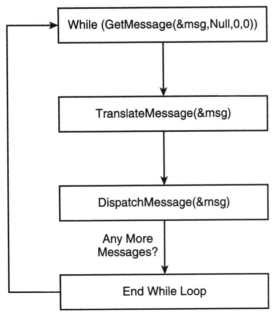

Figure 4.1
The standard `WinMain` is not friendly to a real-time game loop.

and we need a common, run-of-the-mill *procedural* `while` loop that keeps going, and going, and going ... regardless of what's happening. A real-time game loop has to keep running non-stop until the game ends. And in case you were wondering, I'll show you how to create a consistent, regular frame rate in the next chapter. Our goal at this point is to make things run as blindingly fast as possible, and then worry about timing later. Always work on getting something to work first, and then optimize or clean it up it later (if you have time).

Now let's look at another illustration, in Figure 4.2, that shows a new version of `WinMain`, only this time it features a real-time game loop that doesn't just loop through the events but keeps on looping regardless of the events.

WinMain and Looping

The key to making a real-time loop is to modify the `while` loop in `WinMain` so that it runs indefinitely, and then check for messages *inside* the `while` loop. By indefinitely, I mean that the loop will keep running forever unless something interrupts the loop and causes it to exit (by calling `exit` or `return` inside the loop). In addition to using an endless loop, there's an alternative to calling the `GetMessage` function to detect event messages coming in. The alternate function

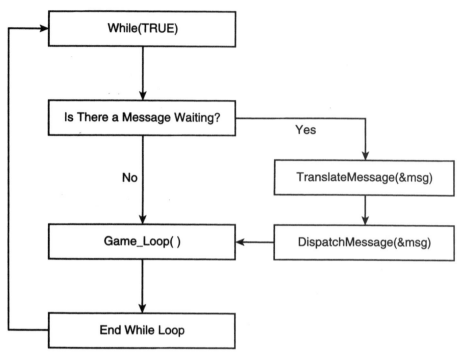

Figure 4.2
The newly modified WinMain is much more friendly to a real-time game loop.

is called PeekMessage. As the name implies, this function can look at incoming messages without necessarily retrieving them out of the message queue.

Now, as you don't want the message queue to just pile up (it will probably crash your program eventually), you want to use PeekMessage in place of GetMessage, regardless of whether there are messages or not. If there are messages, fine, go ahead and process them. Otherwise, just return control to the next line of code. As it turns out, GetMessage is not very polite, and doesn't let us keep the game loop going unless a message is actually sitting in the message queue to be processed. PeekMessage, on the other hand, is polite and will just pass control on to the next statement if no message is waiting.

Time to Take a Peek

Let's take a look at the format of the PeekMessage function:

```
BOOL PeekMessage(
    LPMSG lpMsg,              //pointer to message struct
    HWND hWnd,               //window handle
```

```
UINT wMsgFilterMin,      //first message
UINT wMsgFilterMax,      //last message
UINT wRemoveMsg);        //removal flag
```

Now for a rundown on the parameters:

- **LPMSG lpMsg.** This parameter is a pointer to the message structure that describes the message (type, parameters, and so on).

- **HWND hWnd.** This is a handle to the window that is associated with the event.

- **UINT wMsgFilterMin.** This is the first message that has been received.

- **UINT wMsgFilterMax.** This is the last message that has been received.

- **UINT wRemoveMsg.** This is a flag that determines how the message will be handled after it has been read. This can be PM_NOREMOVE to leave the message in the message queue, or PM_REMOVE to remove the message from the queue after it has been read.

Plugging PeekMessage into WinMain

Okay, now let's make use of PeekMessage so that you can see how this all fits in with writing a game. Here's a new version of the main loop in WinMain with the new PeekMessage function in place (along with a few extra lines that I'll explain shortly).

```
while (TRUE)
{
    if (PeekMessage(&msg, NULL, 0, 0, PM_REMOVE))
    {
        //look for quit message
        if (msg.message = = WM_QUIT)
            break;
        //decode and pass messages on to WndProc
        TranslateMessage(&msg);
        DispatchMessage(&msg);
    }

    //process game loop regardless of Windows messages!
    Game_Run();
}
```

In this new version of the while loop you'll notice that PeekMessage is now called instead of GetMessage, and you'll recognize the PM_REMOVE parameter, which causes any event messages to be pulled out of the queue and processed. In actuality, there are really no messages coming in to a DirectX program (except perhaps WM_QUIT) because most of the processing takes place in the DirectX libraries.

Take a look at the if statement that looks for the WM_QUIT message. This is really the only case that causes the while loop to exit; otherwise, it keeps on running indefinitely.

So, suppose you now have a game loop. What can you do with it? I sneaked in an extra line of code that should have caught your eye, as it is called Game_Run. This function is not part of Windows; in fact, it doesn't even exist yet. You're going to write this function yourself shortly! It will also make more sense in the next chapter when you finally get a chance to start digging into DirectX code.

That said, let's take a look at the finished version of WinMain:

```
int WINAPI WinMain(HINSTANCE  hInstance,
                   HINSTANCE  hPrevInstance,
                   LPSTR      lpCmdLine,
                   int        nCmdShow)
{
    // declare variables
    MSG msg;

    // register the class
    MyRegisterClass(hInstance);

    // initialize application
    if (!InitInstance (hInstance, nCmdShow))
        return FALSE;

    //initialize the game
    Game_Init();

    // main message loop
    while (TRUE)
    {
        if (PeekMessage(&msg, NULL, 0, 0, PM_REMOVE))
        {
```

```
        //look for quit message
        if (msg.message == WM_QUIT)
            break;

        //decode and pass messages on to WndProc
        TranslateMessage(&msg);
        DispatchMessage(&msg);
    }

        //process game loop regardless of Windows messages!
        Game_Run();

    }
    //do cleanup
    Game_End();

    //end program
    return msg.wParam;
}
```

Okay, I admit it; I skipped ahead a little and sneaked something in without warning. What I'm talking about is the unknown function call to Game_Init and a similar call to Game_End. Now, don't get upset—I'm not going to make a habit of dumping new things on you without explanation. But sometimes I think it's interesting to show how something works before really going over it. In this case, what I'm doing is planning ahead a little. I've written enough games to know that initialization is a task best handled before the game loop starts.

State-Driven Games

This is actually one of those annoying sources of debate among die-hard game programmers. Some argue that a game should be state-driven from the start, and all function calls should be abstracted in the extreme so that code is portable to other platforms (for instance, some people write code wherein all the Windows code is hidden away, and they'll then have a similar Mac OS X or Linux version of the O/S code available, at which point it's possible to port much of the game to those platforms without too much difficulty). I'm going to delve into this a *little* just because it's such a good habit to develop! Even while being stressed out over getting a game finished and pounding out code for 16 hours at a time, if you are a true professional, you'll manage that while also sparing some neurons for higher-level things like code management and pondering issues that might come up in the future for your game.

The GameLoop Project

In order to show you how this discussion of real-time programming applies, I'm going to have you create a new project that includes the new version of WinMain and all these new functions that I've been sneaking into the code listings.

Go ahead and create a new Win32 Application like usual, with no sample code included (an empty project). Name the new project GameLoop, as shown in Figure 4.3. Next, open the File menu, select New to bring up the New dialog. Select C++ Source File from the list of available files to add to the project. (Remember to ignore the C++ part and name your file with a .c extension.) Name the new file winmain.cpp and click OK to add the file to your new project, as shown in Figure 4.4. As an option, you can also load the GameLoop project off the CD-ROM.

Source Code for the GameLoop Program

The code I will present here will be the basis for all of the programs that will follow, with only very few changes to come. You might notice quite a few minor improvements from the similar code listing presented in the last chapter. Go ahead and open the winmain.cpp file in the GameLoop project and type in the following code listing. I'll go over it shortly.

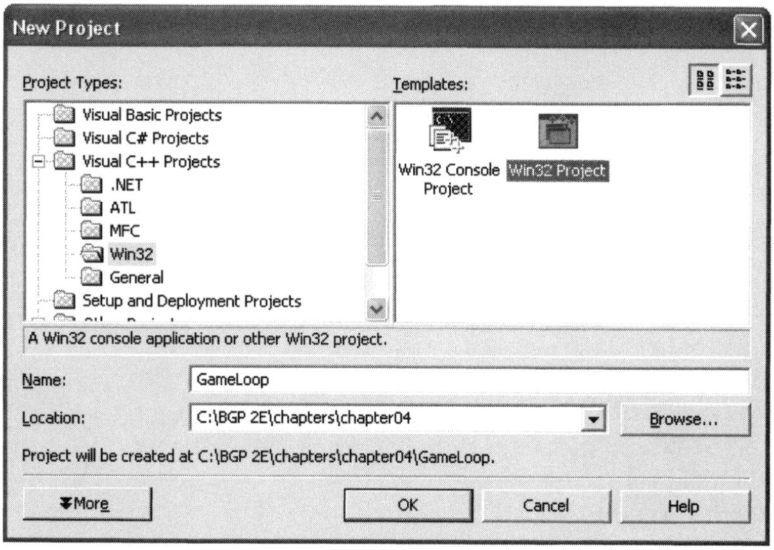

Figure 4.3
Creating a new Win32 Application project called GameLoop

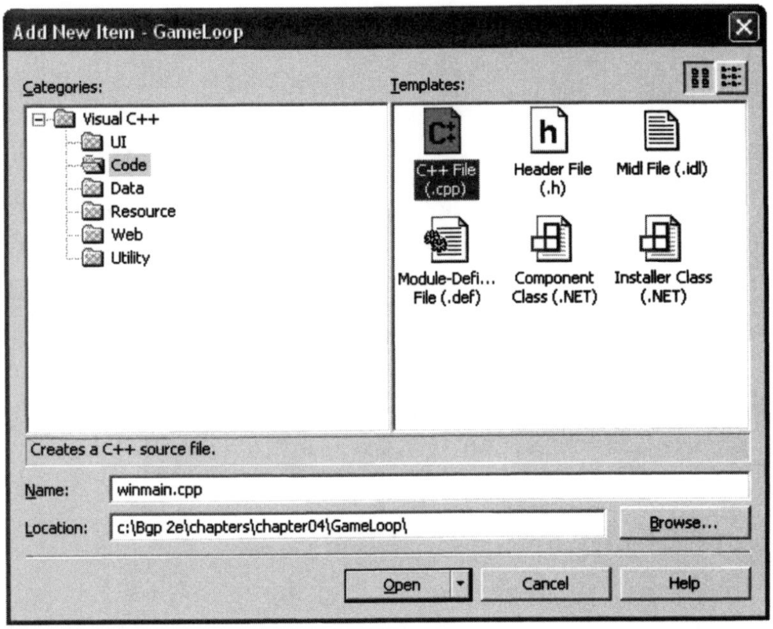

Figure 4.4
Adding the winmain.cpp file to the project

```
// Beginning Game Programming, Second Edition
// Chapter 4
// GameLoop project

#include <windows.h>
#include <winuser.h>
#include <stdio.h>
#include <stdlib.h>
#include <time.h>

#define APPTITLE "Game Loop"

//function prototypes
LRESULT CALLBACK WinProc(HWND,UINT,WPARAM,LPARAM);
ATOM MyRegisterClass(HINSTANCE);
BOOL InitInstance(HINSTANCE,int);
void DrawBitmap(HDC,char*,int,int);
void Game_Init();
void Game_Run();
void Game_End();
```

```
//local variables
HWND global_hwnd;
HDC global_hdc;

//the window event callback function
LRESULT CALLBACK WinProc(HWND hWnd, UINT message, WPARAM wParam, LPARAM lParam)
{
      global_hwnd = hWnd;
      global_hdc = GetDC(hWnd);

      switch (message)
      {
           case WM_DESTROY:
                 PostQuitMessage(0);
                 break;
      }
      return DefWindowProc(hWnd, message, wParam, lParam);
}

//helper function to set up the window properties
ATOM MyRegisterClass(HINSTANCE hInstance)
{
    //create the window class structure
    WNDCLASSEX wc;
    wc.cbSize = sizeof(WNDCLASSEX);

    //fill the struct with info
    wc.style          = CS_HREDRAW | CS_VREDRAW;
    wc.lpfnWndProc    = (WNDPROC)WinProc;
    wc.cbClsExtra     = 0;
    wc.cbWndExtra     = 0;
    wc.hInstance      = hInstance;
    wc.hIcon          = NULL;
    wc.hCursor        = LoadCursor(NULL, IDC_ARROW);
    wc.hbrBackground  = (HBRUSH)GetStockObject(BLACK_BRUSH);
    wc.lpszMenuName   = NULL;
    wc.lpszClassName  = APPTITLE;
    wc.hIconSm        = NULL;

    //set up the window with the class info
    return RegisterClassEx(&wc);
}
```

```
//helper function to create the window and refresh it
BOOL InitInstance(HINSTANCE hInstance, int nCmdShow)
{
    HWND hWnd;

    //create a new window
    hWnd = CreateWindow(
        APPTITLE,               //window class
        APPTITLE,               //title bar
        WS_OVERLAPPEDWINDOW,    //window style
        CW_USEDEFAULT,          //x position of window
        CW_USEDEFAULT,          //y position of window
        500,                    //width of the window
        400,                    //height of the window
    NULL,                   //parent window
        NULL,                   //menu
        hInstance,              //application instance
        NULL);                  //window parameters

    //was there an error creating the window?
    if (!hWnd)
      return FALSE;

    //display the window
    ShowWindow(hWnd, nCmdShow);
    UpdateWindow(hWnd);

    return TRUE;
}

//entry point for a Windows program
int WINAPI WinMain(HINSTANCE hInstance,
                   HINSTANCE hPrevInstance,
                   LPSTR     lpCmdLine,
                   int       nCmdShow)
{
    int done = 0;
    MSG msg;

    // register the class
    MyRegisterClass(hInstance);

    // initialize application
    if (!InitInstance (hInstance, nCmdShow))
      return FALSE;
```

```
    //initialize the game
    Game_Init();

    // main message loop
    while (!done)
    {
        if (PeekMessage(&msg, NULL, 0, 0, PM_REMOVE))
        {
            //look for quit message
            if (msg.message == WM_QUIT)
                done = 1;

            //decode and pass messages on to WndProc
            TranslateMessage(&msg);
            DispatchMessage(&msg);
        }

        //process game loop
        Game_Run();
    }

    //do cleanup
    Game_End();

    return msg.wParam;
}
```

Wait, We're Not Finished Yet!

Okay, there's more to this code listing but I wanted to pause here for a moment because that's the end of the Windows code. It might be better to put these functions in a separate source file, but things are simple enough at this point that doing so isn't necessary. Now let's add the two additional functions to the bottom of the listing:

```
void Game_Init()
{
    //initialize the game...
    //load bitmaps, meshes, textures, sounds, etc.

    //initialize the random number generator
    srand(time(NULL));
}
```

```
void Game_Run()
{
    //this is called once every frame
    //do not include your own loop here!

    int x = 0, y = 0;
    RECT rect;
    GetClientRect(global_hwnd, &rect);

    if (rect.right > 0)
    {
        x = rand() % (rect.right - rect.left);
        y = rand() % (rect.bottom - rect.top);
        DrawBitmap(global_hdc, "c.bmp", x, y);
    }
}

void Game_End()
{
}
```

Hold It, There's One More Detail

Okay, now for one more support function that I threw in just for fun (because I was getting tired of drawing pixels). This function is called DrawBitmap, and does just that—rather slowly, I'll admit. This function is suitable for loading a full background image or a small bitmap, as I do in this program. The function actually loads a bitmap file into memory, does some Windows fuddling with it, and then draws it at a random location on the window (using the window's device context). You would never want to do this in a real game, because it loads the darned bitmap file every single time it goes through the loop! That's insanely slow and wasteful, but it is okay for demonstration purposes because all of the bitmap-related code is located in this function rather than strewn about the rest of the listing. I want you to focus on the game loop and support functions rather than this antiquated bitmap code that we won't even use beyond this chapter.

```
void DrawBitmap(HDC hdcDest, char *filename, int x, int y)
{
    HBITMAP image;
    BITMAP bm;
    HDC hdcMem;
```

```
//load the bitmap image
image = (HBITMAP)LoadImage(0,"c.bmp",IMAGE_BITMAP,0,0,LR_LOADFROMFILE);

//read the bitmap's properties
GetObject(image, sizeof(BITMAP), &bm);

//create a device context for the bitmap
hdcMem = CreateCompatibleDC(global_hdc);
SelectObject(hdcMem, image);

//draw the bitmap to the window (bit block transfer)
BitBlt(
    global_hdc,                  //destination device context
    x, y,                        //x,y location on destination
    bm.bmWidth, bm.bmHeight,     //width,height of source bitmap
    hdcMem,                      //source bitmap device context
    0, 0,                        //start x,y on source bitmap
    SRCCOPY);                    //blit method

//delete the device context and bitmap
DeleteDC(hdcMem);
DeleteObject((HBITMAP)image);
}
```

Note

If this were a book about programming the Windows GDI (graphical device interface), I would certainly go over all of the GDI graphics functions with you in vast detail! But since it's a side note at best, just take the GDI for granted.

Running the GameLoop Program

Alrighty, then! Go ahead and run the program now, and you should see a window appear with a bunch of freaking crazy C bitmaps being blasted onto the window, as shown in Figure 4.5.

The Windows GDI—which is the system that provides you with window handles and device contexts and allows you to draw on windows to build a user interface (or a game that does not use DirectX)—is a step backward, to be blunt. I want to keep moving forward, covering only the aspects of Windows coding necessary to provide a footing for DirectX, so kindly ignore this lapse in my own judgment. I was being nostalgic.

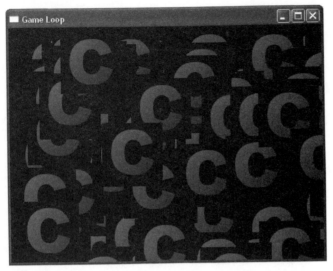

Figure 4.5
The GameLoop program window is filled with C bitmaps.

What You Have Learned

In this chapter you have learned how to write a real-time game loop, and have picked up a few extra tidbits about the Windows GDI along the way. Here are the key points:

■ You learned all about the PeekMessage function.

■ You learned how to modify the main loop in WinMain.

- You added some new functions that will make it easier to write a game.

- You learned a few antiquated skills on how to draw with the GDI (just for fun).

Review Questions

Here are some review questions that will help you to think outside the box and retain some of the information covered in this chapter.

1. What is a real-time game loop?

2. Why do you need to use a real-time loop in a game?

3. What is the main helper function used to create a real-time loop?

4. What Windows API function can you use to draw a bitmap onto the screen?

5. What does DC stand for?

On Your Own

These exercises will challenge you to learn more about the subjects presented in this chapter and will help you to push yourself to see what you are capable of doing on your own.

Exercise 1. The GameLoop program demonstrated how to load and draw a bitmap using the GDI routines. Modify the c.bmp image with a bitmap of your choice and load it into the program instead.

Exercise 2. Modify the GameLoop program so that it draws just a single bitmap that moves around in the window. (Hint: You will need to make sure the bitmap doesn't "fly off" the boundaries of the window.)

PART II

DirectX Programming

The second part of the book covers the basics of DirectX 9 programming. You will learn how to use DirectX Graphics, DirectX Audio, and DirectInput, and will put it all together into a game framework library that can be reused in the remainder of the book's projects (as well as in your own future projects). Here are the chapters you will encounter in Part II:

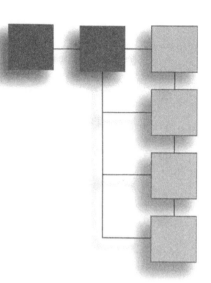

CHAPTER 5

Your First DirectX Graphics Program

This chapter will show you how to write a simple Direct3D program, and is intentionally sparse on the 3D details because the more complicated 3D topics are reserved for Part III of the book. You will learn how to initialize Direct3D and create a device that gives you access to the video card, providing access to the primary surface. You will also learn how to use a back buffer for flicker-free display of graphics. Chapter 6 will take you deeper into the depths of Direct3D's architecture by exploring surfaces, how to draw on them, how to load bitmaps, and how to create animated sprites (which is the basis for a 2D game).

If you are eager to get started with 3D graphics, you can skip ahead to Part III of the book, but I recommend that you stay here and learn the basics first. Before you start loading 3D objects and rendering animated characters on the screen, you need to know the basics of DirectX. In particular, the game framework in Chapter 9 is used in all future chapters, so it's important to understand how the game library works. Much of the game framework is readied in this very chapter, and you will add to it over the next several chapters to make DirectX programming easier.

Here is what you will learn in this chapter:

- How to initialize the Direct3D object.

- How to create a device for accessing the video display.

- How to create a back buffer for flicker-free graphics.

- How to run a Direct3D program in a window.

- How to run a Direct3D program in fullscreen mode.

Getting Started with Direct3D

To use Direct3D or any other component of DirectX, you must be somewhat familiar with how to use headers and library files (standard fare in C programming), because DirectX function calls are stored in header files, and the precompiled DirectX functions are stored in libs. For instance, the Direct3D functions are stored in d3d9.lib, and the way your program "sees" Direct3D is by including the d3d9.h header file using the #include <d3d9.h> directive in your source code files.

I will assume that you have already installed the DirectX 9 Software Development Kit (SDK) for Visual C++ or the separate version of DX9 for Dev-C++. If you have not installed one of these yet, you should do that before reading any further. The DirectX 9 SDK is located on the CD-ROM that accompanies this book in the \DirectX folder, while the Dev-C++ version is located in \dev-cpp. When given the DirectX Runtime Support option, you want to install the debug version for development.

Okay, ready to go?

The Direct3D Interfaces

In order to write a program that uses Direct3D, you must create one variable for the Direct3D interface and another for the graphics device. The Direct3D interface is called LPDIRECT3D9 and the device object is called LPDIRECT3DDEVICE9. You can create the variables like this:

```
LPDIRECT3D9        d3d      = NULL;
LPDIRECT3DDEVICE9 d3ddev    = NULL;
```

The LPDIRECT3D9 object is the big boss of the Direct3D library, the object that controls everything, while LPDIRECT3DDEVICE9 represents the video card. You can probably tell what those objects are by their names. LP means "long pointer," so LPDIRECT3D9 is a long pointer to the DIRECT3D9 object. These definitions are located in the d3d9.h header file, which you must #include in your source code file. Here is how LPDIRECT3D9 is defined:

```
typedef struct IDirect3D9 *LPDIRECT3D9;
```

This may be confusing if you aren't particularly adept with pointers; they can be confusing until you "get it." Pointers are certainly the biggest obstacle to most programmers' mastery of C. When I don't understand something, I prefer to let my subconscious work on it—because my conscious mind just gets in the way sometimes. Seriously—if you don't get it, just start using these pointers and objects and give yourself time. You'll slowly come to understand. One mistake programmers often make is to assume that they must know how something works in order to use it. Not so! Just go ahead and write Direct3D programs; you don't need to know anything about 3D modeling or rendering right away. Practice builds experience, which makes up for a lack of understanding.

IDirect3D9 is an interface; therefore, LPDIRECT3D9 is a long pointer to the Direct3D9 interface. The same goes for LPDIRECT3DDEVICE9, which is a long pointer to the IDirect3DDevice9 interface.

Creating the Direct3D Object

Let me now show you how to initialize the main Direct3D object:

```
d3d = Direct3DCreate9(D3D_SDK_VERSION);
```

This code initializes Direct3D, which means that it is ready to be used. First, you must create the device upon which Direct3D will display output. This is where the d3ddev variable will be used (note that d3d is used to call this function):

```
d3d->CreateDevice(
    D3DADAPTER_DEFAULT,                 //use default video card
    D3DDEVTYPE_HAL,                     //use the hardware renderer
    hWnd,                               //window handle
    D3DCREATE_SOFTWARE_VERTEXPROCESSING, //do not use T&L (for compatibility)
    &d3dpp,                             //presentation parameters
    &d3ddev);                           //pointer to the new device
```

Hardware T&L

If you are a technophile (that is, someone who loves to tinker with gadgets), or rather, if you are a hardcore gamer who loves to argue about video card specifications, then the parameter D3DCREATE_SOFTWARE_VERTEXPROCESSING probably irritated you. If you don't know anything about video cards, then no harm done! But I suspect you make it a habit to keep up to date on all the latest computer technology, right? Well, we all know that "transform and lighting" was the big buzzword of 2002, and all video cards since then have come with T&L. What this really means is that much of the 3D setup work is handled by the video card itself, rather than your computer's central processing unit (CPU).

When 3Dfx came out with the world's first 3D accelerator card for the PC, it took the industry by storm and revolutionized gaming. It would have happened sooner or later anyway, but 3Dfx was first because the company had been building 3D hardware for arcade game machines for years. I remember the first time I saw *Quake* running with 3D acceleration; my jaw dropped.

Having the rendering pipeline reside in the 3D card rather than the CPU is a given at this point. Evolution takes over for a few years and video cards are bumping up the polygon counts and feature sets. Then nVidia ushered in the next revolution by adding the transform and lighting phase of the 3D rendering pipeline to the 3D chip itself, offloading that work from the CPU.

What is transform & lighting, anyway? A *transform* is the manipulation of polygons, while lighting is just like it sounds—adding lighting effects to those polygons. While 3D chips first enhanced games by rendering textured polygons in the hardware (vastly improving quality and speed), T&L added the final touch by having the 3D chip manipulate and light the scene as well. This frees up the CPU for other tasks, like artificial intelligence and game physics—which, in case you haven't noticed, have really taken off in recent years! This is not due to just faster CPUs, but primarily due to the GPU taking the load off.

The last two parameters of CreateDevice specify the device parameters (d3dpp) and the device object (d3ddev). d3dpp must be defined before use, so let's go over it now. There are a lot of options that you can specify for the device, which you can see in Table 5.1.

Table 5.1 Direct3D Presentation Parameters

Variable	Type	Description
BackBufferWidth	UINT	Width of the back buffer
BackBufferHeight	UINT	Height of the back buffer
BackBufferFormat	D3DFORMAT	Format of the back buffer, D3DFORMAT. Pass D3DFMT_UNKNOWN to use desktop format in windowed mode
BackBufferCount	UINT	Number of back buffers
MultiSampleType	D3DMULTISAMPLE_TYPE	Number of multi-sampling levels for full-screen anti-aliasing. Normally pass D3DMULTISAM-PLE_NONE
MultiSampleQuality	DWORD	Quality level of multi-sampling. Normally pass 0
SwapEffect	D3DSWAPEFFECT	Swapping method for back buffer
hDeviceWindow	HWND	Parent window for this device
Windowed	BOOL	Set to TRUE for windowed mode, FALSE for fullscreen mode
EnableAutoDepthStencil	BOOL	Allow D3D to control the depth buffers (normally set to TRUE)
AutoDepthStencilFormat	D3DFORMAT	Format of the depth buffers
Flags	DWORD	Optional flags (normally set to 0)
FullScreen_RefreshRateInHz	UINT	Fullscreen refresh rate (must be 0 for windowed)
PresentationInterval	UINT	Controls the buffer swap rate

First, create a variable of the D3DPRESENT_PARAMETERS struct that is used to set up the device parameters:

```
D3DPRESENT_PARAMETERS d3dpp;
```

and then clear out the struct to zero all values before use:

```
ZeroMemory(&d3dpp, sizeof(d3dpp));
```

Let's take a look at all the possible Direct3D presentation parameters:

There are a lot of options in the d3dpp struct, and a lot of sub-structs within it as well. I'll go over options that you need in order to work through the topics in this chapter, but I may not cover every option (which would amount to information overload). Let's fill in the d3dpp struct with just a few values needed to get a windowed Direct3D program running:

```
d3dpp.Windowed = TRUE;
d3dpp.SwapEffect = D3DSWAPEFFECT_DISCARD;
d3dpp.BackBufferFormat = D3DFMT_UNKNOWN;
```

After these few values have been filled in, you can then call `CreateDevice` to create the primary Direct3D drawing surface.

Taking Direct3D for a Spin

Let's create a sample project to use in this section on Direct3D to get a feel for how a complete Direct3D program works. Create a new Win32 Project type of program and call it d3d_windowed (or whatever name you wish, although this is the name of the project on the CD-ROM). Add a new file, called winmain.cpp, to the empty project. Now let's configure the project for Direct3D.

Note

Remember that this is all basically just C code (rather than C++), even though the filenames all have an extension of .cpp. Visual C++ may complain if the source files don't end with .cpp in some cases.

Adding Direct3D to the Linker

Open the Project menu and select Properties (the last option on the bottom of the menu). The Properties dialog is shown in Figure 5.1.

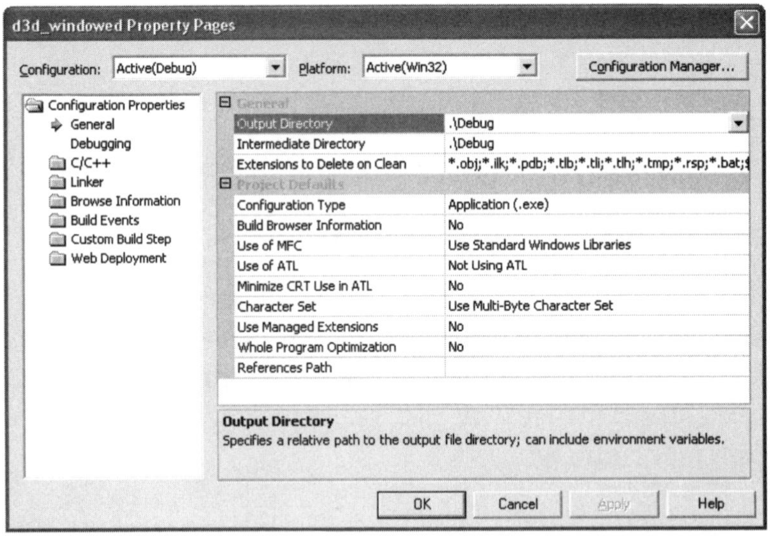

Figure 5.1
The Project Properties dialog for the d3d_windowed project in Microsoft Visual C++

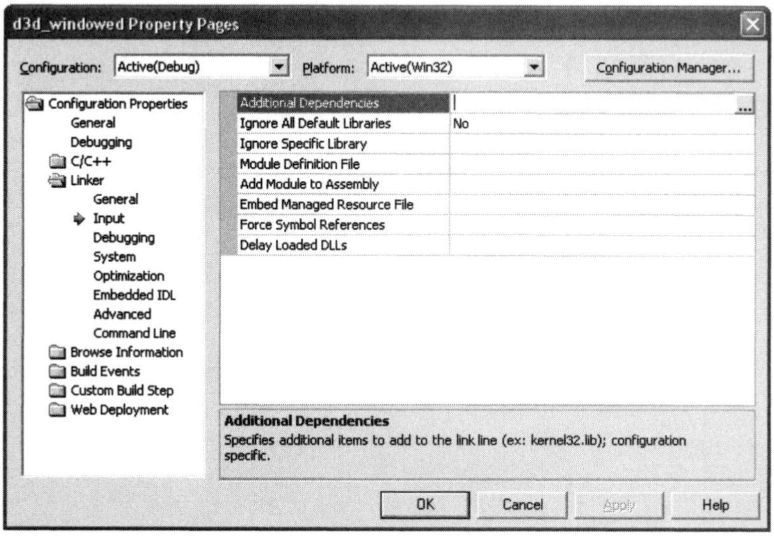

Figure 5.2
Opening the Link tab in the Project Properties dialog

Now, click the Linker item on the list at the left to open up the linker options. You'll notice several sub-items under the Linker tree item, such as General, Input, Debugging, and so on. Select the sub-item called Input under the Linker tree menu, as shown in Figure 5.2.

Pay special attention to the field called Additional Dependencies. This field shows all of the library files that are linked to your program when all of the various source code files are compiled and linked together to form the executable file. If you have a winmain.cpp file in your project, then it is compiled to winmain.obj (which is an object file), which contains the binary instructions that will run on your computer. This is a very low-level binary file that is not readable, so don't even try to open it (you can see the various output files inside the Debug folder, as it is created inside your program's main folder when you compile the program).

Now, let's add the Direct3D library file to the list of libraries. Add "d3d9.lib" to the Additional Dependencies field, as shown in Figure 5.3, and then close the dialog.

Assuming your source code is correct, this is all you need to do to compile a Direct3D program. You have now configured your first DirectX project in Visual C++! This is no easy thing to do, so you should feel like you're making some serious progress—especially if you are new to the C++ language!

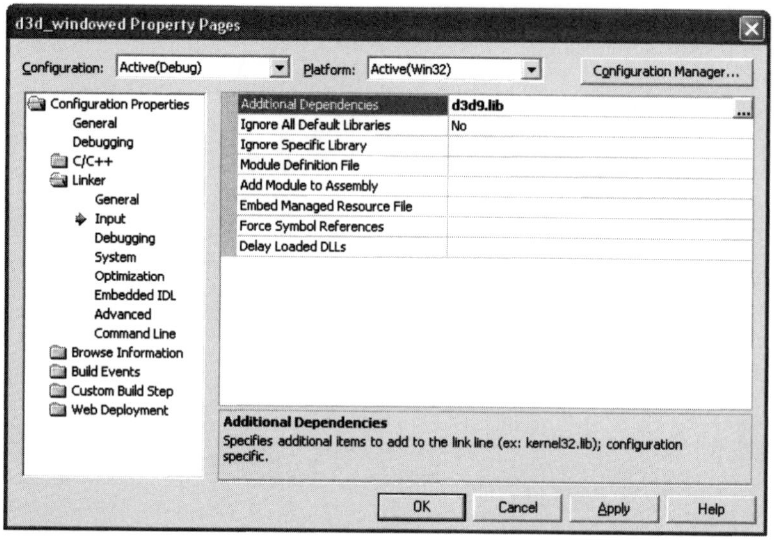

Figure 5.3
Adding d3d9.lib to the Additional Dependencies field.

Typing in the Source Code

Here is the standard Windows code needed to get the program rolling. I'll show you the Direct3D-specific code at the end of this listing.

```
// Beginning Game Programming, Second Edition
// Chapter 5
// d3d_windowed program

//header files to include
#include <d3d9.h>
#include <time.h>

//application title
#define APPTITLE "Direct3D_Windowed"

//forward declarations
LRESULT WINAPI WinProc(HWND,UINT,WPARAM,LPARAM);
ATOM MyRegisterClass(HINSTANCE);
int Game_Init(HWND);
void Game_Run(HWND);
void Game_End(HWND);

//Direct3D objects
```

```
LPDIRECT3D9 d3d = NULL;
LPDIRECT3DDEVICE9 d3ddev = NULL;

//window event callback function
LRESULT WINAPI WinProc( HWND hWnd, UINT msg, WPARAM wParam, LPARAM lParam )
{
    switch( msg )
    {
      case WM_DESTROY:
          Game_End(hWnd);
          PostQuitMessage(0);
          return 0;
    }
    return DefWindowProc( hWnd, msg, wParam, lParam );
}


//helper function to set up the window properties
ATOM MyRegisterClass(HINSTANCE hInstance)
{
    //create the window class structure
    WNDCLASSEX wc;
    wc.cbSize = sizeof(WNDCLASSEX);

    //fill the struct with info
    wc.style            = CS_HREDRAW | CS_VREDRAW;
    wc.lpfnWndProc      = (WNDPROC)WinProc;
    wc.cbClsExtra       = 0;
    wc.cbWndExtra       = 0;
    wc.hInstance        = hInstance;
    wc.hIcon            = NULL;
    wc.hCursor          = LoadCursor(NULL, IDC_ARROW);
    wc.hbrBackground    = (HBRUSH)GetStockObject(WHITE_BRUSH);
    wc.lpszMenuName     = NULL;
    wc.lpszClassName    = APPTITLE;
    wc.hIconSm          = NULL;

    //set up the window with the class info
    return RegisterClassEx(&wc);
}


//entry point for a Windows program
int WINAPI WinMain(HINSTANCE hInstance,
                   HINSTANCE hPrevInstance,
```

```
                LPSTR     lpCmdLine,
                int       nCmdShow)
{
   // declare variables
   MSG msg;

   // register the class
   MyRegisterClass(hInstance);

   // initialize application
   //note--got rid of initinstance
   HWND hWnd;

   //create a new window
   hWnd = CreateWindow(
      APPTITLE,                  //window class
      APPTITLE,                  //title bar
      WS_OVERLAPPEDWINDOW,       //window style
      CW_USEDEFAULT,             //x position of window
      CW_USEDEFAULT,             //y position of window
      500,                       //width of the window
      400,                       //height of the window
      NULL,                      //parent window
      NULL,                      //menu
      hInstance,                 //application instance
      NULL);                     //window parameters

   //was there an error creating the window?
   if (!hWnd)
       return FALSE;

   //display the window
   ShowWindow(hWnd, nCmdShow);
   UpdateWindow(hWnd);

     //initialize the game
 if (!Game_Init(hWnd))
       return 0;

   // main message loop
   int done = 0;
      while (!done)
   {
```

```
    if (PeekMessage(&msg, NULL, 0, 0, PM_REMOVE))
     {
     //look for quit message
     if (msg.message == WM_QUIT)
     {
        MessageBox(hWnd, "Received WM_QUIT message", "WinMain", MB_OK);
        done = 1;
     }

     //decode and pass messages on to WndProc
         TranslateMessage(&msg);
         DispatchMessage(&msg);
     }
    else
     //process game loop (else prevents running after window is closed)
     Game_Run(hWnd);
   }
  return msg.wParam;
}
```

The first thing you might have noticed about this code is that InitInstance is missing. Actually, I just moved the code from this helper function directly into WinMain because the Direct3D code needs access to the window handle (hWnd), and I would prefer to just keep the CreateWindow function right inside WinMain.

There are several more changes in this code listing that make it differ from the GameLoop program that you saw in the last chapter. For one thing, Game_End is called from within WinProc (the window event callback function, as you'll recall) after the WM_DESTROY message. This function actually removes the Direct3D objects and any other things from memory before the program ends. If you want to see the program hang, just terminate the program without first releasing Direct3D—it will keep running in memory, even though the program window is gone! This is what you might call a *bad thing*. Oh, why beat around the bush? This is a *very bad thing*. So, this call to Game_End right inside the callback function ensures that Direct3D is shut down properly before the program ends.

Now let's go over the code to initialize Direct3D. I have put the code you have learned about in this chapter so far inside Game_Init, which is called by WinMain just before the main loop starts running. The calls to MessageBox are for testing purposes, and can be removed once you understand how the program works.

```
int Game_Init(HWND hwnd)
{
  //display init message
  MessageBox(hwnd, "Program is about to start", "Game_Init", MB_OK);

  //initialize Direct3D
  d3d = Direct3DCreate9(D3D_SDK_VERSION);
  if (d3d == NULL)
  {
    MessageBox(hwnd, "Error initializing Direct3D", "Error", MB_OK);
    return 0;
  }

  //set Direct3D presentation parameters
  D3DPRESENT_PARAMETERS d3dpp;
  ZeroMemory(&d3dpp, sizeof(d3dpp));
  d3dpp.Windowed = TRUE;
  d3dpp.SwapEffect = D3DSWAPEFFECT_DISCARD;
  d3dpp.BackBufferFormat = D3DFMT_UNKNOWN;

  //create Direct3D device
  d3d->CreateDevice(
    D3DADAPTER_DEFAULT,
    D3DDEVTYPE_HAL,
    hwnd,
    D3DCREATE_SOFTWARE_VERTEXPROCESSING,
    &d3dpp,
    &d3ddev);

  if (d3ddev == NULL)
  {
    MessageBox(hwnd, "Error creating Direct3D device", "Error", MB_OK);
    return 0;
  }

    //set random number seed
    srand(time(NULL));

  //return okay
  return 1;
}
```

Did you see that first line that calls MessageBox to display a message? I inserted this to demonstrate how things work in the program, how the functions are called, and to demonstrate the ordering of events in a Windows program. If you want to really see how it all works, you may insert similar MessageBox function calls elsewhere in the program. You can insert them basically anywhere except for in the game loop, which you don't really want to interrupt with a message box, as that will mess everything up. Okay, let's take a look at Game_Run to see what happens to draw on the Direct3D display:

```
void Game_Run(HWND hwnd)
{
  //make sure the Direct3D device is valid
  if (d3ddev == NULL)
     return;

  //clear the screen with a green color
  d3ddev->Clear(0, NULL, D3DCLEAR_TARGET, D3DCOLOR_XRGB(0,255,255), 1.0f, 0);

  //start rendering
  if (d3ddev->BeginScene())
  {
     //do something here!

     //stop rendering
     d3ddev->EndScene();
  }

  //display the back buffer on the screen
  d3ddev->Present(NULL, NULL, NULL, NULL);

}
```

First, this function makes sure that the d3ddev (Direct3D device) exists; otherwise, it returns an error. Next, the Clear function is called to clear the back buffer with the color green. This is not just a cosmetic function call to Clear. This literally blanks out the screen before each frame is rendered (and as you will learn later on, this function can also clear the z-buffer used to draw polygons). Imagine that you have a character walking on the screen. At each frame (here within Game_Run) you will change to the next frame of animation, so that over time the character really appears to be walking. Well, if you don't clear the screen first, then each frame of the animation is drawn over the last frame, resulting in a big mess on the screen. That is why Clear is called before the rendering begins: to wipe the slate clean and prepare it for the next frame.

Now for the last part of the program:

```
void Game_End(HWND hwnd)
{
  //display close message
  MessageBox(hwnd, "Program is about to end", "Game_End", MB_OK);

  //release the Direct3D device
  if (d3ddev != NULL)
      d3ddev->Release();

  //release the Direct3D object
  if (d3d != NULL)
      d3d->Release();
}
```

The Game_End function is called from within WinMain, as you'll recall, after a WM_DESTROY message comes in. This usually happens when you close the program window (clicking the small X icon at the top right corner—duh, you knew that, right?).

Running the Program

If you run the program (F5 from Visual C++), you should see a blank window pop up, as shown in Figure 5.4. Hey, it doesn't do much, but you've learned a lot about initializing Direct3D—that baby is ready for some polygons!

Figure 5.4
The Direct3D_Windowed program demonstrates how to initialize Direct3D.

Direct3D in Fullscreen Mode

The next step is to learn how to program Direct3D to run in fullscreen mode, which is how most games run. This requires a change to the CreateWindow function and a few changes to the Direct3D presentation parameters. Using the d3d_windowed program as a basis, you can just make the following changes to make the program run in fullscreen mode.

Tip

It's good to have your game run fullscreen for production, but it's preferable to run the game in windowed mode while you are working on it because in fullscreen mode Direct3D takes control over the screen, and you won't be able to see any error messages that pop up.

Modifying the Code

First, add the following lines up near the top of the code listing:

```
//screen resolution
#define SCREEN_WIDTH 640
#define SCREEN_HEIGHT 480
```

These defines will make it easier to change the video resolution later, if you wish. They also make the code more readable.

Adding Keyboard Support

Because this program will run in fullscreen mode, you need a way to end the program. Without some way to check for keyboard input, the only way to end a program in fullscreen mode is to Alt+Tab out to the desktop, open Task Manager, and terminate the program the hard way. This just will not do, so let me show you a quick and easy solution that will work until I've had a chance to introduce you to DirectInput in a later chapter. Add this code below the last two defines that you inserted into the code:

```
//macros to read the keyboard asynchronously
#define KEY_DOWN(vk_code) ((GetAsyncKeyState(vk_code) & 0x8000) ? 1 : 0)
#define KEY_UP(vk_code)((GetAsyncKeyState(vk_code) & 0x8000) ? 1 : 0)
```

Modifying CreateWindow

Now, down in WinMain, I have made some changes to the CreateWindow function call that you should note (the changes appear in bold):

```
//create a new window
hWnd = CreateWindow(
    APPTITLE,                //window class
    APPTITLE,                //title bar
    WS_EX_TOPMOST | WS_VISIBLE | WS_POPUP,  //window style
    CW_USEDEFAULT,           //x position of window
    CW_USEDEFAULT,           //y position of window
    SCREEN_WIDTH,            //width of the window
    SCREEN_HEIGHT,           //height of the window
    NULL,                    //parent window
    NULL,                    //menu
    hInstance,               //application instance
    NULL);                   //window parameters
```

The CreateWindow function includes the screen width and height defines, but I also made some changes to the WS_OVERLAPPED window style. It now includes the WS_EX_TOPMOST value, which causes the window to take precedence over all other windows. The other two options are WS_VISIBLE and WS_POPUP, which ensure that the window has focus and no longer includes a border or title bar.

Changing the Presentation Parameters

The next change involves the D3DPRESENT_PARAMETERS struct, which directly affects the appearance and capabilities of the Direct3D primary surface. You may recall that the last program set it up with the following three lines:

```
d3dpp.Windowed = TRUE;
d3dpp.SwapEffect = D3DSWAPEFFECT_DISCARD;
d3dpp.BackBufferFormat = D3DFMT_UNKNOWN;
```

There are several other options that I did not set the first time around that are now significant when you are trying to initialize Direct3D in fullscreen mode. Here are the new d3dpp settings with changes in bold (found in Game_Init).

```
d3dpp.Windowed = FALSE;
d3dpp.SwapEffect = D3DSWAPEFFECT_DISCARD;
d3dpp.BackBufferFormat = D3DFMT_X8R8G8B8;
d3dpp.BackBufferCount = 1;
d3dpp.BackBufferWidth = SCREEN_WIDTH;
d3dpp.BackBufferHeight = SCREEN_HEIGHT;
d3dpp.hDeviceWindow = hwnd;
```

Looking for the Escape Key

Okay, just one more change and you'll be on target with this fullscreen program. Scroll down in the code listing to the Game_Run function, which is called by WinMain to update the screen (this is where all rendering and core gameplay will occur). Add the following code to the end of the Game_Run function:

```
//check for escape key (to exit program)
if (KEY_DOWN(VK_ESCAPE))
    PostMessage(hwnd, WM_DESTROY, 0, 0);
```

Now, when the program runs in fullscreen mode, you will have a way to exit out of the program. See, I do plan ahead! The program is now ready to run, so give it a spin.

What You Have Learned

In this chapter, you have learned how to initialize and run a Direct3D program in windowed and fullscreen modes. Here are the key points:

- You learned about the Direct3D interface objects.

- You learned about the CreateDevice function.

- You learned about the Direct3D presentation parameters.

- You learned what settings to use to run Direct3D in windowed mode.

- You learned how to run Direct3D in fullscreen mode.

Review Questions

Here are some review questions to challenge your impressive intellect and see if you have any weaknesses:

1. What is Direct3D?

2. What is the Direct3D interface object called?

3. What is the Direct3D device called?

4. What function do you use to start rendering?

5. What function lets you read from the keyboard asynchronously?

On Your Own

These exercises will challenge you to learn more about the subjects presented in this chapter and will help you to push yourself to see what you are capable of doing on your own.

Exercise 1. Modify the `Direct3D_Windowed` program so that it displays a different color in the background other than green.

Exercise 2. Modify the `Direct3D_Fullscreen` program so that it uses a different resolution other than 640 × 480.

CHAPTER 6

BITMAPS AND SURFACES

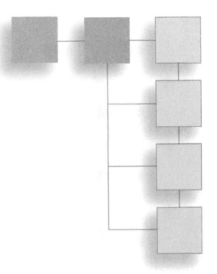

Some of the best games ever made were 2D games that didn't even require an advanced 3D accelerated video card. It is important to learn about 2D graphics because they are the basis for all graphics that are displayed on your monitor—regardless of how those graphics are rendered, game graphics are all converted to an array of pixels on the screen. In this chapter, you will learn about surfaces, which are just regular bitmaps that can be drawn to the screen. So, think back on some of your all-time favorite games. Were they all 3D games? Very likely not—there have been more blockbuster 2D games than there have been of the 3D variety. Rather than compare and contrast the 2D and 3D, it's better to just learn both and then use whichever one your game calls for. A game programmer should know everything in order to create the best games.

Here is what you will learn in this chapter:

- How to create a surface in memory.

- How to fill a surface with color.

- How to load a bitmap image file.

- How to draw a surface on the screen.

Surfaces and Bitmaps

Direct3D uses surfaces for many things. The monitor (shown in Figure 6.1) displays what the video card sends to it, and the video card pulls the video display out of a frame buffer that is sent to the monitor one pixel at a time (they might be in single file, but they move insanely fast!).

The frame buffer is stored in the memory chips on the video card itself (shown in Figure 6.2), and these chips are usually very fast. There was a time when video memory (VRAM) was extremely expensive because it was so fast—much faster than standard system RAM. Now things are somewhat reversed, as the PC's main memory usually has the best technology and the video cards are a step or two behind. The reason for this is because it's difficult to redo the architecture of a video card, which is a very precise and complex circuit board.

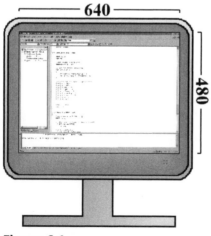

Figure 6.1
A typical monitor

Monitor   **Video Card**

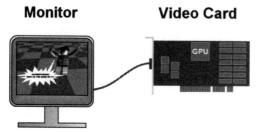

Figure 6.2
The monitor displays the linear array of pixels sent to it by the video card

Frame Buffer   **Monitor**
(in video card)

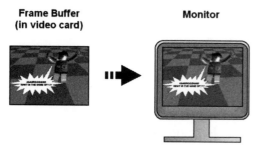

Figure 6.3
The frame buffer in VRAM contains the image that is rendered on the monitor

The PC motherboard, on the other hand, is constantly in a state of flux, as semiconductor companies strive to outdo each other. Video card companies, no matter how competitive they may be, can't gamble on putting six months' worth of effort into a memory technology that fails in the market and is replaced by other types of memory (remember Rambus?). Also, while motherboards are built for a variety of industries and uses—and, thus, have been subject to much experimentation—video cards are built for one thing only: displaying graphics. Therefore, less experimentation goes on with the chips on a video card. After the PC market has decided on a memory standard, it tends to show up on video cards. You may recall when the first DDR (double data rate) memory was used on video cards; it was quite a while after DDR had been initially released.

Where was I? Oh, right! The frame buffer resides in video memory, and represents the image you see on the monitor (as shown in Figure 6.3). So it makes sense that the easiest way to create graphics is to just modify the frame buffer directly; the result is that you see the changes on the screen right away. This is how things work, basically, but I'm leaving out one small detail. You don't want to draw directly on the frame buffer because that causes flicker as your graphics are drawn, erased, moved, and redrawn while the screen is being refreshed.

Instead, what you want to do is draw everything on an offscreen buffer and then blast that "double" or "back" buffer to the screen very quickly. This is called *double buffering.* There are other methods of creating a flicker-free display, such as page flipping, but I tend to prefer a back buffer because it is more straightforward (and a bit easier).

The Primary Surfaces

You might recall from the last chapter that you created a back buffer by setting the presentation parameters. Then, using the `Clear` function, you filled the back buffer with green and then used the `Present` function to refresh the screen. You were using a double/back buffer without even realizing it! That's one nice feature that Direct3D provides—a built-in back buffer. And it makes sense, because double buffering is as common today in games as bread and butter is in your kitchen.

The "frame buffer" that I mentioned earlier is also called the *front buffer,* which makes sense in that the back buffer is copied to it during each frame. Both the front and back buffers are created for you when you configure the presentation parameters and call `CreateDevice`. Isn't that great?

Secondary Offscreen Surfaces

The other type of surface you can use is called a *secondary* or *offscreen* surface. This type of surface is really just an array in memory that looks like a bitmap (where it has a header and then data representing pixels). You can create as many offscreen surfaces as you need for your game; it is common to use hundreds of them while a game is running. The reason is because all of the graphics in a game are stored in surfaces, and these surfaces are copied to the screen in a process called *bit-block transfer.* The common way to refer to this term is "blitter"—you "blit" surfaces to the screen.

You might remember the GameLoop program from Chapter 4 that used a function called `BitBlt` (that I purposely neglected to explain at the time). `BitBlt` is a Windows GDI function for "blitting" bitmaps to device contexts, such as the main window of your program. A device context is sort of like a Direct3D surface, but is more difficult to use (due to the complexity of the Windows GDI). Direct3D surfaces are simple in comparison, as you'll see shortly. In fact, I might use the word *refreshing* to describe them after writing Windows code for so many years.

Creating a Surface

You create a Direct3D surface by first declaring a variable to point to the surface in memory. The surface object is called `LPDIRECT3DSURFACE9`, and you create a variable like so:

```
LPDIRECT3DSURFACE9 surface = NULL;
```

Once you have created a surface, you have a lot of freedom as to what you can do with the surface. You can use the "blitter" to draw bitmaps to the surface (from other surfaces, of course), or you can fill the surface with a color, among other things. If you want to clear the surface prior to drawing on it, for instance, you would use the `ColorFill` function, which has this syntax:

```
HRESULT ColorFill(

    IDirect3DSurface9 *pSurface,
    CONST RECT *pRect,
    D3DCOLOR color
);
```

This usage causes the destination surface to be filled with the color red:

```
d3ddev->ColorFill(surface, NULL, D3DCOLOR_XRGB(255,0,0));
```

Drawing the Surface (Blitting)

Probably the most interesting function, of course, is the blitter. You can blit portions or all of one surface onto another surface (including the back buffer or the screen). The blitter is called `StretchRect` (strange name, huh?). Here is what it looks like:

```
HRESULT StretchRect(

    IDirect3DSurface9 *pSourceSurface,
    CONST RECT *pSourceRect,
    IDirect3DSurface9 *pDestSurface,
    CONST RECT *pDestRect,
    D3DTEXTUREFILTERTYPE Filter
);
```

Well, didn't I tell you that bitmaps were easier to deal with in Direct3D than they are with the Windows GDI? I wasn't kidding. This sweet little function only has five parameters, and it is really easy to use. Let me give you an example:

```
d3ddev->StretchRect(surface, NULL, backbuffer, NULL, D3DTEXF_NONE);
```

This is the easiest way to call the function, assuming that the two surfaces are the same size. If the source surface is smaller than the destination, then it is blitted to the upper-left corner of the destination surface. Of course, this isn't very interesting; when this function is really handy is when you specify the rectangles for the source and destination. The source rectangle can be just a small portion or the entire surface; the same goes for the destination, but you'll usually blit the source somewhere "on" the destination. Here's an example:

```
rect.left = 100;
rect.top = 90;
rect.right = 200;
rect.bottom = 180;
d3ddev->StretchRect(surface, NULL, backbuffer, &rect, D3DTEXF_NONE);
```

This code copies the source surface onto the destination, stretching it into the rectangle at (100, 90, 200, 180), which is 100×90 pixels in size. Regardless of the size of the source surface, as long as it isn't NULL, it will be "stuffed" into the dimensions specified by the destination rectangle.

I've been using backbuffer without first explaining where it came from. No, there is not a global variable called backbuffer that you can freely use! (Although that would be kind of cool.) But it's not a big deal—you can create this variable yourself. It is actually just a pointer to the real back buffer, and you can get this pointer by calling a special function called GetBackBuffer. Boy, was that a tough call, huh? Well, you can't argue with the straightforward approach (which is not Microsoft's usual approach).

```
HRESULT GetBackBuffer(

    UINT iSwapChain,
    UINT BackBuffer,
    D3DBACKBUFFER_TYPE Type,
    IDirect3DSurface9 **ppBackBuffer
);
```

Here is how you might call this function to retrieve a pointer to the back buffer. First, let's create the backbuffer variable (that is, pointer) and then have this fancy GetBackBuffer function "point it" to the real back buffer:

```
LPDIRECT3DSURFACE9 backbuffer = NULL;
d3ddev->GetBackBuffer(0, 0, D3DBACKBUFFER_TYPE_MONO, &backbuffer);
```

Figure 6.4
The Create_Surface program copies random rectangles from an offscreen surface to the screen.

I'll bet you were worried that Direct3D was going to be hard. Well, it all depends on your point of view. You can either be the pessimist and complain about every unknown function in the DirectX 9 SDK help file (which I refer to often), or you can just do what works, use what you learn, and get started writing a game. Granted, you have yet to draw a polygon, but we'll be there soon enough.

The Create_Surface Example

Let's turn this into a sample program so that you can see it all come together nicely. I have written a program called Create_Surface that demonstrates the functions ColorFill, StretchRect, and GetBackBuffer, and, more importantly, shows how to use surfaces! You can see sample output from the program in Figure 6.4. In case you're wondering why there's just one rectangle in the figure: it's because when the program is running, there is only one rectangle on the screen at a time, though it's running so fast there appear to be many on the screen at once.

Go ahead and create a new project called Create_Surface and add a new file to the project called winmain.cpp. Now, as before, go into the Project menu, click on Settings, click on the Linker/Input item, and add d3d9.lib to the Additional Dependencies field.

Ready? Okay, let's do it; here's the code for the program. I've highlighted important lines of code in bold so you can identify them if you're just modifying the Direct3D_Fullscreen from the last chapter (from which this program was originally based).

Note

You can load this project off the CD-ROM or just modify a program from the last chapter and make changes to it, as much of the Windows code remains unchanged.

```
// Beginning Game Programming, Second Edition
// Chapter 6
// Create_Surface program

//header files to include
#include <d3d9.h>
#include <time.h>

//application title
#define APPTITLE "Create_Surface"

//macros to read the keyboard asynchronously
#define KEY_DOWN(vk_code) ((GetAsyncKeyState(vk_code) & 0x8000) ? 1 : 0)
#define KEY_UP(vk_code)((GetAsyncKeyState(vk_code) & 0x8000) ? 1 : 0)

//screen resolution
#define SCREEN_WIDTH 640
#define SCREEN_HEIGHT 480

//forward declarations
LRESULT WINAPI WinProc(HWND,UINT,WPARAM,LPARAM);
ATOM MyRegisterClass(HINSTANCE);
int Game_Init(HWND);
void Game_Run(HWND);
void Game_End(HWND);

//Direct3D objects
LPDIRECT3D9 d3d = NULL;
LPDIRECT3DDEVICE9 d3ddev = NULL;

LPDIRECT3DSURFACE9 backbuffer = NULL;
LPDIRECT3DSURFACE9 surface = NULL;

//window event callback function
LRESULT WINAPI WinProc( HWND hWnd, UINT msg, WPARAM wParam, LPARAM lParam )
{
    switch( msg )
    {
        case WM_DESTROY:
            Game_End(hWnd);
            PostQuitMessage(0);
            return 0;
    }
```

```
        return DefWindowProc( hWnd, msg, wParam, lParam );
}

//helper function to set up the window properties
ATOM MyRegisterClass(HINSTANCE hInstance)
{
    //create the window class structure
    WNDCLASSEX wc;
    wc.cbSize = sizeof(WNDCLASSEX);

    //fill the struct with info
    wc.style         = CS_HREDRAW | CS_VREDRAW;
    wc.lpfnWndProc   = (WNDPROC)WinProc;
    wc.cbClsExtra    = 0;
    wc.cbWndExtra    = 0;
    wc.hInstance     = hInstance;
    wc.hIcon         = NULL;
    wc.hCursor       = LoadCursor(NULL, IDC_ARROW);
    wc.hbrBackground = (HBRUSH)GetStockObject(WHITE_BRUSH);
    wc.lpszMenuName  = NULL;
    wc.lpszClassName = APPTITLE;
    wc.hIconSm       = NULL;

    //set up the window with the class info
    return RegisterClassEx(&wc);
}


//entry point for a Windows program
int WINAPI WinMain(HINSTANCE hInstance,
                   HINSTANCE hPrevInstance,
                   LPSTR     lpCmdLine,
                   int       nCmdShow)
{
    // declare variables
    MSG msg;

    // register the class
    MyRegisterClass(hInstance);

    // initialize application
    HWND hWnd;
```

```
//create a new window
hWnd = CreateWindow(
    APPTITLE,               //window class
    APPTITLE,               //title bar
    WS_EX_TOPMOST | WS_VISIBLE | WS_POPUP,   //window style
    CW_USEDEFAULT,          //x position of window
    CW_USEDEFAULT,          //y position of window
    SCREEN_WIDTH,           //width of the window
    SCREEN_HEIGHT,          //height of the window
    NULL,                   //parent window
    NULL,                   //menu
    hInstance,              //application instance
    NULL);                  //window parameters

//was there an error creating the window?
if (!hWnd)
    return FALSE;

//display the window
ShowWindow(hWnd, nCmdShow);
UpdateWindow(hWnd);

    //initialize the game
if (!Game_Init(hWnd))
    return 0;

// main message loop
int done = 0;
while (!done)
{
    if (PeekMessage(&msg, NULL, 0, 0, PM_REMOVE))
    {
        //look for quit message
        if (msg.message == WM_QUIT)
            done = 1;

        //decode and pass messages on to WndProc
TranslateMessage(&msg);
        DispatchMessage(&msg);
    }
    else
        //process game loop (else prevents running after window is closed)
        Game_Run(hWnd);
}
```

```
        return msg.wParam;
}


int Game_Init(HWND hwnd)
{
    HRESULT result;

    //initialize Direct3D
    d3d = Direct3DCreate9(D3D_SDK_VERSION);
    if (d3d == NULL)
    {
        MessageBox(hwnd, "Error initializing Direct3D", "Error", MB_OK);
        return 0;
    }

    //set Direct3D presentation parameters
    D3DPRESENT_PARAMETERS d3dpp;
    ZeroMemory(&d3dpp, sizeof(d3dpp));

    d3dpp.Windowed = FALSE;
    d3dpp.SwapEffect = D3DSWAPEFFECT_DISCARD;
    d3dpp.BackBufferFormat = D3DFMT_X8R8G8B8;
    d3dpp.BackBufferCount = 1;
    d3dpp.BackBufferWidth = SCREEN_WIDTH;
    d3dpp.BackBufferHeight = SCREEN_HEIGHT;
    d3dpp.hDeviceWindow = hwnd;

    //create Direct3D device
    d3d->CreateDevice(
        D3DADAPTER_DEFAULT,
        D3DDEVTYPE_HAL,
        hwnd,
        D3DCREATE_SOFTWARE_VERTEXPROCESSING,
        &d3dpp,
        &d3ddev);

    if (d3ddev == NULL)
    {
        MessageBox(hwnd, "Error creating Direct3D device", "Error", MB_OK);
        return 0;
    }
```

```
    //set random number seed
    srand(time(NULL));

    //clear the backbuffer to black
    d3ddev->Clear(0, NULL, D3DCLEAR_TARGET, D3DCOLOR_XRGB(0,0,0), 1.0f, 0);

    //create pointer to the back buffer
    d3ddev->GetBackBuffer(0, 0, D3DBACKBUFFER_TYPE_MONO, &backbuffer);

    //create surface
    result = d3ddev->CreateOffscreenPlainSurface(
        100,                  //width of the surface
        100,                  //height of the surface
        D3DFMT_X8R8G8B8,      //surface format
        D3DPOOL_DEFAULT,      //memory pool to use
        &surface,             //pointer to the surface
        NULL);                //reserved (always NULL)

    if (!result)
        return 1;

    //return okay
    return 1;
}

void Game_Run(HWND hwnd)
{
    RECT rect;
    int r,g,b;

    //make sure the Direct3D device is valid
    if (d3ddev == NULL)
        return;

    //start rendering
    if (d3ddev->BeginScene())
    {
        //fill the surface with random color
        r = rand() % 255;
        g = rand() % 255;
        b = rand() % 255;
        d3ddev->ColorFill(surface, NULL, D3DCOLOR_XRGB(r,g,b));
```

```
    //copy the surface to the backbuffer
    rect.left = rand() % SCREEN_WIDTH/2;
    rect.right = rect.left + rand() % SCREEN_WIDTH/2;
    rect.top = rand() % SCREEN_HEIGHT;
    rect.bottom = rect.top + rand() % SCREEN_HEIGHT/2;
    d3ddev->StretchRect(surface, NULL, backbuffer, &rect, D3DTEXF_NONE);

    //stop rendering
    d3ddev->EndScene();
  }

  //display the back buffer on the screen
  d3ddev->Present(NULL, NULL, NULL, NULL);

  //check for escape key (to exit program)
  if (KEY_DOWN(VK_ESCAPE))
      PostMessage(hwnd, WM_DESTROY, 0, 0);
}

void Game_End(HWND hwnd)
{
    //free the surface
    surface->Release();

    //release the Direct3D device
    if (d3ddev != NULL)
        d3ddev->Release();

    //release the Direct3D object
    if (d3d != NULL)
        d3d->Release();
}
```

Note

Isn't it astonishing how little this program changed from the last one? For this reason, I will not repeat all the Windows code any longer from this point forward, but will simply include the necessary code to demonstrate the topic at hand. I will leave it to you to open an existing project and modify it to suit. I recommend the Direct3D_Fullscreen program, which is an excellent example that is suitable as a basis for all future programs. In case you were wondering, this code will become the game foundation that you'll assemble later on, and all the repeated code will be moved into a reusable source code file. Then you'll be able to spend all your time just writing DirectX code rather than dealing with the Windows code. But we aren't quite there yet. . . .

Loading Bitmaps from Disk

The next step is to load a bitmap file from disk into a surface and then draw the bitmap on the screen (via the back buffer, of course). Unfortunately, Direct3D does not have any function for loading a bitmap file, so you'll have to write your own bitmap loader.

<Indeterminate pause>. Just kidding!

Actually, what I was thinking at this very moment was Balki Bartokamous from the TV show *Perfect Strangers,* and his famous quote: "Don't be reedeeculose!" Writing your own bitmap loader, for a program running on the Windows O/S: yes, that *is* ridiculous.

However, Direct3D really doesn't know how to load a bitmap. Fortunately, there is a helper library called *D3DX* (which stands for *Direct3D extensions*) that provides many helpful functions, including one to load a bitmap into a surface. The only stipulation is that you must add the #include <d3dx.h> include statement to your program, and you must also add d3dx9.lib to the project settings. No big whoop.

Note

Why is it that whenever a Microsoft project manager or marketing manager can't think of a good name for a new product, they just call it "X" something? The whole "X" thing was trendy in the '90s, but it's really retro at this point... i.e. *Xbox...* we get the joke, *DirectX box.* Now that's just hilarious.

The function we're interested in is called D3DXLoadSurfaceFromFile, which has this syntax:

```
HRESULT D3DXLoadSurfaceFromFile(

    LPDIRECT3DSURFACE9 pDestSurface,
    CONST PALETTEENTRY* pDestPalette,
    CONST RECT* pDestRect,
    LPCTSTR pSrcFile,
    CONST RECT* pSrcRect,
    DWORD Filter,
    D3DCOLOR ColorKey,
    D3DXIMAGE_INFO* pSrcInfo
);
```

Table 6.1 Graphics File Formats

Extension	Format
.bmp	Windows Bitmap (standard)
.dds	DirectDraw Surface (DirectX 7)
.dib	Windows Device Independent Bitmap
.jpg	Joint Photographic Experts Group (JPEG)
.png	Portable Network Graphics
.tga	Truevision Targa

Okay, now for the good part. Not only can this great function load a standard Windows bitmap file, it can also load a bunch more formats! Table 6.1 has the list.

As usual, many of these parameters will be NULL, so it's not as difficult as it appears (although when I see any function with more than six parameters, my eyes tend to glaze over ...).

The Load_Bitmap Program

Let's write a short program to demonstrate how to load a bitmap file into a surface and draw it on the screen. First of all, you don't need to type in all that code again; you can just make the noted changes to the Create_Surface program, so I'll just list the code that's necessary to make the changes. Second, I need to show you how to configure the project for D3DX. Open the Project Settings dialog, click the Link tab, and type both **d3d9.lib** and **d3dx9.lib** into the Additional Dependencies field, as shown in Figure 6.5.

The first thing you need to do is add the #include <d3dx9.h> to the code as shown:

```
//header files to include
#include <d3d9.h>
#include <d3dx9.h>
#include <time.h>

//application title
#define APPTITLE "Load_Bitmap"
```

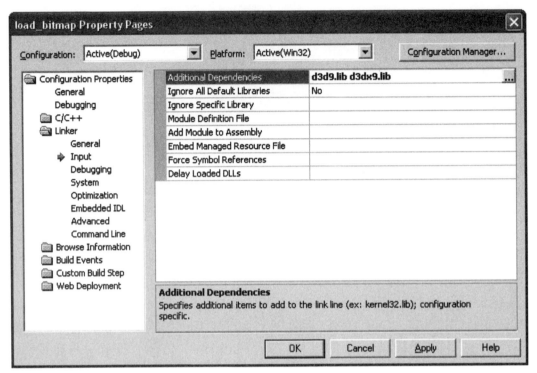

Figure 6.5
Adding support for the D3DX library to the project

Now scroll on down to the Game_Init function and make the changes noted in bold (deleting any lines of code that no longer belong from the previous project). Most of the code remains unchanged.

```
int Game_Init(HWND hwnd)
{
    HRESULT result;

    //initialize Direct3D
    d3d = Direct3DCreate9(D3D_SDK_VERSION);
    if (d3d == NULL)
    {
        MessageBox(hwnd, "Error initializing Direct3D", "Error", MB_OK);
        return 0;
    }

    //set Direct3D presentation parameters
    D3DPRESENT_PARAMETERS d3dpp;
    ZeroMemory(&d3dpp, sizeof(d3dpp));
```

```
d3dpp.Windowed = FALSE;
d3dpp.SwapEffect = D3DSWAPEFFECT_DISCARD;
d3dpp.BackBufferFormat = D3DFMT_X8R8G8B8;
d3dpp.BackBufferCount = 1;
d3dpp.BackBufferWidth = SCREEN_WIDTH;
d3dpp.BackBufferHeight = SCREEN_HEIGHT;
d3dpp.hDeviceWindow = hwnd;

//create Direct3D device
d3d->CreateDevice(
    D3DADAPTER_DEFAULT,
    D3DDEVTYPE_HAL,
    hwnd,
    D3DCREATE_SOFTWARE_VERTEXPROCESSING,
    &d3dpp,
    &d3ddev);

if (d3ddev == NULL)
{
    MessageBox(hwnd, "Error creating Direct3D device", "Error", MB_OK);
    return 0;
}

//set random number seed
srand(time(NULL));

//clear the backbuffer to black
d3ddev->Clear(0, NULL, D3DCLEAR_TARGET, D3DCOLOR_XRGB(0,0,0), 1.0f, 0);

//create pointer to the back buffer
d3ddev->GetBackBuffer(0, 0, D3DBACKBUFFER_TYPE_MONO, &backbuffer);

//create surface
result = d3ddev->CreateOffscreenPlainSurface(
    640,                  //width of the surface
    480,                  //height of the surface
    D3DFMT_X8R8G8B8,      //surface format
    D3DPOOL_DEFAULT,      //memory pool to use
    &surface,             //pointer to the surface
    NULL);                //reserved (always NULL)

if (result != D3D_OK)
    return 1;
```

```
//load surface from file
result = D3DXLoadSurfaceFromFile(
    surface,            //destination surface
    NULL,               //destination palette
    NULL,               //destination rectangle
    "legotron.bmp",     //source filename
    NULL,               //source rectangle
    D3DX_DEFAULT,       //controls how image is filtered
    0,                  //for transparency (0 for none)
    NULL);              //source image info (usually NULL)

//make sure file was loaded okay
if (result != D3D_OK)
    return 1;

//draw surface to the backbuffer
d3ddev->StretchRect(surface, NULL, backbuffer, NULL, D3DTEXF_NONE);

//return okay
return 1;
}
```

There are a few changes that need to be made to Game_Run, mainly involving the removal of some code because no screen updates will take place after the image has been drawn.

```
void Game_Run(HWND hwnd)
{
    //make sure the Direct3D device is valid
    if (d3ddev == NULL)
        return;

    //start rendering
    if (d3ddev->BeginScene())
    {
        //create pointer to the back buffer
        d3ddev->GetBackBuffer(0, 0, D3DBACKBUFFER_TYPE_MONO, &backbuffer);

        //draw surface to the backbuffer
        d3ddev->StretchRect(surface, NULL, backbuffer, NULL, D3DTEXF_NONE);

        //stop rendering
        d3ddev->EndScene();
    }
```

Figure 6.6
The Load_Bitmap program loads a bitmap image into a Direct3D surface and then blits it to the screen.

```
    //display the back buffer on the screen
    d3ddev->Present(NULL, NULL, NULL, NULL);

    //check for escape key (to exit program)
    if (KEY_DOWN(VK_ESCAPE))
        PostMessage(hwnd, WM_DESTROY, 0, 0);
}
```

The complete source listing and project for the program are included on the CD-ROM in \sources\chapter06\load_bitmap. When you run the program, you should see the bitmap shown in Figure 6.6 fill the screen.

What You Have Learned

In this chapter you learned how to create and manipulate surfaces. Here are the key points:

- You learned how to create a surface.

- You were able to fill the surface with random colors.

- You found out how to load a bitmap image from disk into a surface, with support for many graphics file formats.

- You learned how to draw whole and partial surfaces onto the screen.

Review Questions

Here are some review questions to dash your self-image and shatter your motivation.

1. What is the name of the primary Direct3D object?

2. What is the Direct3D device called?

3. What is the name of the Direct3D surface object?

4. What function can you use to draw images to the screen?

5. What is the term that describes copying images to a surface?

On Your Own

These exercises will help to reinforce the material you have learned today. It may not stick, but it's worth a shot!

Exercise 1. The Load_Bitmap program loads a bitmap file and displays it on the screen. Use what you have learned about StretchRect to draw only a portion of the bitmap image to the screen.

Exercise 2. You have been recruited by the Star League to defend the frontiers against the Zurg. Using the knowledge you have learned in this chapter, write a simple game to demonstrate your worthiness to continue reading this book.

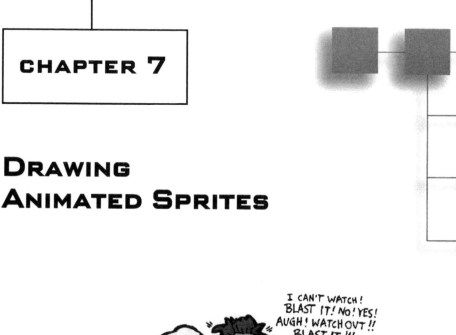

CHAPTER 7

DRAWING ANIMATED SPRITES

This chapter will teach you how to create and use sprites, which are suitable for creating 2D games, in the Direct3D environment. Sprites are small bitmaps (usually transparent) that are displayed on the screen and represent the objects in the game, such as a spaceship or a turtle-stomping plumber. All 2D games use sprites, as well as solid bitmaps that are called "tiles," which are used to fill in the background scene of a typical 2D game.

Here is what you will learn in this chapter:

- How to create a sprite and load a bitmap into a sprite surface.

- How to control the animation of a sprite.

- How to move a sprite on the screen.

Drawing Animated Sprites

There are two ways to draw a sprite with Direct3D. Both methods require that you keep track of the sprite's position, size, speed, and other properties on your own, so the logistics are not relevant. The simpler of the two methods is to load a sprite image into a D3D surface (which you learned about in the last chapter) and then draw the sprite using StretchRect. The more difficult—but more powerful—method is to use a special object called D3DXSprite to handle sprites in Direct3D. D3DXSprite uses textures rather than surfaces to hold the sprite image, so using it requires a slightly different approach than what you learned in the last chapter. However, loading a bitmap image into a texture is no more difficult than loading an image into a surface. I will cover the simple method of drawing sprites in this chapter, and then go over D3DXSprite in Chapter 8.

The Anim_Sprite Project

In the last chapter, I hinted about creating a game framework. The purpose of a framework is to make it easier to get started on each new game project; with a framework, you don't have to re-create an entire DirectX 9 project from scratch. The framework should have source code files with helper functions that assist with initializing Direct3D, DirectInput, DirectSound, and so on, along with functions for loading bitmaps into surfaces and textures, among other things. In this chapter, you will get started working on that framework, as you now have enough information to put it all together. Another reason to create a framework is that the single code listings are getting quite long, and most of it is repeated code.

While creating this new project that demonstrates sprite animation, you will again learn by repetition and will also encounter some new functions. I will explain how it all works after you have created the project, so that you'll have some exposure to the code before learning about the theory.

Configuring the Project

Let's start working on this framework by putting the code with which you are now intimately familiar into more logical, organized source code files that will work together to make it possible to write DirectX 9 games. First of all, fire up Visual C++. Create a new project by opening the File menu and selecting New. The new project is called Anim_Sprite and is a standard Win32 Project with an empty project workspace, as usual.

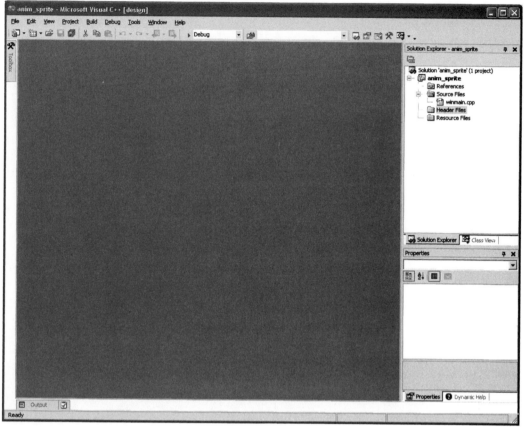

Figure 7.1
The new Anim_Sprite project.

Next, add a new source code file to the project called winmain.cpp. Figure 7.1 shows the project at this stage; it looks like all the previous projects you have worked on thus far.

I'll go over the steps for adding the DirectX libraries to the project again: First go into the Project menu and select Properties to bring up the Project Properties dialog, shown in Figure 7.2.

Add the Direct3D libraries to the list of library files in the linker settings page. Click the Link tab and add the two entries d3d9.lib and d3dx9.lib, as shown in Figure 7.3.

That's all you need to do to officially add Direct3D support to your program. In the next few chapters, as I take you on a tour of DirectInput and DirectSound (with DirectMusic), you'll learn how to add support for these libraries as well,

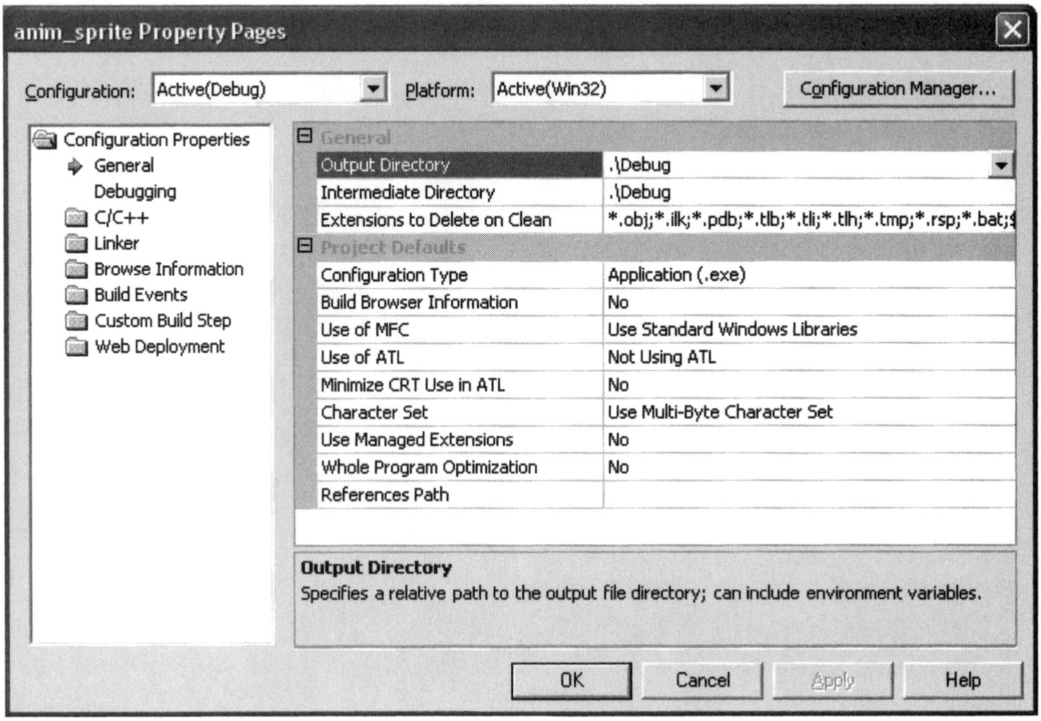

Figure 7.2
The Project Properties dialog.

and when the time comes, we'll also write new source code files for these DirectX components that will be added to the framework.

Source Code Files

As you have already added the winmain.cpp file to the project, let's start there. Just note that you'll be adding several more source code files and header files to the project shortly. The source for the winmain.cpp file this time will include *only* the Windows-specific code and nothing else. There will not be any DirectX or game loops here because I'm isolating the Windows, DirectX, and game code. I think you will love the result—it gets the clutter out of your game's source file. It's hard enough to design and program a game—with the several hundred variables that you must keep track of (in a typical small- to medium-sized game) in your head—without having to deal with all the logistical code as well.

Now then, here is the code for winmain.cpp. Note that it isn't exactly the same as the code you've seen in previous chapters because function calls are now being made to functions you haven't written yet (but we'll get to them soon!).

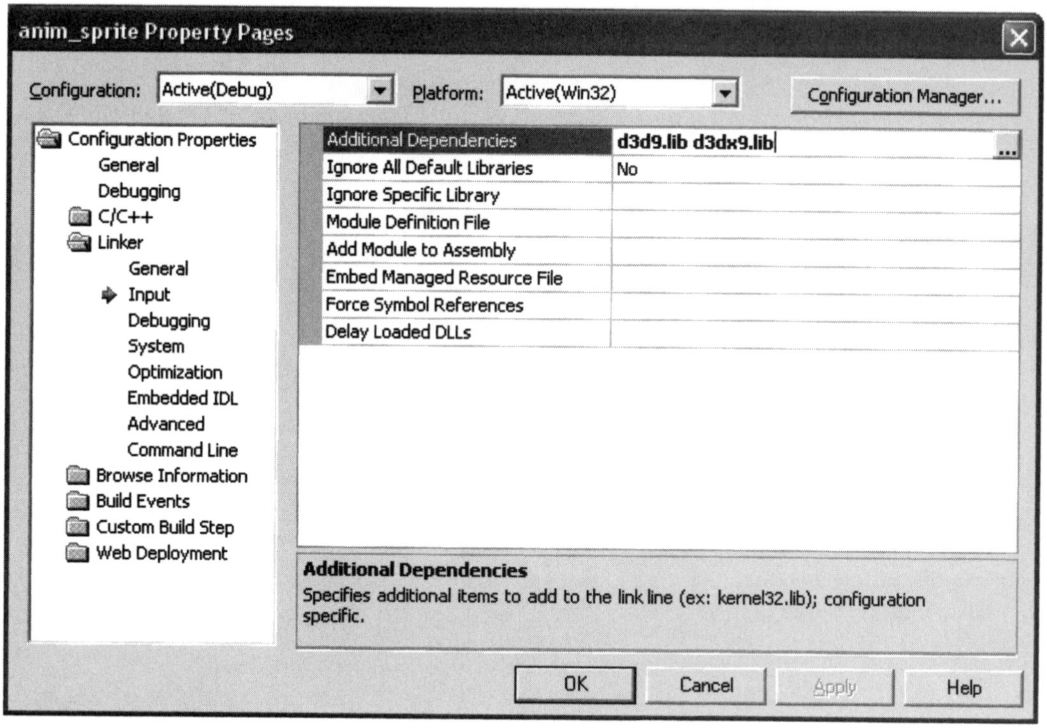

Figure 7.3
Adding the Direct3D libraries to the project.

winmain.cpp

```
// Beginning Game Programming, Second Edition
// Chapter 7
// winmain.cpp - Windows framework source code file

#include <d3d9.h>
#include <d3dx9.h>
#include <time.h>
#include <stdio.h>
#include "dxgraphics.h"
#include "game.h"

//window event callback function
LRESULT WINAPI WinProc( HWND hWnd, UINT msg, WPARAM wParam, LPARAM lParam )
{
    switch( msg )
    {
      case WM_DESTROY:
          //release the Direct3D device
```

```
                    if (d3ddev != NULL)
                        d3ddev->Release();

                    //release the Direct3D object
                    if (d3d != NULL)
                        d3d->Release();

                    //call the "front-end" shutdown function
                    Game_End(hWnd);

                    //tell Windows to kill this program
                    PostQuitMessage(0);
                    return 0;
            }
        return DefWindowProc( hWnd, msg, wParam, lParam );
}


//helper function to set up the window properties
ATOM MyRegisterClass(HINSTANCE hInstance)
{
        //create the window class structure
        WNDCLASSEX wc;
        wc.cbSize = sizeof(WNDCLASSEX);

        //fill the struct with info
        wc.style            = CS_HREDRAW | CS_VREDRAW;
        wc.lpfnWndProc      = (WNDPROC)WinProc;
        wc.cbClsExtra       = 0;
        wc.cbWndExtra       = 0;
        wc.hInstance        = hInstance;
        wc.hIcon            = NULL;
        wc.hCursor          = LoadCursor(NULL, IDC_ARROW);
        wc.hbrBackground    = (HBRUSH)GetStockObject(BLACK_BRUSH);
        wc.lpszMenuName     = NULL;
        wc.lpszClassName    = APPTITLE;
        wc.hIconSm          = NULL;

        //set up the window with the class info
        return RegisterClassEx(&wc);
}


//entry point for a Windows program
int WINAPI WinMain(HINSTANCE hInstance,
```

```
                    HINSTANCE        hPrevInstance,
                    LPSTR            lpCmdLine,
                    int              nCmdShow)
{
    MSG msg;
    HWND hWnd;

    // register the class
    MyRegisterClass(hInstance);

    //set up the screen in windowed or fullscreen mode?
    DWORD style;
    if (FULLSCREEN)
        style = WS_EX_TOPMOST | WS_VISIBLE | WS_POPUP;
    else
      style = WS_OVERLAPPED;

    //create a new window
    hWnd = CreateWindow(
        APPTITLE,              //window class
        APPTITLE,              //title bar
        style,                 //window style
        CW_USEDEFAULT,         //x position of window
        CW_USEDEFAULT,         //y position of window
        SCREEN_WIDTH,          //width of the window
        SCREEN_HEIGHT,         //height of the window
        NULL,                  //parent window
        NULL,                  //menu
        hInstance,             //application instance
        NULL);                 //window parameters

        //was there an error creating the window?
        if (!hWnd)
            return FALSE;

        //display the window
        ShowWindow(hWnd, nCmdShow);
        UpdateWindow(hWnd);

        if (!Init_Direct3D(hWnd, SCREEN_WIDTH, SCREEN_HEIGHT, FULLSCREEN))
            return 0;

            //initialize the game
```

```
if (!Game_Init(hWnd))
{
    MessageBox(hWnd, "Error initializing the game", "Error", MB_OK);
    return 0;
}

// main message loop
int done = 0;
while (!done)
{
    if (PeekMessage(&msg, NULL, 0, 0, PM_REMOVE))
    {
        //look for quit message
        if (msg.message == WM_QUIT)
            done = 1;

        //decode and pass messages on to WndProc
        TranslateMessage(&msg);
        DispatchMessage(&msg);
    }
    else
        //process game loop (prevents running after window is closed)
        Game_Run(hWnd);
}
return msg.wParam;
}
```

dxgraphics.h

Now open the Project menu and select Add New Item to bring up the Add New Item dialog. Select Header File (.h) from the list and type **dxgraphics.h** in the file name field, as shown in Figure 7.4.

Here is the code listing for dxgraphics.h. After you have added this file to the project, the workspace will look like that in Figure 7.5.

```
#ifndef _DXGRAPHICS_H
#define _DXGRAPHICS_H

//function prototypes
int Init_Direct3D(HWND, int, int, int);
LPDIRECT3DSURFACE9 LoadSurface(char *, D3DCOLOR);

//variable declarations
extern LPDIRECT3D9 d3d;
```

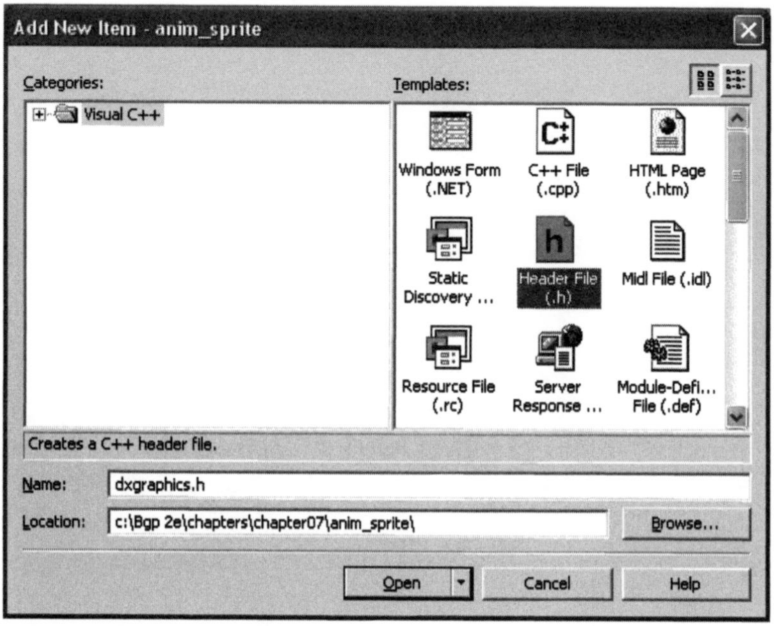

Figure 7.4
Adding a new header file to the project.

```
extern LPDIRECT3DDEVICE9 d3ddev;
extern LPDIRECT3DSURFACE9 backbuffer;

#endif
```

dxgraphics.cpp

In like manner, add another source code file, called dxgraphics.cpp, to the project. This will contain the actual functions defined in the header file above. Here is the source code for the dxgraphics.cpp file:

```
// Beginning Game Programming, 2nd Edition
// Chapter 7
// dxgraphics.cpp - Direct3D framework source code file

#include <d3d9.h>
#include <d3dx9.h>
#include "dxgraphics.h"

//variable declarations
LPDIRECT3D9 d3d = NULL;
LPDIRECT3DDEVICE9 d3ddev = NULL;
LPDIRECT3DSURFACE9 backbuffer = NULL;
```

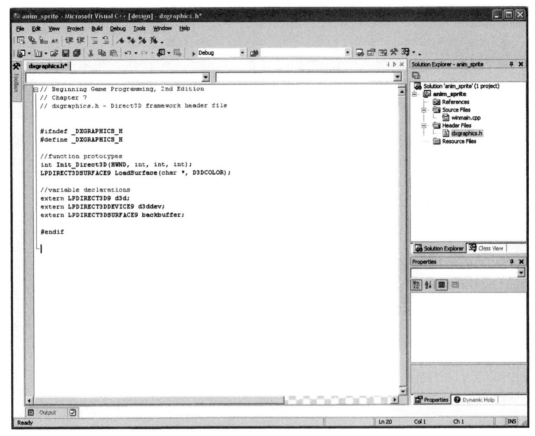

Figure 7.5
The Anim_Sprite project now includes dxgraphics.h.

```
int Init_Direct3D(HWND hwnd, int width, int height, int fullscreen)
{
    //initialize Direct3D
    d3d = Direct3DCreate9(D3D_SDK_VERSION);
    if (d3d == NULL)
    {
        MessageBox(hwnd, "Error initializing Direct3D", "Error", MB_OK);
        return 0;
    }

    //set Direct3D presentation parameters
    D3DPRESENT_PARAMETERS d3dpp;
    ZeroMemory(&d3dpp, sizeof(d3dpp));

    d3dpp.Windowed = (!fullscreen);
```

```
    d3dpp.SwapEffect = D3DSWAPEFFECT_COPY;
    d3dpp.BackBufferFormat = D3DFMT_X8R8G8B8;
    d3dpp.BackBufferCount = 1;
    d3dpp.BackBufferWidth = width;
    d3dpp.BackBufferHeight = height;
    d3dpp.hDeviceWindow = hwnd;
    d3dpp.EnableAutoDepthStencil = TRUE;
    d3dpp.AutoDepthStencilFormat = D3DFMT_D16;
    d3dpp.PresentationInterval    = D3DPRESENT_INTERVAL_IMMEDIATE;

    //create Direct3D device
    d3d->CreateDevice(
        D3DADAPTER_DEFAULT,
        D3DDEVTYPE_HAL,
        hwnd,
        D3DCREATE_SOFTWARE_VERTEXPROCESSING,
        &d3dpp,
        &d3ddev);

    if (d3ddev == NULL)
    {
        MessageBox(hwnd, "Error creating Direct3D device", "Error", MB_OK);
        return 0;
    }

    //clear the backbuffer to black
    d3ddev->Clear(0, NULL, D3DCLEAR_TARGET, D3DCOLOR_XRGB(0,0,0), 1.0f, 0);

    //create pointer to the back buffer
    d3ddev->GetBackBuffer(0, 0, D3DBACKBUFFER_TYPE_MONO, &backbuffer);

    return 1;
}

LPDIRECT3DSURFACE9 LoadSurface(char *filename, D3DCOLOR transcolor)
{
    LPDIRECT3DSURFACE9 image = NULL;
    D3DXIMAGE_INFO info;
    HRESULT result;

    //get width and height from bitmap file
    result = D3DXGetImageInfoFromFile(filename, &info);
    if (result != D3D_OK)
        return NULL;
```

```
    //create surface
    result = d3ddev->CreateOffscreenPlainSurface(
        info.Width,          //width of the surface
        info.Height,         //height of the surface
        D3DFMT_X8R8G8B8,     //surface format
        D3DPOOL_DEFAULT,     //memory pool to use
        &image,              //pointer to the surface
        NULL);               //reserved (always NULL)

    if (result != D3D_OK)
        return NULL;

    //load surface from file into newly created surface
    result = D3DXLoadSurfaceFromFile(
        image,               //destination surface
        NULL,                //destination palette
        NULL,                //destination rectangle
        filename,            //source filename
        NULL,                //source rectangle
        D3DX_DEFAULT,        //controls how image is filtered
        transcolor,          //for transparency (0 for none)
        NULL);               //source image info (usually NULL)

    //make sure file was loaded okay
    if (result != D3D_OK)
        return NULL;

    return image;
}
```

Well that's all there is to the Windows and DirectX code thus far. As you can see, there's still a long way to go, and we'll fill in more details over the next few chapters. For now, let's focus on the specific code for the Anim_Sprite program.

game.h
Add another Header File (.h) item to the project and name it game.h. Here is the source code listing for game.h.

```
#ifndef _GAME_H
#define _GAME_H

#include <d3d9.h>
#include <time.h>
#include <stdio.h>
```

```
#include <stdlib.h>
#include "dxgraphics.h"

//application title
#define APPTITLE "Anim_Sprite"

//screen setup
#define FULLSCREEN 1
#define SCREEN_WIDTH 640
#define SCREEN_HEIGHT 480

//macros to read the keyboard asynchronously
#define KEY_DOWN(vk_code) ((GetAsyncKeyState(vk_code) & 0x8000) ? 1 : 0)
#define KEY_UP(vk_code)((GetAsyncKeyState(vk_code) & 0x8000) ? 1 : 0)

//function prototypes
int Game_Init(HWND);
void Game_Run(HWND);
void Game_End(HWND);

//sprite structure
typedef struct {
    int x,y;
    int width,height;
    int movex,movey;
    int curframe,lastframe;
    int animdelay,animcount;
} SPRITE;

#endif
```

game.cpp

Alrighty, then—we're finally at the code that is the whole point of all this work, the game.cpp file. Add a new C++ File (.cpp) to the project using the Project menu and name the file game.cpp. Here is the code to type into this file.

```
#include "game.h"

LPDIRECT3DSURFACE9 kitty_image[7];
SPRITE kitty;

//timing variable
long start = GetTickCount();
```

```
//initializes the game
int Game_Init(HWND hwnd)
{
    char s[20];
    int n;

    //set random number seed
    srand(time(NULL));

    //load the sprite animation
    for (n=0; n<6; n++)
    {
        sprintf(s,"cat%d.bmp",n+1);
        kitty_image[n] = LoadSurface(s, D3DCOLOR_XRGB(255,0,255));
        if (kitty_image[n] == NULL)
            return 0;
    }


    //initialize the sprite's properties
    kitty.x = 100;
    kitty.y = 150;
    kitty.width = 96;
    kitty.height = 96;
    kitty.curframe = 0;
    kitty.lastframe = 5;
    kitty.animdelay = 2;
    kitty.animcount = 0;
    kitty.movex = 8;
    kitty.movey = 0;

    //return okay
    return 1;
}

//the main game loop
void Game_Run(HWND hwnd)
{
    RECT rect;

    //make sure the Direct3D device is valid
    if (d3ddev == NULL)
        return;
```

```
//after short delay, ready for next frame?
//this keeps the game running at a steady frame rate
if (GetTickCount() - start >= 30)
{
    //reset timing
    start = GetTickCount();


    //move the sprite
    kitty.x += kitty.movex;
    kitty.y += kitty.movey;


     //"warp" the sprite at screen edges
    if (kitty.x > SCREEN_WIDTH - kitty.width)
        kitty.x = 0;
    if (kitty.x < 0)
        kitty.x = SCREEN_WIDTH - kitty.width;


    //has animation delay reached threshold?
    if (++kitty.animcount > kitty.animdelay)
    {
        //reset counter
          kitty.animcount = 0;

        //animate the sprite
        if (++kitty.curframe > kitty.lastframe)
            kitty.curframe = 0;
    }
}


//start rendering
if (d3ddev->BeginScene())
{

    //erase the entire background
    d3ddev->ColorFill(backbuffer, NULL, D3DCOLOR_XRGB(0,0,0));

    //set the sprite's rect for drawing
    rect.left = kitty.x;
    rect.top = kitty.y;
    rect.right = kitty.x + kitty.width;
    rect.bottom = kitty.y + kitty.height;
```

```
        //draw the sprite
        d3ddev->StretchRect(kitty_image[kitty.curframe], NULL,
            backbuffer, &rect, D3DTEXF_NONE);

    //stop rendering
    d3ddev->EndScene();
  }

  //display the back buffer on the screen
  d3ddev->Present(NULL, NULL, NULL, NULL);

  //check for escape key (to exit program)
  if (KEY_DOWN(VK_ESCAPE))
      PostMessage(hwnd, WM_DESTROY, 0, 0);
}

//frees memory and cleans up before the game ends
void Game_End(HWND hwnd)
{
    int n;

    //free the surface
    for (n=0; n<6; n++)
        kitty_image[n]->Release();
}
```

The end result of adding all these new source files to the project is shown in Figure 7.6.

The Sprite Artwork

Obviously, before you can run the program you'll need the source artwork that I have used. When you run the program, it should look like Figure 7.7.

This animated cat has six frames of high-quality animation and looks quite good running across the screen. The artwork is part of a free sprite library called SpriteLib, created by Ari Feldman, a talented artist who runs a Web site at http://www.flyingyogi.com. Ari released SpriteLib to help budding game programmers get started without having to worry too much about content while learning. There are literally hundreds of sprites (both static and animated) and background tiles included in SpriteLib, and Ari adds to it now and then. Visit his Web site to download the complete SpriteLib, because only a few examples are included with this book.

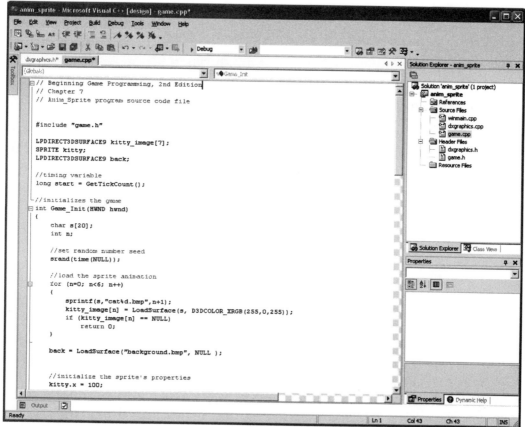

```
// Beginning Game Programming, 2nd Edition
// Chapter 7
// Anim_Sprite program source code file


#include "game.h"

LPDIRECT3DSURFACE9 kitty_image[7];
SPRITE kitty;
LPDIRECT3DSURFACE9 back;

//timing variable
long start = GetTickCount();

//initializes the game
int Game_Init(HWND hwnd)
{
    char s[20];
    int n;

    //set random number seed
    srand(time(NULL));

    //load the sprite animation
    for (n=0; n<6; n++)
    {
        sprintf(s,"cat%d.bmp",n+1);
        kitty_image[n] = LoadSurface(s, D3DCOLOR_XRGB(255,0,255));
        if (kitty_image[n] == NULL)
            return 0;
    }

    back = LoadSurface("background.bmp", NULL );


    //initialize the sprite's properties
    kitty.x = 100;
```

Figure 7.6
The completed Anim_Sprite project has five source code files.

Figure 7.7
The Anim_Sprite program draws an animated cat on the screen.

Tip

The home of Ari Feldman's SpriteLib is at http://www.flyingyogi.com.

The six frames of the animated cat sprite are shown in Figure 7.8. You can copy the files off the CD-ROM to the project folder on your hard drive in order to run this program.

These six catxx.bmp files are each 96 × 96 pixels in size, and have a pink background with an RGB value of (255,0,255). If you refer back to the Game_Init function given previously, you will notice that the call to LoadSurface included a color value for the second parameter:

```
//load the sprite animation
for (n=0; n<6; n++)
{
    sprintf(s,"cat%d.bmp",n+1);
    kitty_image[n] = LoadSurface(s, D3DCOLOR_XRGB(255,0,255));
    if (kitty_image[n] == NULL)
        return 0;
}
```

The color value represented by D3DCOLOR_XRGB(255,0,255) is that pink color. But why does the LoadSurface function need to worry about the background color? After all, this program doesn't even use transparency (check the next chapter for that). You specify the transparent color so the StretchRect function will render the transparent color as black (note that StretchRect does not handle true transparency). This is convenient because then you can use any color you want while editing the sprite to offset it from the background, and it will be rendered in black when loaded into the game.

Do you want to see how the cat will look when drawn over a background other than black? Okay, here are a few small modifications you can make to the program to add a background. I have included a background.bmp file in the folder for this project already, so it's ready to go if you copy it off the CD-ROM.

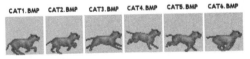

Figure 7.8
The animated cat sprite has six frames.

First, add the following line up near the top of the game.cpp with the other variable declarations:

```
LPDIRECT3DSURFACE9 back;
```

Next, in Game_Init, add the line of code to load the background bitmap into this new surface:

```
back = LoadSurface("background.bmp", D3DCOLOR_XRGB(255,0,255));
```

Next, down in Game_Run, comment out the ColorFill line and replace it with a call to StretchRect, as shown here:

```
//d3ddev->ColorFill(backbuffer, NULL, D3DCOLOR_XRGB(0,0,0));
d3ddev->StretchRect(back, NULL, backbuffer, NULL, D3DTEXF_NONE);
```

Finally, add a line to Game_End to free the memory used by the background surface:

```
back->Release();
```

Now go ahead and run the program again, this time with a background showing; the screen should look something like Figure 7.9. Why all this discussion if the cat isn't even being drawn with transparency? Because we're just dealing with raw surfaces, translating the background color of your sprite into black is the best we

Figure 7.9
The cat is being animated over a colorful background. Note the lack of transparency.

can do at this point. But stay tuned, as I'll cover true sprite transparency (and a lot of other interesting features) in the next chapter.

Naturally, you can use black for the background "transparent" color of your sprites in the first place, but the point here is that most people don't use black—they use an alternate color that is easier to see when editing the source image. To see what the surface would look like without manipulating the transparent color, you can modify the call to D3DXLoadSurfaceFromFile in dxgraphics.cpp (which you may recall from Chapter 6).

Note the second-to-last parameter, transcolor. If you change this to 0, then recompile and run the program, Direct3D will ignore the so-called "transparent" color of the image and just draw it natively. See Figure 7.10.

```
result = D3DXLoadSurfaceFromFile(
    image,            //destination surface
    NULL,             //destination palette
    NULL,             //destination rectangle
    filename,         //source filename
    NULL,             //source rectangle
    D3DX_DEFAULT,     //controls how image is filtered
    transcolor,       //for transparency (0 for none)
    NULL);            //source image info (usually NULL)
```

Figure 7.10
The cat is being drawn without regard to the "transparent" color.

Concept Art

Most sprites are rendered from 3D models today. It is rare to come across a game that features all hand-drawn artwork. Why? Because a 3D model can be rotated, textured, and manipulated easily after it has been created, while a 2D drawing is permanent. It is a simple matter to apply battle damage textures to a 3D model and then render out another frame for the game to use. I don't have room to discuss the complete process of creating concept art and turning it into game characters in this meager chapter. But I can give you a few examples.

Figure 7.11 is a concept drawing that I commissioned for an RPG. This was an early concept of a character that would have been a female archer. The drawing was made by Jessica K. Fuerst.

Pixel artists or 3D modelers use the concept drawings to construct the 2D images and 3D models for the game. Concept art is very important because it helps you to think through your designs and really brings the characters to life. If you are not a talented artist or can't afford to pay an artist to draw concept art for your game, then at least try to come up with your own pencil-and-paper drawings—the process of drawing is almost as important as the end result.

Figure 7.11
Concept drawing of a female archer character for an RPG. Image courtesy of Jessica K. Fuerst.

Figure 7.12
Concept drawing of another fantasy character for an RPG. Image courtesy of Eden Celeste.

Figure 7.12 is a painting of a female fantasy character, drawn by Eden Celeste, that inspired some ideas for another RPG character. Sometimes browsing online art galleries is a good way to derive inspiration for your game. Many artists are willing to work for hire or sell some of their existing work to you for use in a game.

Animated Sprites Explained

Now that you've had some exposure to the source code for a program that draws an animated sprite on the screen, I'll go over the key aspects of this program to help fill in any gaps in your understanding of it.

First of all, by presenting the practical application before the theory, I am assuming that you know a little about games already and have the background to understand what it is that makes up a game—at least in principle. A *sprite* is a small bitmapped image that is drawn on the screen and represents a character or object in a game. Sprites can be used for inanimate objects like trees and rocks, or animated game characters like a hero/heroine in a role-playing game. One thing is certain in the modern world of game development: Sprites are reserved exclusively for the 2D realm. You will not find a sprite in a 3D game, unless that sprite is being drawn "over" the 3D rendered game scene, as with a heads-up display or bitmapped font. For instance, in a multi-player game with a chat feature, the text messages appearing on the screen from other players are usually

Figure 7.13
A bitmapped font used to print text on the screen in a game.

Figure 7.14
A tank sprite with animated treads, courtesy of Ari Feldman.

drawn as individual letters, each treated as a sprite. Figure 7.13 shows an example of a bitmapped font stored in a bitmap file.

A sprite is typically stored in a bitmap file as a series of tiles, each tile representing a single frame of that sprite's animation sequence. An animation might look less like movement than a change of direction, as in the case of an airplane or spaceship in a shoot-'em-up game. Figure 7.14 shows a tank sprite that faces in a single direction but includes animated treads for movement.

Now what if you wanted that tank to face other directions as well as animate? As you can imagine, the number of frames can increase exponentially as you add a new frame of animation for each direction of travel. Figure 7.15 shows a non-animated tank that has been rotated in 32 directions for a very smooth turning rate. Unfortunately, when you add the moving tank treads, those 32 frames suddenly become 32 * 8 = 256 frames! It would be difficult to program a tank with so many frames, and how would you store them in the bitmap file? Linearly, most likely, in rows and columns. A better solution is usually to reduce the number of frames until you get the game finished, and then perhaps (if you are so inclined) add more precision and detail to the animation.

MechCommander (MicroProse, FASA Studios) was one of the most highly animated video games ever made, and were it not for the terrible AI in this game and unrealistic difficulty level, I would have considered it among my all-time favorite games. The fascinating thing about *MechCommander* is that it is a highly detailed

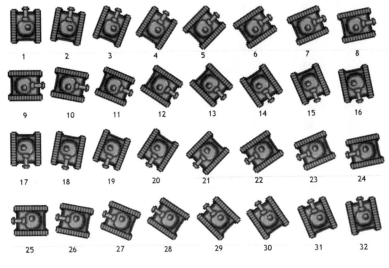

Figure 7.15
A 32-frame rotation of the tank sprite (not animated), courtesy of Ari Feldman.

2D sprite-based game. Every single mech in the game is a 2D sprite stored in a series of bitmap files. The traditional 2D nature of this game becomes amazing when you consider that the game featured about 100,000 frames! Imagine the amount of time it took to first model the mechs with a 3D modeler (like *3ds max*), and then render out 100,000 snapshots of various angles and positions, and then resize and add the final touches to each sprite.

Note

In August of 2006, Microsoft released the source code to *MechCommander 2*, along with all of the game's resources (artwork, etc). You can download the complete code for the game (which is powered by DirectX) from here: http://www.microsoft.com/downloads/details.aspx?familyid= 6D790CDE-C3E5-46BE-B3A5-729581269A9C&displaylang=en. I found this link by Googling for "mechcommander 2 source code".

Another common type of sprite is the platformer game sprite, shown in Figure 7.16. Programming a platform game is more difficult than programming a shoot-'em-up, but the results are usually worth the extra work.

The SPRITE Struct

The key to this program is the SPRITE struct defined in game.h:

```
//sprite structure
typedef struct {
    int x,y;
```

Figure 7.16
An animated platform game character, courtesy of Ari Feldman.

```
    int width,height;
    int movex,movey;
    int curframe,lastframe;
    int animdelay,animcount;
} SPRITE;
```

The obvious members of this struct are x, y, width, and height. What may not be so obvious is movex and movey. These member variables are used to update the x and y position of the sprite during each frame update. The curframe and lastframe variables help to keep track of the current frame of animation for the sprite. curframe is updated during each iteration through the game loop, and when it has reached lastframe it is looped back to zero. The animdelay and animcount variables work with the previous two in order to adjust the timing of a particular sprite. If the animation frame is updated every single time through the game's main loop, then the animation will run too fast. You don't want to slow down the frame rate of the game just to keep animation at a reasonable rate, so the alternative is to delay updating the frame by a set value.

The "kitty" sprite is defined like this:

```
LPDIRECT3DSURFACE9 kitty_image[7];
SPRITE kitty;
```

The sprite is initialized in the Game_Init function and set to the following values:

```
//initialize the sprite's properties
kitty.x = 100;
kitty.y = 150;
kitty.width = 96;
kitty.height = 96;
kitty.curframe = 0;
kitty.lastframe = 5;
```

```
kitty.animdelay = 2;
kitty.animcount = 0;
kitty.movex = 8;
kitty.movey = 0;
```

The Game Loop

The Game_Run function *is* the game loop, so always remember that it must process a single screen update and that is all! Don't ever put a while loop here or the game will probably just lock up (because control will not return to WinMain).

There are two parts to the Game_Run function. The first part should move and animate the sprite(s) in the game. The second part should draw the sprite(s) to the screen. The reason that a screen update is divided into two parts (one for logic, the other for screen refresh) is because you don't want to take too much processing time in between the BeginScene and EndScene calls, so keep the code there to the minimum required to update the graphics and leave other processing tasks for either before or after the screen update.

The key lines of code that you should pay attention to are those that move the sprite, keep the sprite on the screen, and animate the sprite:

```
//move the sprite
kitty.x += kitty.movex;
kitty.y += kitty.movey;

//"warp" the sprite at screen edges
if (kitty.x > SCREEN_WIDTH - kitty.width)
    kitty.x = 0;
if (kitty.x < 0)
        kitty.x = SCREEN_WIDTH - kitty.width;

//has animation delay reached threshold?
if (++kitty.animcount > kitty.animdelay)
{
    //reset counter
    kitty.animcount = 0;

    //animate the sprite
    if (++kitty.curframe > kitty.lastframe)
        kitty.curframe = 0;
}
```

Do you see how convenient the sprite movement and animation code is when you utilize the SPRITE struct? This code is generic enough to be put into a separate function that can be passed a specific SPRITE variable to update multiple sprites in a game (something I'll get into in the next chapter).

What You Have Learned

In this chapter you have forged ahead in learning how to program 2D surfaces and sprites in Direct3D! Take heart if you are not entirely confident of all this new information, though, because learning it is no simple feat! If you have any doubts, I recommend reading this chapter again before forging ahead to the next one, which deals with advanced sprite programming. Don't balk at all the 2D graphics discussions here; I encourage you to keep learning because this is the foundation for the 3D chapters to come! Here are the key points:

- You learned how to create a 2D surface that is rendered by Direct3D.

- You created a sprite and learned how to associate it with a surface.

- You learned about timing and how to slow down the game.

- You learned about animation and animated a running cat on the screen.

- You learned a thing or two about transparency.

Review Questions

These questions will challenge you to study this chapter further, if necessary.

1. What is the benefit of having concept drawings for a game?

2. What is the name of the surface object in Direct3D?

3. What function should you use to draw a surface on the screen?

4. What D3DX helper function do you use to load a bitmap image into a surface?

5. Where can you find a good collection of free sprites on the Web?

On Your Own

The following exercises will help you to think outside the box and push the limits of your understanding of this material.

Exercise 1. The Anim_Sprite program draws an animated cat on the screen. Modify the bitmaps and the program so that it draws a different animated sprite.

Exercise 2. Modify the Anim_Sprite program so that the cat runs twice as fast, without adjusting the frame rate limiter (`start` and `GetTickCount`). Modify the program again so the sprite moves half as fast as it did originally.

CHAPTER 8

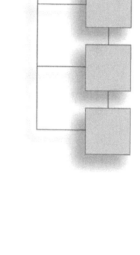

Advanced Sprite Programming

This chapter takes the subject of sprites to the next level. By utilizing textures rather than surfaces it is possible to draw a sprite transparently; other special effects are also possible. This chapter will provide you with a truly robust and reusable set of sprite routines that will be useful in future projects. This chapter is rounded out with a discussion of collision detection, which makes it possible to detect when two sprites have overlapped or collided with each other.

Here is what you will learn in this chapter:

- How to use the D3DXSprite object.

- How to load a texture.

- How to draw a transparent sprite.

- How to test for sprite collisions.

Drawing Transparent Sprites

The D3DXSprite object is really a wonderful surprise for any programmer planning to write a 2D game using Direct3D. One of the benefits of doing so is that you have a full 3D renderer at your disposal while using 2D functions that are every bit as fast as previous implementations (such as the old DirectDraw). By treating a sprite as a texture and rendering the sprite as a rectangle (comprised of two triangles, as is the case with all 3D rectangles), you have the ability to transform the sprite!

By *transform* I mean you can move the sprite with full 3D hardware acceleration. You can draw the sprite transparently by specifying an alpha color in the source bitmap that represents transparent pixels. Black (0,0,0) is a common color to use for transparency, but it is not a very good color to use. Why? Because it's hard to tell which pixels are transparent and which are simply dark in color. A better color to use is pink (255,0,255) because it is seldom used in game graphics and shows up brightly in the source image. You can instantly spot the transparent pixels in such an image.

Obviously, the D3DXSprite method is the way to go, but I'm going to cover the simpler method as well because it may be helpful in some circumstances to use non-transparent images—for instance, to draw a tiled background.

Creating a Sprite Handler Object

The D3DXSprite object is just a sprite handler that includes a function to draw sprites from a texture (with various transformations). Here is how you might declare it:

```
LPD3DXSPRITE sprite_handler;
```

You can then initialize the object by calling the D3DXCreateSprite function. What this does, basically, is attach the sprite handler to your primary Direct3D object and device so that it knows how to draw sprites on the back buffer.

```
HRESULT WINAPI D3DXCreateSprite(

    LPDIRECT3DDEVICE9 pDevice,
    LPD3DXSPRITE *ppSprite
);
```

And here is an example of how you might invoke this function:

```
result = D3DXCreateSprite(d3ddev, &sprite_handler);
```

Starting the Sprite Handler

I'll go over loading a sprite image shortly, but for the time being, let me show you how to use D3DXSprite. When you have called BeginScene from your primary Direct3D device, you can start drawing sprites. The first thing you must do is lock the surface so that the sprites can be drawn. You do this by calling the D3DXSprite.Begin function, which has this format:

```
HRESULT Begin(
    DWORD Flags
);
```

The flags parameter is required and will usually be D3DXSPRITE_ALPHABLEND, which draws sprites with transparency support. Here is an example:

```
sprite_handler->Begin(D3DXSPRITE_ALPHABLEND);
```

Drawing a Sprite

Drawing a sprite is a little more complicated than simply blitting the image using a source and destination rectangle, as was the case with surfaces in the last chapter. However, D3DXSprite just uses a single function, Draw, for all of the transformation options, so once you understand how this function works you can perform transparency, scaling, and rotation by just altering the parameters. Here is the declaration for the Draw function:

```
HRESULT Draw(

    LPDIRECT3DTEXTURE9 pTexture,
    CONST RECT *pSrcRect,
    CONST D3DXVECTOR3 *pCenter,
    CONST D3DXVECTOR3 *pPosition,
    D3DCOLOR Color
);
```

The first parameter is the most important one, because it specifies the texture to use for the source image of the sprite. The second parameter is also important, because you can use it to grab "tiles" out of the source image and thus store all of your sprite's animation frames in a single bitmap file (more on that later in this chapter). The third parameter specifies the center point from which rotation takes place. The fourth parameter specifies the position of the sprite, and this is typically where you set the x and y value. The last parameter specifies the color alterations to be made on the sprite image as it is drawn (and doesn't affect transparency).

The D3DXVECTOR3 is a new data type released with DirectX 9.0b, and includes three member variables: x, y, and z.

```
typedef struct D3DXVECTOR3 {
    FLOAT x;
    FLOAT y;
    FLOAT z;
} D3DXVECTOR3;
```

The first two, x and y, are the only ones you'll need to move the sprite on the 2D surface of the screen. I will show you an example of how to use Draw in a sample program shortly.

Stopping the Sprite Handler

After you have finished drawing sprites, but before you have called EndScene, you must call D3DXSprite.End to unlock the surface for other processes to use. Here is the syntax:

```
HRESULT End(VOID);
```

Usage is fairly obvious because the function is so short:

```
sprite_handler->End();
```

Loading the Sprite Image

The first thing that you should be aware of is that D3DXSprite uses a texture rather than a surface to store the sprite image. So, while the LPDIRECT3DSURFACE9 object was used in the last chapter for sprites, in this chapter you will use the LPDIRECT3DTEXTURE9 object instead. If I were creating a tile-based scrolling arcade game like *Super Mario World* or *R-Type* or *Mars Matrix*, I would use a surface to draw (and scroll) the background, but I would use a texture for the foreground sprites that represent the game characters/spaceships/enemies, as the case may be. There really is no performance benefit to using a surface over a texture, because your expensive video card (with an advanced 3D chip) will render your sprites on the screen using a hardware texture-mapping system that is light-years faster than anything you could do with software. Gone are the days when a 2D sprite blitter was written in assembly language! Today, we let Direct3D draw our sprites.

The first thing you must do to create a D3DXSprite is to create a texture object into which the sprite's bitmap image is loaded:

```
LPDIRECT3DTEXTURE9 texture = NULL;
```

The next thing you need to do is grab the resolution out of the bitmap file (assuming you have the sprite bitmap ready to go) using the D3DXGetImage-InfoFromFile function:

```
D3DXIMAGE_INFO info;
result = D3DXGetImageInfoFromFile("image.bmp", &info);
```

If the file exists, then you will have the Width and Height, which are useful for the next step. Next, you load the sprite's image from a bitmap file directly into a texture in a single step using the D3DXCreateTextureFromFileEx function:

```
HRESULT WINAPI D3DXCreateTextureFromFileEx(

    LPDIRECT3DDEVICE9 pDevice,
    LPCTSTR pSrcFile,
    UINT Width,
    UINT Height,
    UINT MipLevels,
    DWORD Usage,
    D3DFORMAT Format,
    D3DPOOL Pool,
    DWORD Filter,
    DWORD MipFilter,
    D3DCOLOR ColorKey,
    D3DXIMAGE_INFO *pSrcInfo,
    PALETTEENTRY *pPalette,
    LPDIRECT3DTEXTURE9 *ppTexture
);
```

Don't worry too much about all these parameters, as most of them are filled in with default values and NULLs. The only thing left to do, then, is to write a little function that puts all of this information together and returns a texture for you. Here is that function, which I have called LoadTexture (creative, aren't I?):

```
LPDIRECT3DTEXTURE9 LoadTexture(char *filename, D3DCOLOR transcolor)
{
    //the texture pointer
    LPDIRECT3DTEXTURE9 texture = NULL;

    //the struct for reading bitmap file info
    D3DXIMAGE_INFO info;

    //standard Windows return value
    HRESULT result;

    //get width and height from bitmap file
    result = D3DXGetImageInfoFromFile(filename, &info);
    if (result != D3D_OK)
        return NULL;

    //create the new texture by loading a bitmap image file
    D3DXCreateTextureFromFileEx(
        d3ddev,                 //Direct3D device object
        filename,               //bitmap filename
        info.Width,             //bitmap image width
        info.Height,            //bitmap image height
        1,                      //mip-map levels (1 for no chain)
        D3DPOOL_DEFAULT,        //the type of surface (standard)
        D3DFMT_UNKNOWN,         //surface format (default)
        D3DPOOL_DEFAULT,        //memory class for the texture
        D3DX_DEFAULT,           //image filter
        D3DX_DEFAULT,           //mip filter
        transcolor,             //color key for transparency
        &info,                  //bitmap file info (from loaded file)
        NULL,                   //color palette
        &texture );             //destination texture

    //make sure the bitmap texture was loaded correctly
    if (result != D3D_OK)
        return NULL;

    return texture;
}
```

As texturing will be discussed more in Part III, I will skip over a detailed explanation of this function for now. Make use of it to load sprites at this point and we'll go over it again later. Remember to always ignore things that you don't immediately need and move on toward getting what you do need accomplished. Only return to look over the advanced options when you have the time, willingness, and ability to do so.

Drawing Transparent Sprites

Now that you understand how D3DXSprite works with Direct3D textures to draw a transparent sprite (at least, that's the theory!), let's write a short program to show how to pull it all together. You can load the project off the CD-ROM if you wish, or you can modify the Anim_Sprite project from the previous chapter. I'll assume you're going to create a new project from scratch. After all, that's the best way to learn. Figure 8.1 shows the Trans_Sprite program.

Creating the Trans_Sprite Project

First of all, fire up Visual C++ and create a new Win32 Project, and give it the name Trans_Sprite. Next, open the Project menu and select Properties to bring

Figure 8.1
The Trans_Sprite program demonstrates how to draw transparent sprites with Direct3D.

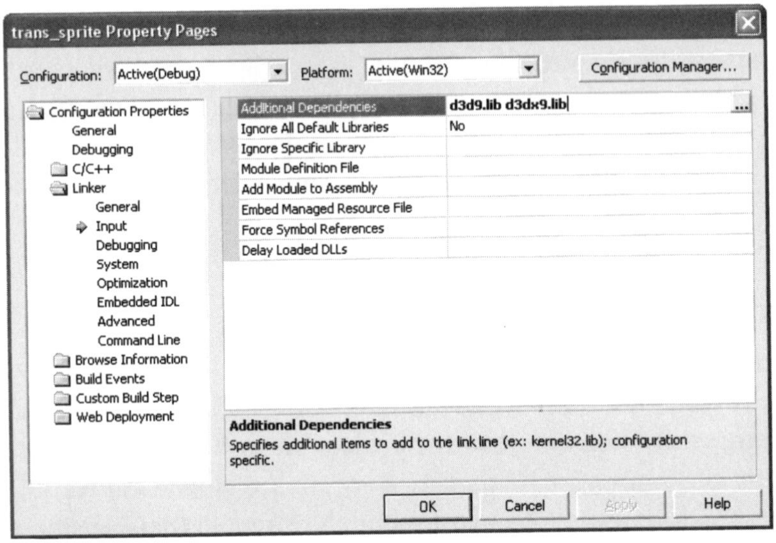

Figure 8.2
Adding support for Direct3D to the project

up the Project Properties dialog. Click the Linker/Input item and add d3d9.lib and d3dx9.lib to the Additional Dependencies field, as shown in Figure 8.2.

Next, you need to copy the following files from the Anim_Sprite folder from Chapter 7 into your new project folder:

- winmain.cpp

- dxgraphics.h

- dxgraphics.cpp

You can add game.h and game.cpp if you wish, but I recommend just creating them from scratch because most of the code in these two key files will change from one project to the next. To add them, open the Project menu and select Add New Item to add new source code files. Select Header File (.h) for the game.h file, and select Source File (.cpp) for the game.cpp file.

game.h

Now that you have re-created a project that supports the game framework (which currently just includes the Windows and Direct3D code, but in time will include other DirectX components), it's time to write the "real" code for this program. Here is the code for game.h:

```
#ifndef _GAME_H
#define _GAME_H

#include <d3d9.h>
#include <d3dx9.h>
#include <d3dx9math.h>
#include <time.h>
#include <stdio.h>
#include <stdlib.h>
#include "dxgraphics.h"

//application title
#define APPTITLE "Trans_Sprite"

//screen setup
#define FULLSCREEN 0           //0 = windowed, 1 = fullscreen
#define SCREEN_WIDTH 640
#define SCREEN_HEIGHT 480

//macros to read the keyboard asynchronously
#define KEY_DOWN(vk_code) ((GetAsyncKeyState(vk_code) & 0x8000) ? 1 : 0)
#define KEY_UP(vk_code)((GetAsyncKeyState(vk_code) & 0x8000) ? 1 : 0)

//function prototypes
int Game_Init(HWND);
void Game_Run(HWND);
void Game_End(HWND);

//sprite structure
typedef struct {
    int x,y;
    int width,height;
    int movex,movey;
    int curframe,lastframe;
    int animdelay,animcount;
} SPRITE;

#endif
```

game.cpp

Here is the main code for the Trans_Sprite program, which is entered into the game.cpp source code file:

```
#include "game.h"

LPDIRECT3DTEXTURE9 kitty_image[7];
SPRITE kitty;
LPDIRECT3DSURFACE9 back;
LPD3DXSPRITE sprite_handler;

HRESULT result;

//timing variable
long start = GetTickCount();

//initializes the game
int Game_Init(HWND hwnd)
{
    char s[20];
    int n;

    //set random number seed
    srand(time(NULL));

    //create sprite handler object
    result = D3DXCreateSprite(d3ddev, &sprite_handler);
    if (result != D3D_OK)
        return 0;

    //load the sprite animation
    for (n=0; n<6; n++)
    {
        //set up the filename
        sprintf(s,"cat%d.bmp",n+1);

        //load texture with "pink" as the transparent color
        kitty_image[n] = LoadTexture(s, D3DCOLOR_XRGB(255,0,255));
        if (kitty_image[n] == NULL)
        return 0;
    }

    //load the background image
    back = LoadSurface("background.bmp", NULL);

    //initialize the sprite's properties
    kitty.x = 100;
```

```
        kitty.y = 150;
        kitty.width = 96;
        kitty.height = 96;
        kitty.curframe = 0;
        kitty.lastframe = 5;
        kitty.animdelay = 2;
        kitty.animcount = 0;
        kitty.movex = 8;
        kitty.movey = 0;

        //return okay
        return 1;
    }

    //the main game loop
    void Game_Run(HWND hwnd)
    {
        //make sure the Direct3D device is valid
        if (d3ddev == NULL)
            return;

            //after short delay, ready for next frame?
            //this keeps the game running at a steady frame rate
            if (GetTickCount() - start >= 30)
            {
                //reset timing
                start = GetTickCount();

                //move the sprite
                kitty.x += kitty.movex;
                kitty.y += kitty.movey;

                //"warp" the sprite at screen edges
                if (kitty.x > SCREEN_WIDTH - kitty.width)
                    kitty.x = 0;
                if (kitty.x < 0)
                    kitty.x = SCREEN_WIDTH - kitty.width;

                //has animation delay reached threshold?
                if (++ kitty.animcount > kitty.animdelay)
            {
                    //reset counter
                    kitty.animcount = 0;
```

```
                //animate the sprite
                if (++kitty.curframe > kitty.lastframe)
                    kitty.curframe = 0;
            }
        }

    //start rendering
    if (d3ddev->BeginScene())
    {
        //erase the entire background
        d3ddev->StretchRect(back, NULL, backbuffer, NULL, D3DTEXF_NONE);

        //start sprite handler
        sprite_handler->Begin(D3DXSPRITE_ALPHABLEND);

        //create vector to update sprite position
          D3DXVECTOR3 position((float)kitty.x, (float)kitty.y, 0);

        //draw the sprite
        sprite_handler->Draw(
            kitty_image[kitty.curframe],
            NULL,
            NULL,
            &position,
            D3DCOLOR_XRGB(255,255,255));

        //stop drawing
        sprite_handler->End();

    //stop rendering
    d3ddev->EndScene();
    }

    //display the back buffer on the screen
    d3ddev->Present(NULL, NULL, NULL, NULL);

    //check for escape key (to exit program)
    if (KEY_DOWN(VK_ESCAPE))
        PostMessage(hwnd, WM_DESTROY, 0, 0);

}

//frees memory and cleans up before the game ends
```

```
void Game_End(HWND hwnd)
{
    int n;

    for (n=0; n<6; n++)
        if (kitty_image[n] != NULL)
            kitty_image[n]->Release();

    if (back != NULL)
        back->Release();

    if (sprite_handler != NULL)
        sprite_handler->Release();
}
```

Modifying dxgraphics.h

Now we need to add support for loading of textures to the framework file called dxgraphics.h. This file is already in your project, so you can simply open it and add the new line of code that will make the LoadTexture function visible throughout the project.

Add the following line of code to dxgraphics.h in the function prototypes section:

```
LPDIRECT3DTEXTURE9 LoadTexture(char *, D3DCOLOR);
```

After you have added the line, the prototypes section should look like this:

```
//function prototypes
int Init_Direct3D(HWND, int, int, int);
LPDIRECT3DSURFACE9 LoadSurface(char *, D3DCOLOR);
LPDIRECT3DTEXTURE9 LoadTexture(char *, D3DCOLOR);
```

Modifying dxgraphics.cpp

Now that you have defined the new LoadTexture function so the rest of the program can use it, you'll need to open the dxgraphics.cpp file and add the actual function to this file.

```
LPDIRECT3DTEXTURE9 LoadTexture(char *filename, D3DCOLOR transcolor)
{
    //the texture pointer
    LPDIRECT3DTEXTURE9 texture = NULL;
```

```
//the struct for reading bitmap file info
D3DXIMAGE_INFO info;

//standard Windows return value
HRESULT result;

//get width and height from bitmap file
result = D3DXGetImageInfoFromFile(filename, &info);
if (result != D3D_OK)
    return NULL;

//create the new texture by loading a bitmap image file
  D3DXCreateTextureFromFileEx(
        d3ddev,              //Direct3D device object
        filename,            //bitmap filename
        info.Width,          //bitmap image width
        info.Height,         //bitmap image height
        1,                   //mip-map levels (1 for no chain)
        D3DPOOL_DEFAULT,     //the type of surface (standard)
        D3DFMT_UNKNOWN,      //surface format (default)
        D3DPOOL_DEFAULT,     //memory class for the texture
        D3DX_DEFAULT,        //image filter
        D3DX_DEFAULT,        //mip filter
        transcolor,          //color key for transparency
        &info,               //bitmap file info (from loaded file)
        NULL,                //color palette
        &texture );          //destination texture

//make sure the bitmap texture was loaded correctly
if (result != D3D_OK)
    return NULL;

return texture;
}
```

Drawing an Animated Sprite

Up to this point, you have been learning about creating, manipulating, and drawing sprites using just a single bitmap image for each frame of animation (at least, for those sprites that are animated). This is a good way to learn about sprite programming, but it is not very efficient. For one thing, your game will have probably hundreds of bitmap files to load, which takes a long time.

Figure 8.3
The caveman character has eight running frames and four jumping frames of animation.

A much better way to handle sprites is by storing the sprite images in a single tiled bitmap image. I hinted about this in the last chapter, when I showed you some tiled images of a tank sprite and a running caveman character, shown in Figure 8.3.

Working with Sprite Sheets

The trick to capturing a tile is understanding that the source image is made up of rows and columns of tiles—and in the context of a sprite, we call this tiled image a *sprite sheet*. What you want to do is figure out the upper left corner of where the tile is located in the bitmap image and then copy from that source a rectangle based on the width and height of the sprite.

First, you need to figure out the left, or x, position of the tile. You do that by using the modulus operator, %. Modulus returns the remainder of a division. So, for instance, if the current frame is 20, and there are only five columns in the bitmap, then modulus will give you the horizontal starting position of the tile (when you multiply it by the width of the sprite). Calculating the top edge of the tile is then simply a matter of dividing the current frame by the number of columns, and multiplying the result by the sprite height. If there are five columns across, then tile 20 will be in row 4, column 5. Here is the pseudo-code:

```
left = (current frame % number of columns) * sprite width
top  = (current frame / number of columns) * sprite height
```

The actual code used in the Tiled_Sprite program looks like this (note the use of the sprite width and height in the calculation for the left and top as well as for then calculating the right and bottom edges of the source rectangle):

```
left = (curframe % columns) * width;
top = (curframe / columns) * height;
right = left + width;
bottom = top + height;
```

The Tiled_Sprite Program

Here is the source code for the Tiled_Sprite program, which demonstrates how to animate a sprite based on a single bitmap image. The output from the program is shown in Figure 8.4. You will want to type this code into the game.cpp file, assuming you are using the same type of framework that we've been building up to this point (with the dxgraphics.h, dxgraphics.cpp, and other files in our small game library).

```
#include "game.h"

LPDIRECT3DTEXTURE9 caveman_image;
SPRITE caveman;
LPDIRECT3DSURFACE9 back;
LPD3DXSPRITE sprite_handler;

HRESULT result;

//timing variable
long start = GetTickCount();
```

Figure 8.4
The Tiled_Sprite program demonstrates how to use a tiled bitmap image for sprite animation.

```
//initializes the game
int Game_Init(HWND hwnd)
{
    //set random number seed
    srand(time(NULL));

    //create sprite handler object
    result = D3DXCreateSprite(d3ddev, &sprite_handler);
    if (result != D3D_OK)
        return 0;

    //load texture with "pink" as the transparent color
    caveman_image = LoadTexture("caveman.bmp", D3DCOLOR_XRGB(255,0,255));
    if (caveman_image == NULL)
        return 0;

    //load the background image
    back = LoadSurface("background.bmp", NULL);

    //initialize the sprite's properties
    caveman.x = 100;
    caveman.y = 180;
    caveman.width = 50;
    caveman.height = 64;
    caveman.curframe = 1;
    caveman.lastframe = 11;
    caveman.animdelay = 3;
    caveman.animcount = 0;
    caveman.movex = 5;
    caveman.movey = 0;

    //return okay
    return 1;
}

//the main game loop
void Game_Run(HWND hwnd)
{
    //make sure the Direct3D device is valid
    if (d3ddev == NULL)
        return;

        //after short delay, ready for next frame?
```

```
//this keeps the game running at a steady frame rate
if (GetTickCount() - start >= 30)
{
    //reset timing
    start = GetTickCount();

    //move the sprite
    caveman.x += caveman.movex;
    caveman.y += caveman.movey;

    //"warp" the sprite at screen edges
    if (caveman.x > SCREEN_WIDTH - caveman.width)
        caveman.x = 0;
    if (caveman.x < 0)
        caveman.x = SCREEN_WIDTH - caveman.width;

    //has animation delay reached threshold?
    if (++ caveman.animcount > caveman.animdelay)
    {
        //reset counter
        caveman.animcount = 0;

        //animate the sprite
        if (++ caveman.curframe > caveman.lastframe)
            caveman.curframe = 1;
    }
}

//start rendering
if (d3ddev->BeginScene())
{
    //erase the entire background
    d3ddev->StretchRect(back, NULL, backbuffer, NULL, D3DTEXF_NONE);

    //start sprite handler
    sprite_handler->Begin(D3DXSPRITE_ALPHABLEND);

    //create vector to update sprite position
    D3DXVECTOR3 position((float)caveman.x, (float)caveman.y, 0);

    //configure the rect for the source tile
    RECT srcRect;
    int columns = 8;
```

```
            srcRect.left = (caveman.curframe % columns) * caveman.width;
            srcRect.top = (caveman.curframe / columns) * caveman.height;
            srcRect.right = srcRect.left + caveman.width;
            srcRect.bottom = srcRect.top + caveman.height;

            //draw the sprite
            sprite_handler->Draw(
               caveman_image,
               &srcRect,
               NULL,
               &position,
               D3DCOLOR_XRGB(255,255,255));

            //stop drawing
            sprite_handler->End();

        //stop rendering
        d3ddev->EndScene();
    }

    //display the back buffer on the screen
    d3ddev->Present(NULL, NULL, NULL, NULL);

    //check for escape key (to exit program)
    if (KEY_DOWN(VK_ESCAPE))
        PostMessage(hwnd, WM_DESTROY, 0, 0);

}

//frees memory and cleans up before the game ends
void Game_End(HWND hwnd)
{

    if (caveman_image != NULL)
        caveman_image->Release();

    if (back != NULL)
        back->Release();

    if (sprite_handler != NULL)
        sprite_handler->Release();
}
```

Collision Detection

So far you have learned how to draw sprites onto the screen, but it takes more to make a game than simply the ability to draw. A real game has sprites that interact, where bullets and rockets hit enemy ships and cause them to explode, and sprites that must navigate a maze without going through walls, and sprites that can run and jump over crates and land on top of enemy characters (such as how Mario jumps onto turtles in *Super Mario World* to knock them out).

All of these situations require the ability to detect when two sprites have collided, or touched each other. Sprite collision really opens up the world of game programming and makes it possible for you to build a real game! The key to collision testing is to identify where two sprites are on the screen, and then compare their bounding boxes (or rectangles). That is why this type of collision testing is called *bounding box collision detection*.

Testing for Collisions

If you know the location of both sprites, and you know their widths and heights, then it should be possible to create a temporary rectangle variable (using Windows' RECT structure) containing the bounds of each sprite. Here is an example using the SPRITE struct that you have been using so far (which contains a sprite's x, y, width, and height properties).

```
RECT rect1;
rect1.left = sprite1.x + 1;
rect1.top = sprite1.y + 1;
rect1.right = sprite1.x + sprite1.width-1;
rect1.bottom = sprite1.y + sprite1.height-1;
```

Notice that the rectangle's left and top properties have been set to the sprite's x and y values. Likewise, the rectangle's bottom-right corner has been set using the width and height of the sprite. Thus, a RECT has been populated with the sprite's physical location on the screen.

To actually put this code to use, we'll call on a Windows API function. The function is extremely helpful, because it performs the collision test for us with a single call! The function is called IntersectRect. It accepts two RECT variables and simply returns 0 for false, or 1 for true (which indicates that the sprites are intersecting—or colliding). This function also returns the union of the two sprites—the portions that overlapped—although we aren't interested in this information (a simple yes or no will suffice!).

Let's take a look at a function that creates two RECT variables and then calls on IntersectRect to see if they have collided. This function is called Collision, and is very reusable.

```
int Collision(SPRITE sprite1, SPRITE sprite2)
{
    RECT rect1;
    rect1.left = sprite1.x + 1;
    rect1.top = sprite1.y + 1;
    rect1.right = sprite1.x + sprite1.width-1;
    rect1.bottom = sprite1.y + sprite1.height-1;

    RECT rect2;
    rect2.left = sprite2.x + 1;
    rect2.top = sprite2.y + 1;
    rect2.right = sprite2.x + sprite2.width-1;
    rect2.bottom = sprite2.y + sprite2.height-1;

    RECT dest;
    return IntersectRect(&dest, &rect1, &rect2);
}
```

The CollisionTest Program

The CollisionTest program source code is shown on the following page. This program is based on the previous projects in this chapter, utilizing the following reusable source files:

- winmain.cpp

- dxgraphics.cpp

- dxgraphics.h

- game.h

This program is really neat, as it loads up a ball sprite and draws 50 balls on the screen at a time, performing collision testing among all of them. Whenever two balls collide, the program causes them to rebound off of each other realistically. A whole screen full of them can get quite crazy as a result! Figure 8.5 shows the output of this program. The following code should be typed into the game.cpp source code file of our framework/template project that you've been building. You may create a whole new project or simply replace the code in game.cpp from an earlier project.

Figure 8.5
The CollisionTest program demonstrates collision detection.

```
// Beginning Game Programming, Second Edition
// Chapter 8
// CollisionTest program

#include "game.h"

//number of balls on the screen
#define NUMBALLS 50

typedef enum _DIRS
{
   NONE = -1,
   ABOVE = 0,
   LEFT = 1,
   BELOW = 2,
   RIGHT = 3
} DIRS;

//misc variables
LPDIRECT3DTEXTURE9 ball_image;
SPRITE balls[NUMBALLS];
LPDIRECT3DSURFACE9 back;
```

```
LPD3DXSPRITE sprite_handler;
HRESULT result;

//timing variable
long start = GetTickCount();

int Collision(SPRITE sprite1, SPRITE sprite2)
{
   RECT rect1;
   rect1.left = sprite1.x + 1;
   rect1.top = sprite1.y + 1;
   rect1.right = sprite1.x + sprite1.width-1;
   rect1.bottom = sprite1.y + sprite1.height-1;

   RECT rect2;
   rect2.left = sprite2.x + 1;
   rect2.top = sprite2.y + 1;
   rect2.right = sprite2.x + sprite2.width-1;
   rect2.bottom = sprite2.y + sprite2.height-1;

   RECT dest;
   return IntersectRect(&dest, &rect1, &rect2);
}

DIRS Orientation(SPRITE sprite1, SPRITE defendent)
{
   RECT r;
   r.left = sprite1.x + 1;
   r.top = sprite1.y9 + 1;
   r.right = sprite1.x + sprite1.width-1;
   r.bottom = sprite1.y + sprite1.height-1;

    int centerx = defendent.x + defendent.width/2;
    int centery = defendent.y + defendent.height/2;

   if (centery < r.top)
         return ABOVE;

   if (centery > r.bottom)
         return BELOW;

   if (centerx < r.left)
         return LEFT;
```

```
    if (centerx > r.right)
            return    RIGHT;

    return NONE;
}

void MoveBalls()
{
    int n,m;
    DIRS dir;

    for (n=0; n<NUMBALLS; n++)
    {
        balls[n].x += balls[n].movex;
        balls[n].y += balls[n].movey;

        //bounce the ball at screen edges
        if (balls[n].x > SCREEN_WIDTH - balls[n].width)
        {
            balls[n].x -= balls[n].width;
            balls[n].movex *= -1;
        }
        else if (balls[n].x < 0)
        {
            balls[n].x += balls[n].width;
            balls[n].movex *= -1;
        }

        if (balls[n].y > SCREEN_HEIGHT - balls[n].height)
        {
            balls[n].y -= balls[n].height;
            balls[n].movey *= -1;
        }
        else if (balls[n].y < 0)
        {
            balls[n].y += balls[n].height;
            balls[n].movey *= -1;
        }

        //check for collision with other balls
        for (m=0; m<NUMBALLS; m++)
        {
```

```
          //ignore current ball (can't collide with self)
          if (n != m)
          {
            if (Collision(balls[n], balls[m]))
            {
              //argh! we collided!
              dir = Orientation(balls[n], balls[m]);
              switch (dir)
              {
                case ABOVE: //this one is shared below
                case BELOW:
                  balls[n].movey *= -1;
                  balls[m].movey *= -1;
                  break;
                case LEFT: //this one is shared below
                case RIGHT:
                  balls[n].movex *= -1;
                  balls[m].movex *= -1;
                  break;
              } //switch
            } //collision
          } //if
      } //for m
   } //for n
}

void DrawBalls()
{
   int n;
   D3DXVECTOR3 position(0,0,0);  //ball position vector

   //draw the balls
   for (n=0; n<NUMBALLS; n ++)
   {
     position.x = (float)balls[n].x;
     position.y = (float)balls[n].y;
     sprite_handler->Draw(
       ball_image,
       NULL,
       NULL,
       &position,
       D3DCOLOR_XRGB(255,255,255));
   }
}
```

```
//initializes the game
int Game_Init(HWND hwnd)
{
   int n;

   //set random number seed
   srand(time(NULL));

   //create sprite handler object
   result = D3DXCreateSprite(d3ddev, &sprite_handler);
   if (result != D3D_OK)
       return 0;

   //load the background image
   back = LoadSurface("background.bmp", NULL);
   if (back == NULL)
       return 0;

   //load the ball sprite
   ball_image = LoadTexture("ball.bmp", D3DCOLOR_XRGB(255,0,255));
   if (ball_image == NULL)
       return 0;

   //set the balls' properties
   for (n=0; n<NUMBALLS; n ++)
   {
      balls[n].x = rand() % SCREEN_WIDTH;
      balls[n].y = rand() % SCREEN_HEIGHT;
      balls[n].width = 12;
      balls[n].height = 12;
      balls[n].movex = 1 + rand() % 6;
      balls[n].movey = rand() % 12 - 6;
   }

   //return okay
   return 1;
}

//the main game loop
void Game_Run(HWND hwnd)
{
   //make sure the Direct3D device is valid
   if (d3ddev == NULL)
       return;
```

```
        //after short delay, ready for next frame?
        //this keeps the game running at a steady frame rate
        if (GetTickCount() - start >= 30)
        {
            //reset timing
            start = GetTickCount();

            //move the ball sprites
            MoveBalls();
        }

        //start rendering
        if (d3ddev->BeginScene())
        {
            //erase the entire background
            d3ddev->StretchRect(back, NULL, backbuffer, NULL, D3DTEXF_NONE);

            //start sprite handler
            sprite_handler->Begin(D3DXSPRITE_ALPHABLEND);

            //draw the sprites
            DrawBalls();

            //stop drawing
            sprite_handler->End();

            //stop rendering
            d3ddev->EndScene();
        }

        //display the back buffer on the screen
        d3ddev->Present(NULL, NULL, NULL, NULL);

        //check for escape key (to exit program)
        if (KEY_DOWN(VK_ESCAPE))
            PostMessage(hwnd, WM_DESTROY, 0, 0);
}

//frees memory and cleans up before the game ends
void Game_End(HWND hwnd)
{

    if (ball_image != NULL)
        ball_image->Release();
```

```
    if (back != NULL)
        back->Release();

    if (sprite_handler != NULL)
        sprite_handler->Release();


}
```

What You Have Learned

In this chapter, you have learned how to use D3DXSprite to draw transparent sprites in Direct3D. Here are the key points:

- You learned how to create the D3DXSprite object.

- You learned how to load a texture from a bitmap file.

- You learned how to draw a transparent sprite.

- You learned how to grab sprite animation frames out of a single bitmap.

- You learned how to test for sprite collisions.

Review Questions

Here are some review questions to see how much you have retained from this chapter.

1. What is the name of the DirectX object used to handle sprites?

2. What function is used to load a bitmap image into a texture object?

3. What function do you use to create the sprite object?

4. What is the name of the D3DX function that draws a sprite?

5. What is the D3DX texture object called?

On Your Own

The following exercises will help to challenge your grasp of the information presented in this chapter.

Exercise 1. The Trans_Sprite program animates a running cat on the screen. Modify the program so that it uses a new background of your own design, and change the animation rate of the cat sprite.

Exercise 2. The Tiled_Sprite program features a running caveman. Modify the caveman's movement rate and animation rate so that he runs really fast!

CHAPTER 9

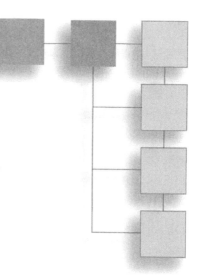

JAMMING WITH DIRECTX AUDIO

Sound and music are vital parts of any game; they help to really make the game feel more immersive and can add an enormous amount of emotion to a game. There is just a completely different reaction to any type of game when it features dynamic, powerful sound effects and appropriate background music. This chapter will show you how to use DirectSound to audibly enhance a game and give it some mood.

Here is what you will learn in this chapter:

- How to initialize DirectSound.

- How to load a wave file.

- How to play a static sound with mixing.

- How to play a looping sound with mixing.

Using DirectSound

DirectSound is the DirectX component that handles all sound output for your game, and features a multi-channel sound mixer. Basically, you just tell DirectSound to play a sound and it takes care of all the details (including combining that sound with any currently playing sounds).

The code required to create, initialize, load, and play a wave file using Direct-Sound is even more involved than the bitmap and sprite code you learned about in the last several chapters. For this reason, and in the interest of re-inventing the wheel, I will show you how to use Microsoft's own wrapper for DirectSound. Using a wrapper is generally against my own instincts as a programmer, as I prefer to know everything about the code I'm using, and often prefer to write my own rather than use someone else's code. However, there comes a time when, in the interest of time, you have to give in and use what's already available. After all, DirectX itself is a game library written by someone else, and it makes no sense to adhere to a strict philosophy in game programming when all it does is slow you down. It's okay if you are writing mostly C, as I am doing in this book, because once in a while you may be required to delve a little into C++ in order to re-use code. In this case, we'll use the DirectSound Utility classes–but I have chosen not to go into detail on how they work. You might think of it as going over an SDK, such as DirectX itself—there is a lot of code that you don't understand, but as long as it works, you can work on your game without worrying about it.

The latest releases of the DirectX SDK provide a new version of the DirectSound Utility library, called DXUTsound. We won't be using this because it has too many support files with it. Instead, we'll use an older version that I hung onto from a previous version of DirectX 9.0c. The old "DXUT" version of Direct-Sound is found in a file called dsutil.cpp (and it depends on only dsutil.h and dxutil.h, nothing more). You will need to include these three files in your game projects in order to use the DirectSound wrapper.

Note

There is nothing wrong with using a wrapper when time is of the essence or when something is too complicated for you to write yourself. If you would like to learn absolutely everything about DirectX Audio, I recommend you acquire a copy of *Beginning Game Audio Programming*, by Mason McCuskey (also published by Thomson Course Technology PTR). This book goes over every detail of the DirectSound interfaces and shows you how to create a more robust and powerful sound library for your game projects.

Note

Three files are required for the programs in this chapter to compile: dxutil.h, dsutil.h, and dsutil.cpp. These files are available in the chapter09\play_sound project folder on the CD-ROM. When you create any new project that uses sound, just include these three files with your project. Later, when we create the dxaudio.cpp and dxaudio.h files, you'll want to include those in any new project you create as well. In the latest DirectX SDK, Microsoft is now distributing a new version of these files under the new name of *DXUT* (which you can find in the DirectX SDK Documentation for C++ in the Programs menu).

The new DXUT has many file dependencies that I did not want to include for our meager needs here. So, I am using the DirectSound helper classes from the old version of the DXUT framework library, as they are self-contained. Everything Microsoft touches becomes hopelessly complicated, so it's often easier to work with earlier versions of the code, as in this case.

There are three classes defined in dsutil that we're interested in here:

CSoundManager	The primary DirectSound device.
CSound	Used to create DirectSound buffers.
CWaveFile	Helps load a wave file into a CSound buffer.

Initializing DirectSound

The first thing to do in order to use DirectSound is create an instance of the CSoundManager class (which creates an "object" of the "class").

```
CSoundManager *dsound = new CSoundManager();
```

The next step requires you to call the Initialize function to initialize the DirectSound manager:

```
dsound->Initialize(window_handle, DSSCL_PRIORITY);
```

The first parameter is the window handle for your program, while the second parameter specifies the DirectSound cooperative level, of which there are three choices:

DSSCL_NORMAL. Shares sound device with other programs.

DSSCL_PRIORITY. Gains higher priority over sound device (recommended for games).

DSSCL_WRITEPRIMARY. Provides access to modify the primary sound buffer.

The most common cooperative level is DSSCL_PRIORITY, which gives your game a higher priority on the sound device than other programs that may be running.

Creating a Sound Buffer

After you have initialized the DirectSound manager (via CSoundManager), you will then usually load all of the sound effects for your game. You access sound effects using CSound pointer variables that are declared like this:

```
CSound *wave;
```

The CSound object that you create is a wrapper for a secondary sound buffer called LPDIRECTSOUNDBUFFER8 that, thanks to dsutil, you do not need to program yourself.

Loading a Wave File

The sound mixer created and managed by DirectSound might be thought of as the primary buffer for sound. Like Direct3D, the primary buffer is where output occurs. But in the case of DirectSound, the secondary buffers are sound data rather than bitmap data, and you play a sound by calling Play (which I'll go over shortly).

Loading a wave file into a DirectSound secondary buffer involves a simple single-line function call rather than a multi-page code listing to initialize the sound buffer, open the wave file, read it into memory, and configure all of the parameters. The CSoundManager object that you create has the function you need to load a wave file. It is called Create:

```
HRESULT Create(
    CSound** ppSound,
    LPTSTR strWaveFileName,
    DWORD dwCreationFlags = 0,
    GUID guid3DAlgorithm = GUID_NULL,
    DWORD dwNumBuffers = 1
);
```

The first parameter specifies the CSound object that you want to use for the newly loaded wave sound. The second parameter is the filename. The remaining parameters can be left at their defaults, meaning you really only need to call this function with two parameters. Here is an example:

```
result = dsound->Create(&wave, "snicker.wav");
```

Tip

Beginning Game Audio Programming explains the wave file format and goes into extensive detail on how to load a wave file from scratch.

Playing a Sound

You are free to play sounds as often as you want without worrying about the sound mixing, ending the sound playback, or any other details, because DirectSound itself handles all of those details for you. Within the CSound class itself is a function called Play that will play the sound for you. Here is what that function looks like:

```
HRESULT Play(
    DWORD dwPriority = 0,
    DWORD dwFlags = 0,
    LONG lVolume = 0,
    LONG lFrequency = -1,
    LONG lPan = 0
);
```

The first parameter is the priority, which is an advanced option and should always be set to zero. The second parameter specifies whether you want the sound to loop, meaning that it will restart at the beginning and continue playing every time it reaches the end of the wave data. If you want to play the sound with looping, use DSBPLAY_LOOPING for this parameter. The last three parameters specify the volume, frequency, and panning (left to right) of the sound, which are also usually left at their defaults, but you may experiment with them if you wish.

Here is an example of how you would usually call this function, first with normal playback. You can either fill in the parameters or leave them out entirely if you want to use the defaults.

```
wave->Play();
```

And here is how you would use looping:

```
wave->Play(0, DSBPLAY_LOOPING);
```

To stop playback of a sound while it is playing, use the Stop function. This function is particularly useful with looping sounds, which will go on forever unless you specifically stop or reset the sound by playing it again without the looping parameter.

```
HRESULT Stop();
```

An example usage of this function couldn't be much simpler:

```
wave->Stop();
```

Testing DirectSound

Let's write a simple demo to test the DirectSound code you have learned how to write in this chapter. As DirectSound is an entirely new component, we need to add it to the so-called "framework" by creating a new header and source code file for the new code. I'll show you how to create the project from scratch, add all the necessary files, and type in the code for the new DirectSound functions you learned about (but have yet to put into practice). After the basic project is ready to go, I'll go over the code for a sample program that bounces a hundred balls on the screen with looping and static sound effects. The Play_Sound program is shown in Figure 9.1.

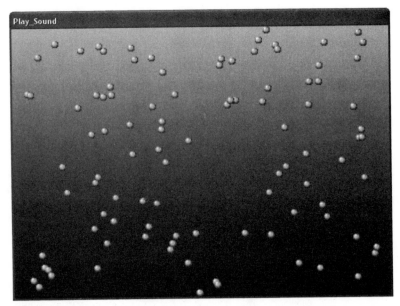

Figure 9.1
The Play_Sound program demonstrates how to use DirectSound.

Creating the Project

I'll show you how to create this entire project from scratch. Although you can open an existing project and modify it, I recommend you follow along and create one from scratch because doing so is good practice and there are a lot of steps involved.

Fire up Visual C++. Open the File menu and select New to bring up the New dialog. Make sure the Projects tab is selected. Choose Win32 Application for the project type, and type **Play_Sound** for the project name. Click OK to close the dialog and create the new project. As usual, don't let Visual C++ add any files for you.

Copying the Reusable Source Files

Next, copy the support files from a previous project into the new folder that was created for the project you just created. Here are the files you will need:

- winmain.cpp
- dxgraphics.h
- dxgraphics.cpp
- game.h
- game.cpp

The game.h and game.cpp files will be replaced with entirely new code, but it doesn't hurt to copy the files to your new project, as that's easier than creating the new files from the New dialog.

Copying the DirectSound Utility Files

The next step is somewhat annoying but it is necessary for using the dsutil support classes, which, as you have learned, greatly simplifies the otherwise very complex DirectSound library. There are three files that must be copied to your project folder and added to your project:

- dxutil.h
- dsutil.h
- dsutil.cpp

Inserting the Copied Files into Your Project

After you have copied these files to your new project folder, you can add them to your project in Visual C++ by opening the Project menu and selecting Add Existing Item. This will bring up the Add Existing Item dialog shown in Figure 9.2.

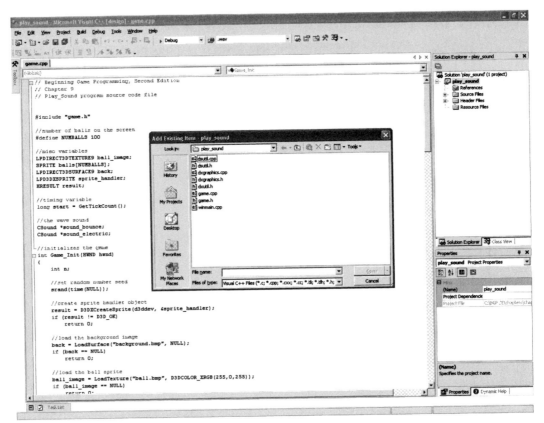

Figure 9.2
Adding an existing file to the project.

Following are listed all of the files that should have been copied to your new project folder that you should select to insert into your project:

- winmain.cpp

- dxgraphics.h

- dxgraphics.cpp

- game.h

- game.cpp

- dsutil.cpp

- dxutil.h

- dsutil.h

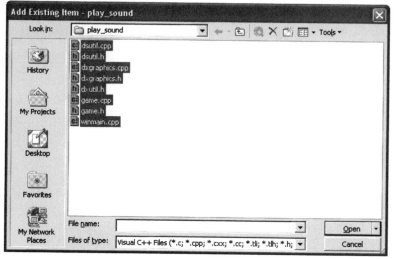

Figure 9.3
Selecting the files to be inserted into the project.

Figure 9.3 shows all of the files selected in the file selection dialog.

You can verify that your project is configured correctly by referring to Figure 9.4, which shows the Solution Explorer loaded with all of the necessary files.

Adding DirectX Library References

Next, let's configure the project for the various DirectX libraries that are required. Open the Project menu and select Properties to bring up the Project Property Pages dialog. Select the Linker tree menu item on the left, and select the Linker/Input page, shown in Figure 9.5.

Here are the lib filenames to add to the Additional Dependencies field on the Project Property Pages dialog:

- d3d9.lib

- d3dx9.lib

- dsound.lib

- dxguid.lib

- dxerr9.lib

- winmm.lib

Figure 9.4
The framework files have been added to the project.

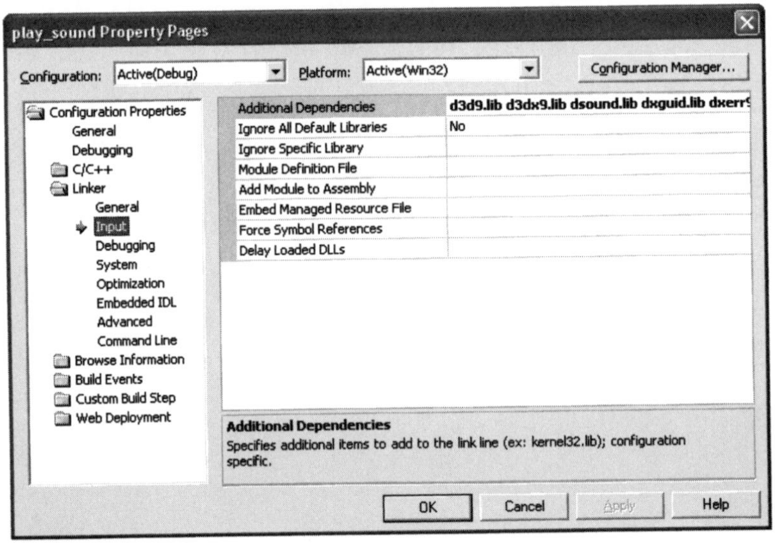

Figure 9.5
Adding DirectX library references to the list of library modules in the Project Settings dialog.

That's a long list of lib files for the project, but just think: it will get even longer when you learn about DirectInput in the next chapter! Actually, we won't be adding many more files to the list.

But hang on a minute! Before you can compile this program, there are a few more things that must be done first.

Creating the DirectX Audio Support Files

Your new Play_Sound project is now ready for the DirectSound code. I have put together the DirectSound helper code we went over earlier in the chapter and placed it inside two files:

- dxaudio.h
- dxaudio.cpp

The header file will include the definitions for the DirectSound functions you'll need to load and play sounds in your game. This just makes it easier to work with the CSoundManager and CSound classes (which are provided by the DirectSound Utility library).

Creating dxaudio.h

Open the Project menu and select Add New Item to bring up the Add New Item dialog. Select Header File (.h) and type **dxaudio.h** for the filename, as shown in Figure 9.6. Click OK to add the new file to your project.

Here is the code for the dxaudio.h file:

```
#ifndef _DXAUDIO_H
#define _DXAUDIO_H 1

#include "dsutil.h"

//primary DirectSound object
extern CSoundManager *dsound;

//function prototypes
int Init_DirectSound(HWND);
CSound *LoadSound(char *);
void PlaySound(CSound *);
```

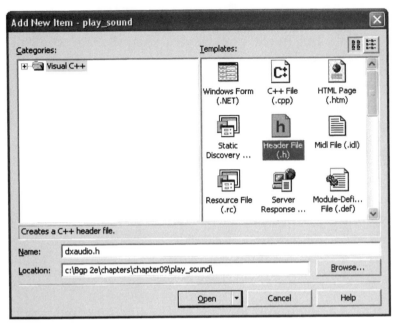

Figure 9.6
Adding the new dxaudio.h file to the project.

```
void LoopSound(CSound *);
void StopSound(CSound *);

#endif
```

Creating dxaudio.cpp

Open the Project menu again and select Add New Item to bring up the Add New Item dialog. Select C++ File (.cpp) and type **dxaudio.cpp** for the filename, as shown in Figure 9.7. Click OK to add the new file to your project.

Here is the code for the dxaudio.cpp file:

```
#include "dxaudio.h"

CSoundManager *dsound;

int Init_DirectSound(HWND hwnd)
{
   HRESULT result;

   //create DirectSound manager object
   dsound = new CSoundManager();
```

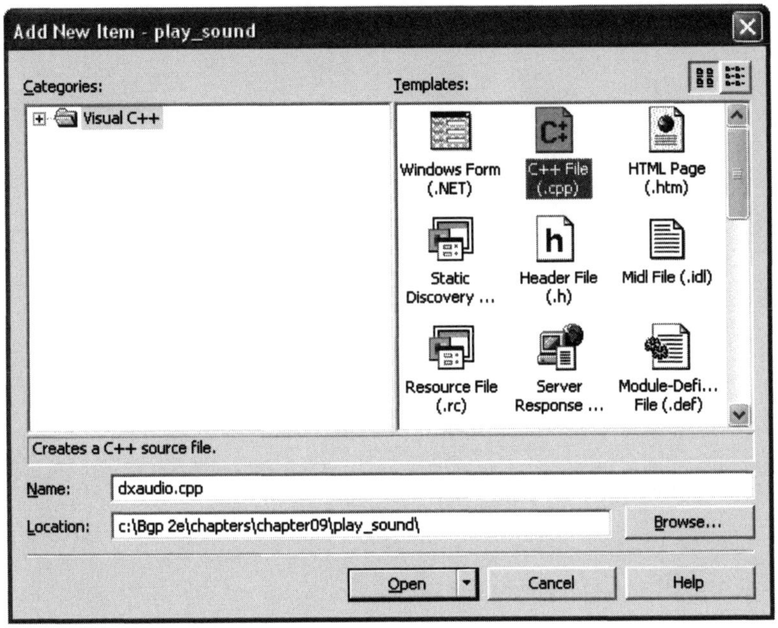

Figure 9.7
Adding the new dxaudio.cpp file to the project.

```cpp
    //initialize DirectSound
    result = dsound->Initialize(hwnd, DSSCL_PRIORITY);
    if (result != DS_OK)
        return 0;

    //set the primary buffer format
    result = dsound->SetPrimaryBufferFormat(2, 22050, 16);
    if (result != DS_OK)
        return 0;

    //return success
    return 1;
}

CSound *LoadSound(char *filename)
{
    HRESULT result;

    //create local reference to wave data
    CSound *wave;

    //attempt to load the wave file
```

```
    result = dsound->Create(&wave, filename);
    if (result != DS_OK)
        return NULL;

    //return the wave
    return wave;
}

void PlaySound(CSound *sound)
{
    sound->Play();
}

void LoopSound(CSound *sound)
{
    sound->Play(0, DSBPLAY_LOOPING);
}

void StopSound(CSound *sound)
{
    sound->Stop();
}
```

Tweaking the Framework Code

The next subject is more a matter of personal preference than it is a requirement. I personally like to stuff as much logistical code away as possible and let the "framework" (I use that word loosely because it is not quite a wrapper and not quite a game engine, but just a way of organizing the DirectX code) handle it. So, you can follow this step to add the DirectSound initialization to WinMain or you can call the Init_DirectSound function from your main initialization routine in the game, instead. I prefer to add it to WinMain, so here is how to do that.

Adding DirectSound Initialization to winmain.cpp

Open winmain.cpp in your project. Scroll down to the WinMain function until you find the beginning of the while loop, which looks like this:

```
// main message loop
int done = 0;
while (!done)
```

Just above that, you'll see the Direct3D initialization and game initialization code. You can insert the DirectSound initialization before or after either of those two other initialization lines, as long as it comes before the while loop.

```
//initialize DirectSound
if (!Init_DirectSound(hWnd))
{
   MessageBox(hWnd, "Error initializing DirectSound", "Error", MB_OK);
   return 0;
}
```

Note

If you ever get totally, completely, absolutely lost during the tutorial to create this project, feel free to save yourself the headache and just load the project off the CD-ROM (which you should have copied to your hard drive already, if you have been working through the examples in each chapter).

Adding the Game Files

Okay, this has been quite a long process, but if you have followed along and performed each step along the way, then you should now have a project that is ready to compile. Unfortunately, the game.h and game.cpp files contain source code from a previous project that has nothing to do with DirectSound! So, conveniently, these files are already in your project—you just need to open them up and replace the code.

game.h

Here is the code for the game.h file. Just delete all of the existing code and replace it with the code listed here, or make selective replacements if you are relatively sure you won't make any mistakes. It's usually safer to wipe all of the code lines, but you can leave the conditional compiler statements in place (such as #ifndef...).

```
#ifndef _GAME_H
#define _GAME_H 1

//windows/directx headers
#include <d3d9.h>
#include <d3dx9.h>
#include <dxerr9.h>
#include <dsound.h>
#include <windows.h>
#include <time.h>
#include <stdio.h>
#include <stdlib.h>
```

```
//framework-specific headers
#include "dxgraphics.h"
#include "dxaudio.h"

//application title
#define APPTITLE "Play_Sound"

//screen setup
#define FULLSCREEN 0      //0 = windowed, 1 = fullscreen
#define SCREEN_WIDTH 640
#define SCREEN_HEIGHT 480

//macros to read the keyboard asynchronously
#define KEY_DOWN(vk_code) ((GetAsyncKeyState(vk_code) & 0x8000) ? 1 : 0)
#define KEY_UP(vk_code)((GetAsyncKeyState(vk_code) & 0x8000) ? 1 : 0)

//function prototypes
int Game_Init(HWND);
void Game_Run(HWND);
void Game_End(HWND);

//sprite structure
typedef struct {
    int x,y;
    int width,height;
    int movex,movey;
    int curframe,lastframe;
    int animdelay,animcount;
    int scalex, scaley;
    int rotation, rotaterate;
} SPRITE;

#endif
```

game.cpp

You'll also need to replace the code in game.cpp with the following code listing. The projects are really completely different, so I don't expect that you'll be able to just selectively replace the code with the listing given here. However, you can give it a try if you wish. If all else fails, you can copy the completed game.cpp file off the CD-ROM and insert it into the project, all ready to go.

```
#include "game.h"
//number of balls on the screen
#define NUMBALLS 100

//misc variables
LPDIRECT3DTEXTURE9 ball_image;
SPRITE balls[NUMBALLS];
LPDIRECT3DSURFACE9 back;
LPD3DXSPRITE sprite_handler;
HRESULT result;

//timing variable
long start = GetTickCount();

//the wave sound
CSound *sound_bounce;
CSound *sound_electric;

//initializes the game
int Game_Init(HWND hwnd)
{
    int n;

    //set random number seed
    srand(time(NULL));

    //create sprite handler object
    result = D3DXCreateSprite(d3ddev, &sprite_handler);
    if (result != D3D_OK)
        return 0;

    //load the background image
    back = LoadSurface("background.bmp", NULL);
    if (back == NULL)
        return 0;

    //load the ball sprite
    ball_image = LoadTexture("ball.bmp", D3DCOLOR_XRGB(255,0,255));
    if (ball_image == NULL)
        return 0;

    //set the balls' properties
    for (n=0; n<NUMBALLS; n++)
```

```
   {
      balls[n].x = rand() % SCREEN_WIDTH;
      balls[n].y = rand() % SCREEN_HEIGHT;
      balls[n].width = 12;
      balls[n].height = 12;
      balls[n].movex = 1 + rand() % 6;
      balls[n].movey = rand() % 12 - 6;
   }

   //load bounce wave file
   sound_bounce = LoadSound("bounce.wav");
   if (sound_bounce == NULL)
      return 0;

   //load the electric wave file
   sound_electric = LoadSound("electric.wav");
   if (sound_electric == NULL)
      return 0;

   //return okay
   return 1;
}

//the main game loop
void Game_Run(HWND hwnd)
{
   D3DXVECTOR3 position(0,0,0);   //ball position vector
   int n;
   int playing = 0;

   //make sure the Direct3D device is valid
   if (d3ddev == NULL)
      return;

      //after short delay, ready for next frame?
      //this keeps the game running at a steady frame rate
      if (GetTickCount() - start >= 30)
      {
         //reset timing
         start = GetTickCount();

         //move the ball sprites
         for (int n=0; n<NUMBALLS; n++)
```

```
        {
           balls[n].x += balls[n].movex;
           balls[n].y += balls[n].movey;

           //bounce the ball at screen edges
           if (balls[n].x > SCREEN_WIDTH - balls[n].width)
           {
              balls[n].x -= balls[n].width;
              balls[n].movex *= -1;
              PlaySound(sound_bounce);
           }
           else if (balls[n].x < 0)
           {
              balls[n].x += balls[n].width;
              balls[n].movex *= -1;
              PlaySound(sound_bounce);
           }

           if (balls[n].y > SCREEN_HEIGHT - balls[n].height)
           {
              balls[n].y -= balls[n].height;
              balls[n].movey *= -1;
              PlaySound(sound_bounce);
           }
           else if (balls[n].y < 0)
           {
              balls[n].y += balls[n].height;
              balls[n].movey *= -1;
              PlaySound(sound_bounce);
           }
        }
    }

    //start rendering
    if (d3ddev->BeginScene())
    {
        //erase the entire background
        d3ddev->StretchRect(back, NULL, backbuffer, NULL, D3DTEXF_NONE);

        //start sprite handler
        sprite_handler->Begin(D3DXSPRITE_ALPHABLEND);

        //draw the balls
        for (n=0; n<NUMBALLS; n++)
```

```
          {
            position.x = (float)balls[n].x;
            position.y = (float)balls[n].y;
            sprite_handler->Draw(
               ball_image,
               NULL,
               NULL,
               &position,
               D3DCOLOR_XRGB(255,255,255));
          }

          //stop drawing
          sprite_handler->End();

       //stop rendering
       d3ddev->EndScene();
    }

    //display the back buffer on the screen
    d3ddev->Present(NULL, NULL, NULL, NULL);

    //check for escape key (to exit program)
    if (KEY_DOWN(VK_ESCAPE))
       PostMessage(hwnd, WM_DESTROY, 0, 0);

    //spacebar plays the electric sound
    if (KEY_DOWN(VK_SPACE))
       LoopSound(sound_electric);

    //enter key stops the electric sound
    if (KEY_DOWN(VK_RETURN))
       StopSound(sound_electric);
}

//frees memory and cleans up before the game ends
void Game_End(HWND hwnd)
{

    if (ball_image != NULL)
       ball_image->Release();

    if (back != NULL)
       back->Release();
```

```
    if (sprite_handler != NULL)
        sprite_handler->Release();

    if (sound_bounce != NULL)
        delete sound_bounce;

    if (sound_electric != NULL)
        delete sound_electric;

}
```

Running the Program

When you run the program, you are presented with either a windowed or full-screen display. I recommend running all of the sample programs in fullscreen mode—refer to the setting in game.h that affects this:

```
#define FULLSCREEN 0      //0 = windowed, 1 = fullscreen
```

Figure 9.8 shows the output of the Play_Sound program.

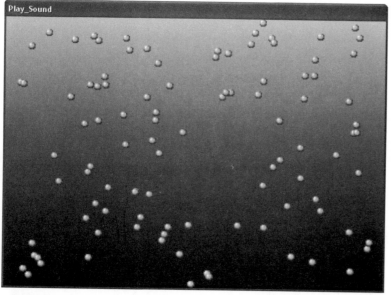

Figure 9.8
The Play_Sound program output.

When you run the program, be aware of how to start and stop the looping sound (which sounds like electricity). Press the spacebar to start the looping sound, and press Enter to stop the sound. All the while, the annoying balls are bouncing all over the screen and making an uproar in the process!

What You Have Learned

This chapter explained how to use some relatively painless DirectSound support routines included in the DirectX SDK to make DirectSound programming easier. Here are the key points:

■ You learned how to initialize the DirectSound object.

■ You learned how to load a wave file into a sound buffer.

■ You learned how to play and stop a sound, with or without looping.

■ You learned a little bit about sound mixing.

■ You got some practice working on a project with many files.

■ You learned about the value of code re-use.

Review Questions

These questions will help to challenge your understanding of the chapter:

1. What is the name of the primary DirectSound class used in this chapter?

2. What is a secondary sound buffer?

3. What is the secondary sound buffer called in dsutil.h?

4. What is the option called that causes a sound to play with looping?

5. For reference, what is the name of the function that draws a surface to the screen?

On Your Own

The following exercises will help you to think outside the box and push your limits, which will increase your capacity for retention.

Exercise 1. The Play_Sound program played a sound effect every time a small ball hit the edge of the screen. Modify the program so that it draws a different number of balls of your choosing (instead of 100).

Exercise 2. The Play_Sound program plays just a single sound when a ball sprite hits an edge. Modify the program by adding three more wave files, with associated code to load them, so that when a ball strikes the top, left, right, or bottom edge of the screen, it plays a different sound for each.

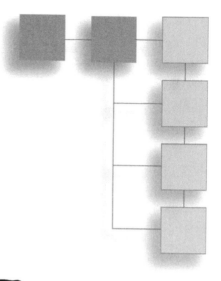

CHAPTER 10

HANDLING INPUT DEVICES

Welcome to the virtual interface chapter! In the coming pages, you will learn how to use DirectInput to program the keyboard and mouse to provide your games with support for the most common input devices.

Here is what you will learn in this chapter:

- How to create the primary DirectInput object.

- How to create DirectInput devices.

- How to write a keyboard handler.

- How to write a mouse handler.

The Keyboard

The keyboard is the standard input device for all games, even for those that don't specifically use the keyboard, so it is a given that your games will use the keyboard one way or another. If nothing else, you should allow the user to exit your game or at least bring up some sort of in-game menu by pressing the Escape key (that's the standard). Programming the keyboard using DirectInput is not difficult, but you do need to initialize DirectInput first.

The primary DirectInput object is called `IDirectInput8`; you can reference it directly or using the `LPDIRECTINPUT8` pointer data type. Why is the number "8" attached to these interfaces? Because, like DirectSound, DirectInput has not changed since the last major revision of DirectX, which was version 8.1. Kind of makes you wonder why we're at a full version upgrade to 9.0c already (and very likely beyond that by the time you read this).

The DirectInput library file is called dinput8.lib, so be sure to add this file to the linker options in the Project Settings dialog along with the other libs. I'll assume that you read the last chapter and learned how to set up the project to support DirectX and the game framework you've been building up to this point. If you have any question about how to set up the project at this point in the book, refer to the last chapter for a complete overview and tutorial. In this chapter, I'll have you add a new component to the framework for DirectInput using two new files (dxinput.h and dxinput.cpp).

DirectInput Object and Device

Okay, you are familiar with the drill of initializing the DirectX components, so let's learn how to scan the keyboard for button input. You will want to first define the primary DirectInput object used by your program along with the object for the device:

```
LPDIRECTINPUT8 dinput;
```

```
LPDIRECTINPUTDEVICE8 dinputdev;
```

After defining the variables, you can then call `DirectInputCreate8` to initialize DirectInput. The function has this format:

```
HRESULT WINAPI DirectInput8Create(
    HINSTANCE hinst,
    DWORD dwVersion,
```

```
    REFIID riidltf,
    LPVOID *ppvOut,
    LPUNKNOWN punkOuter
);
```

This function just creates the primary DirectInput object that you pass to it. The first parameter is the instance handle for the current program. A convenient way to get the current instance when it is not immediately available (normally this is only found in `WinMain`) is by using the `GetModuleHandle` function. The second parameter is the DirectInput version, which is always passed as `DIRECTINPUT_VERSION`, defined in dinput.h. The third parameter is a reference identifier for the version of DirectInput that you want to use. At present, this value is `IID_IDirectInput8`. The fourth parameter is a pointer to the primary=DirectInput object pointer (note the double pointer here), and the fifth parameter is always `NULL`. Here is an example of how you might call this function:

```
HRESULT result = DirectInput8Create(
    GetModuleHandle(NULL),
    DIRECTINPUT_VERSION,
    IID_IDirectInput8,
    (void**)&dinput,
    NULL);
```

After initializing the object, you can then use the object to create a new DirectInput device by calling the `CreateDevice` function:

```
HRESULT CreateDevice(
    REFGUID rguid,
    LPDIRECTINPUTDEVICE *lplpDirectInputDevice,
    LPUNKNOWN pUnkOuter
);
```

The first parameter is a value that specifies the type of object you want to create (such as the keyboard or mouse). Here are the values you can use for this parameter:

- GUID_SysKeyboard

- GUID_SysMouse

The second parameter is your device pointer that receives the address of the DirectInput device handler. The third parameter is always `NULL`. Here is how you might call this function:

```
result = dinput->CreateDevice(GUID_SysKeyboard, &dikeyboard, NULL);
```

Initializing the Keyboard

Once you have the DirectInput object and device object for the keyboard, you can then initialize the keyboard handler to prepare it for input. The next step is to set the keyboard's data format, which instructs DirectInput how to pass the data back to your program. It is abstracted in this way because there are hundreds of input devices on the market with a myriad of features, so there has to be a uniform way to read them all.

Setting the Data Format

The `SetDataFormat` specifies how the data format is set.

```
HRESULT SetDataFormat(
     LPCDIDATAFORMAT lpdf
);
```

The single parameter to this function specifies the device type. For the keyboard, you want to pass the value of `c_dfDIKeyboard` as this parameter. The constant for a mouse would be `c_dfDIMouse`. Here, then, is a sample function call:

```
HRESULT result = dikeyboard->SetDataFormat(&c_dfDIKeyboard);
```

Note that you do not need to define `c_dfDIKeyboard` yourself, as it is defined in dinput.h.

Setting the Cooperative Level

The next step is to set the cooperative level, which determines how much of the keyboard DirectInput will give your program by way of priority. To set the cooperative level, you call the `SetCooperativeLevel` function:

```
HRESULT SetCooperativeLevel(
     HWND hwnd,
     DWORD dwFlags
);
```

The first parameter is the window handle. The second parameter is the interesting one, as it specifies the priority that your program will have over the keyboard or mouse. The most common values to pass when working with the keyboard are

DISCL_NONEXCLUSIVE and DISCL_FOREGROUND. If you try to gain exclusive use of the keyboard, DirectInput will probably complain, so ask for non-exclusive access with priority as the foreground application in order to give your game the most control over the keyboard. So, then, here is how you might call the function:

```
HRESULT result = dikeyboard->SetCooperativeLevel(hwnd,
    DISCL_NONEXCLUSIVE | DISCL_FOREGROUND);
```

Acquiring the Device

The last step in initializing the keyboard is to acquire the keyboard device using the Acquire function:

```
HRESULT Acquire(VOID);
```

If the function returns a positive value (DI_OK) then you have successfully acquired the keyboard and are ready to start checking for key presses.

An important point that I should make here is that you *must* unacquire the keyboard before your game ends or it will leave DirectInput and the keyboard handler in an unknown state. Windows and DirectInput will probably take care of cleaning up after you, but it really depends on the version of Windows that the user is running. Believe it or not, there are still computers running Windows 98 and ME, despite these operating systems being quite out of date. Windows 2000 is quite a bit more stable, as is XP and 2003, but you shouldn't leave anything to chance. It's best to unacquire the device before your game ends. Each DirectInput device has an Unacquire function with the following format:

```
HRESULT Unacquire(VOID);
```

Reading Key Presses

Somewhere in your game loop you need to poll the keyboard to update its key values. Speaking of keys, it is up to you to define the array of keys that are to be populated with the keyboard device status, like this:

```
char keys[256];
```

You must poll the keyboard to fill in this array of characters, and to do that you call the GetDeviceState function. This function is used for all devices regardless of type, so it is standard for all input devices:

```
HRESULT GetDeviceState(
  DWORD cbData,
```

```
    LPVOID lpvData
);
```

The first parameter is the size of the device state buffer to be filled with data. The second parameter is a pointer to the data. In the case of the keyboard, here is how you would call this function:

```
dikeyboard->GetDeviceState(sizeof(keys), (LPVOID)&keys);
```

After polling the keyboard, you can then check the keys array for values corresponding to the DirectInput key codes.

Here is how you would check for the ESCAPE key:

```
if (keys[DIK_ESCAPE] & 0x80)
{
   //ESCAPE key was pressed, so do something!
}
```

The Mouse

Once you have written a handler for the keyboard, it is a piece of cake to support the mouse as well, because the code is very similar, and it shares the DirectInput object and device pointers. So let's jump ahead and learn about the mouse interface. First, define the mouse device:

```
LPDIRECTINPUTDEVICE8 dimouse;
```

Next, create the mouse device:

```
result = dinput->CreateDevice(GUID_SysMouse, &dimouse, NULL);
```

Initializing the Mouse

So, let's assume DirectInput is all squared away, and now you want to add a mouse handler. The next step is to set the data format for the mouse, which instructs DirectInput how to pass the data back to your program. It functions in exactly the same way for the mouse as it does for the keyboard.

Setting the Data Format

The SetDataFormat function looks like this:

```
HRESULT SetDataFormat(
    LPCDIDATAFORMAT lpdf
);
```

The single parameter to this function specifies the device type. The constant for your mouse is c_dfDIMouse. Here, then, is a sample function call:

```
HRESULT result = dimouse->SetDataFormat(&c_dfDIMouse);
```

Note, again, that you do not need to define c_dfDIMouse, as it is defined in dinput.h.

Setting the Cooperative Level

The next step is to set the cooperative level, which determines how much priority over the mouse DirectInput will give your program. To set the cooperative level, you call the SetCooperativeLevel function:

```
HRESULT SetCooperativeLevel(
    HWND hwnd,
    DWORD dwFlags
);
```

The first parameter is the window handle. The second parameter is the interesting one, as it specifies the priority that your program will have over the mouse. The most common values to pass when working with the mouse are DISCL_ EXCLUSIVE and DISCL_FOREGROUND (which has the added benefit of hiding the stock Windows cursor from view). Here is how to call this function:

```
HRESULT result = dimouse->SetCooperativeLevel(hwnd,
    DISCL_EXCLUSIVE | DISCL_FOREGROUND);
```

Acquiring the Device

The last step is to acquire the mouse device using the Acquire function. If the function returns DI_OK, then you have successfully acquired the mouse and are ready to start checking for movement and button presses.

As with the keyboard device, you must also unacquire the mouse device after you are done using it, or else you could leave DirectInput in an unstable state:

```
HRESULT Unacquire(VOID);
```

Reading the Mouse

Somewhere in your game loop you need to poll the mouse to update the mouse position and button status. You poll the mouse using the GetDeviceState function:

```
HRESULT GetDeviceState(
    DWORD cbData,

    LPVOID lpvData
);
```

The first parameter is the size of the device state buffer to be filled with data. The second parameter is a pointer to the data. There is a struct available for your use in polling the mouse:

```
DIMOUSESTATE mouse_state;
```

Here is how you would fill the DIMOUSESTATE struct by calling the GetDeviceState function:

```
dimouse->GetDeviceState(sizeof(mouse_state), (LPVOID)&mouse_state);
```

The struct looks like this:

```
typedef struct DIMOUSESTATE {
    LONG 1X;
    LONG 1Y;
    LONG 1Z;
    BYTE rgbButtons[4];
} DIMOUSESTATE;
```

There is an alternate struct available for your use when you want to support complex mouse devices with more than four buttons, in which case the button array is doubled in size but the struct is otherwise the same:

```
typedef struct DIMOUSESTATE2 {
    LONG 1X;
    LONG 1Y;
    LONG 1Z;
    BYTE rgbButtons[8];
} DIMOUSESTATE2;
```

After polling the mouse, you can then check the mouse_state struct for x and y motion and button presses. You can check for mouse movement, also called *mickeys*, using the 1X and 1Y member variables. What are mickeys? *Mickeys* represent motion of the mouse rather than an absolute position, so you must keep track of the old position if you want to use these mouse-positioning values to draw your own pointer. Mickeys are a convenient way of handling mouse motion because you can continue to move in a single direction and the mouse will continue to report movement, even if the "pointer" would have reached the edge of the screen.

As you can see from the struct, the rgbButtons array holds the result of button presses. If you want to check for a specific button (starting with 0 for button 1), here is how you might do that:

```
button_1 = obj.rgbButtons[0] & 0x80;
```

A more convenient method of detecting button presses is by using a define:

```
#define BUTTON_DOWN(obj, button) (obj.rgbButtons[button] & 0x80)
```

By using the define, you can check for button presses like so:

```
button_1 = BUTTON_DOWN(mouse_state, 0);
```

Paddle Game

That about sums up the keyboard and mouse. Are you ready to put it into practice with a sample program? As this is the last chapter in Part II on the subject of the DirectX library, I have something of a surprise for you. After adding DirectInput to the game framework, I'm going to show you a game called *Paddle Game* that could be the basis for a complete *Breakout* or *Arkanoid*-style game that you can modify and tweak to come up with your own design. Figure 10.1 shows *Paddle Game* running. The game supports both the keyboard and mouse and is ready for your own enhancements! Using the Collision function that I'll go over with you shortly, you'll be able to add your own blocks to the game in order to let the ball "bash" them.

The New Framework Code for DirectInput

Now, while you're working on this *Paddle Game* project, is a good time to update the game framework to add DirectInput support to it.

winmain.cpp

Unfortunately, changes must be made to WinMain again. It would be nice if you didn't have to open up winmain.cpp any more, but in the interest of encapsulating

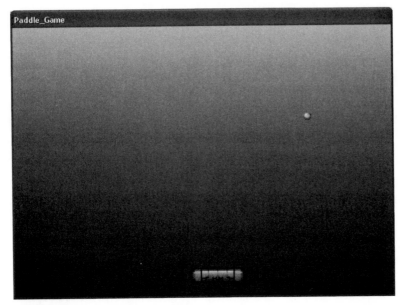

Figure 10.1
Paddle Game is a near-complete game that demonstrates how to use DirectInput to read the keyboard and mouse.

the game framework completely and removing all initialization code from Game_Init, it's a necessary step.

Add #include "dxinput.h" to the includes section in winmain.cpp.

Add the following DirectInput initialization code to the WinMain function just before the main while loop with the other DirectX initialization code.

```
//initialize DirectInput
if (!Init_DirectInput(hwnd))
{
  MessageBox(hWnd, "Error initializing DirectInput", "Error", MB_OK);
  return 0;
}
```

Next, look for the WinProc function and add the following code to the WM_DESTROY event code:

```
//release input objects
Kill_Keyboard();
Kill_Mouse();
if (dinput != NULL) dinput->Release();
```

Come to think of it, we neglected to free up the DirectSound object here! Well, it never hurts to fill in missing cleanup code all at once when you're about done with a project, so here goes:

```
if (dsound != NULL) dsound->Release();
```

I know all this modification is a pain, but the end result is a framework in which the logistical code is all tied up in supporting source code files and your actual game code is isolated and more accessible. In a nutshell: you can focus on gameplay rather than Windows and DirectX.

Caution

If you have any trouble with the updates in this chapter, just refer to Chapter 9, which explained how to create the project from scratch. I won't cover all of that information here again. If you get really lost, then you can load the completed project off the CD-ROM, in which case you should pay attention to the `Game_Init`, `Game_Run`, and `Game_End` functions. Just be sure to add dinput8.lib to the linker options in your project.

dxinput.h

Add a new file to your project called dxinput.h. This is the header file for the DirectInput framework. Here is the code for this file:

```
#ifndef _DXINPUT_H
#define _DXINPUT_H 1

#include <dinput.h>

//function prototypes
int Init_DirectInput(HWND);
int Init_Keyboard(HWND);
void Poll_Keyboard();
int Key_Down(int);
void Kill_Keyboard();
void Poll_Mouse();
int Init_Mouse(HWND);
int Mouse_Button(int);
int Mouse_X();
int Mouse_Y();
void Kill_Mouse();

//DirectInput objects, devices, and states
extern LPDIRECTINPUT8 dinput;
```

```
extern LPDIRECTINPUTDEVICE8 dimouse;
extern LPDIRECTINPUTDEVICE8 dikeyboard;
extern DIMOUSESTATE mouse_state;

#endif
```

dxinput.cpp

Add another new file to the project, and this time name it dxinput.cpp. This file contains the source code for the keyboard and mouse handlers to add DirectInput support to your games.

```
#include "dxinput.h"

#define BUTTON_DOWN(obj, button) (obj.rgbButtons[button] & 0x80)

LPDIRECTINPUT8 dinput;
LPDIRECTINPUTDEVICE8 dimouse;
LPDIRECTINPUTDEVICE8 dikeyboard;
LPDIRECTINPUTDEVICE8 dijoystick;
DIMOUSESTATE mouse_state;

//keyboard input
char keys[256];

int Init_DirectInput(HWND hwnd)
{
    //initialize DirectInput object
    HRESULT result = DirectInput8Create(
        GetModuleHandle(NULL),
        DIRECTINPUT_VERSION,
        IID_IDirectInput8,
        (void**)&dinput,
        NULL);

    if (result != DI_OK)
        return 0;

    //initialize the mouse
    result = dinput->CreateDevice(GUID_SysMouse, &dimouse, NULL);
    if (result != DI_OK)
        return 0;
```

```
   //initialize the keyboard
   result = dinput->CreateDevice(GUID_SysKeyboard, &dikeyboard, NULL);
   if (result != DI_OK)
       return 0;

   //clean return
   return 1;
}

int Init_Mouse(HWND hwnd)
{
   //set the data format for mouse input
   HRESULT result = dimouse->SetDataFormat(&c_dfDIMouse);
   if (result != DI_OK)
       return 0;

   //set the cooperative level
   //this will also hide the mouse pointer
   result = dimouse->SetCooperativeLevel(hwnd,
       DISCL_EXCLUSIVE | DISCL_FOREGROUND);
   if (result != DI_OK)
       return 0;

   //acquire the mouse
   result = dimouse->Acquire();
   if (result != DI_OK)
       return 0;

   //give the go-ahead
   return 1;
}

int Mouse_X()
{
    return mouse_state.lX;
}

int Mouse_Y()
{
    return mouse_state.lY;
}
```

```
int Mouse_Button(int button)
{
   return BUTTON_DOWN(mouse_state, button);
}

void Poll_Mouse()
{
    dimouse->GetDeviceState(sizeof(mouse_state), (LPVOID)&mouse_state);
}

void Kill_Mouse()
{
   if (dimouse != NULL)
  {
     dimouse->Unacquire();
     dimouse->Release();
     dimouse = NULL;
  }
}

int Init_Keyboard(HWND hwnd)
{
  //set the data format for mouse input
  HRESULT result = dikeyboard->SetDataFormat(&c_dfDIKeyboard);
  if (result != DI_OK)
      return 0;

  //set the cooperative level
  result = dikeyboard->SetCooperativeLevel(hwnd,
      DISCL_NONEXCLUSIVE | DISCL_FOREGROUND);
  if (result != DI_OK)
      return 0;

  //acquire the mouse
  result = dikeyboard->Acquire();
  if (result != DI_OK)
      return 0;

  //give the go-ahead
  return 1;
 }

 void Poll_Keyboard()
 {
```

```
    dikeyboard->GetDeviceState(sizeof(keys), (LPVOID)&keys);
}

int Key_Down(int key)
{
    return (keys[key] & 0x80);
}

void Kill_Keyboard()
{
    if (dikeyboard != NULL)
    {
        dikeyboard->Unacquire();
        dikeyboard->Release();
        dikeyboard = NULL;
    }
}
```

The Paddle Game Source Code

Whew, another batch of changes done to add the latest DirectX component to the framework! Aren't you glad that's over? You might be wondering why this is all necessary—is it just a waste of paper and time, or is there a point to it?

Of course there's a point, or I wouldn't have put you through it. Code re-use is the key to becoming a professional programmer. You simply cannot rewrite code again and again and expect to have any time to get real work done. The source code files you have created thus far provide a game framework that greatly reduces the amount of work you must do to write a Windows/DirectX game. And we're talking about a full-blown Direct3D 9.0b game, at that! What? We haven't even gone into 3D yet?

I've been holding off on 3D for a reason: it's a little more complicated. I wanted to have this basis of code (the framework) ready to go before diving headfirst into the 3D code because otherwise we'd be swimming in reams of code right now. The 3D chapters that follow will be easy to understand and grasp because I'm not getting into any 3D math, but there is a lot of code involved when you're working with Direct3D.

Okay, where were we? Oh, yeah, *Paddle Game*! For reference, Figure 10.2 shows the project workspace for the *Paddle Game* project as it should appear at this point. If you are still lost, go ahead and load the project off the CD-ROM so you can at least keep up with the discussion.

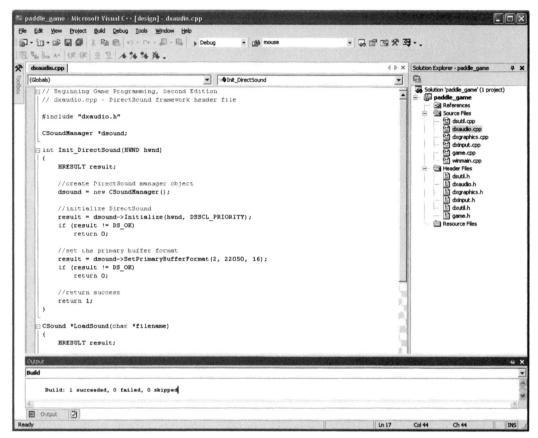

Figure 10.2
The project workspace for the *Paddle Game* project

game.h

Here is the header file for the game.

```
#ifndef _GAME_H
#define _GAME_H 1

//windows/directx headers
#include <d3d9.h>
#include <d3dx9.h>
#include <dxerr9.h>
#include <dsound.h>
#include <dinput.h>
#include <windows.h>
#include <time.h>
```

```
#include <stdio.h>
#include <stdlib.h>

//framework-specific headers
#include "dxgraphics.h"
#include "dxaudio.h"
#include "dxinput.h"

//application title
#define APPTITLE "Paddle_Game"

//screen setup
#define FULLSCREEN 0        //0 = windowed, 1 = fullscreen
#define SCREEN_WIDTH 640
#define SCREEN_HEIGHT 480

//function prototypes
int Game_Init(HWND);
void Game_Run(HWND);
void Game_End(HWND);

//sprite structure
typedef struct {
    int x,y;
    int width,height;
    int movex,movey;
    int curframe,lastframe;
    int animdelay,animcount;
    int scalex, scaley;
    int rotation, rotaterate;
} SPRITE;

#endif
```

game.cpp

Here is the source code for the *Paddle Game* project. I will explain key parts of the code at the end of the listing.

```
#include "game.h"

//background image
LPDIRECT3DSURFACE9 back;
```

```
//sprite handler
LPD3DXSPRITE sprite_handler;

//ball sprite
LPDIRECT3DTEXTURE9 ball_image;
SPRITE ball;

//paddle sprite
LPDIRECT3DTEXTURE9 paddle_image;
SPRITE paddle;

//the wave sound
CSound *sound_bounce;
CSound *sound_hit;

//misc
long start = GetTickCount();
HRESULT result;

//initializes the game
int Game_Init(HWND hwnd)
{
  //set random number seed
  srand(time(NULL));

  //initialize mouse
  if (!Init_Mouse(hWnd))
  {
    MessageBox(hWnd, "Error initializing the mouse", "Error", MB_OK);
    return 0;
  }

  //initialize keyboard
  if (!Init_Keyboard(hWnd))
  {
    MessageBox(hWnd, "Error initializing the keyboard", "Error", MB_OK);
    return 0;
  }

  //create sprite handler object
  result = D3DXCreateSprite(d3ddev, &sprite_handler);
  if (result != D3D_OK)
      return 0;
```

```
    //load the background image
    back = LoadSurface("background.bmp", NULL);
    if (back == NULL)
        return 0;

    //load the ball sprite
    ball_image = LoadTexture("ball.bmp", D3DCOLOR_XRGB(255,0,255));
    if (ball_image == NULL)
        return 0;

    //set the ball's properties
    ball.x = 400;
    ball.y = 200;
    ball.width = 12;
    ball.height = 12;
    ball.movex = 8;
    ball.movey = -8;


    //load the paddle sprite
    paddle_image = LoadTexture("paddle.bmp", D3DCOLOR_XRGB(255,0,255));
    if (paddle_image == NULL)
        return 0;

    //set paddle properties
    paddle.x = 300;
    paddle.y = SCREEN_HEIGHT - 50;
    paddle.width = 90;
    paddle.height = 26;

    //load bounce wave file
    sound_bounce = LoadSound("bounce.wav");
    if (sound_bounce == NULL)
        return 0;

    //load the hit wave file
    sound_hit = LoadSound("hit.wav");
    if (sound_hit == NULL)
        return 0;


    //return okay
    return 1;
}
```

```
int Collision(SPRITE sprite1, SPRITE sprite2)
{
    RECT rect1;
    rect1.left = sprite1.x+1;
    rect1.top = sprite1.y+1;
    rect1.right = sprite1.x + sprite1.width-1;
    rect1.bottom = sprite1.y + sprite1.height-1;

    RECT rect2;
    rect2.left = sprite2.x+1;
    rect2.top = sprite2.y+1;
    rect2.right = sprite2.x + sprite2.width-1;
    rect2.bottom = sprite2.y + sprite2.height-1;

    RECT dest;
    return IntersectRect(&dest, &rect1, &rect2);
}

//the main game loop
void Game_Run(HWND hwnd)
{
    //ball position vector
    D3DXVECTOR3 position(0,0,0);

    //make sure the Direct3D device is valid
    if (d3ddev == NULL)
        return;

    //update mouse and keyboard
    Poll_Mouse();
    Poll_Keyboard();

    //after short delay, ready for next frame?
    //this keeps the game running at a steady frame rate
    if (GetTickCount() - start >= 30)
    {
        //reset timing
        start = GetTickCount();

        //move the ball sprite
        ball.x += ball.movex;
        ball.y += ball.movey;
```

```
   //bounce the ball at screen edges
   if (ball.x > SCREEN_WIDTH - ball.width)
{
   ball.x -= ball.width;
   ball.movex *= -1;
   PlaySound(sound_bounce);
}
else if (ball.x < 0)
{
      ball.x += ball.width;
      ball.movex *= -1;
      PlaySound(sound_bounce);
}

if (ball.y > SCREEN_HEIGHT - ball.height)
{
      ball.y -= ball.height;
      ball.movey *= -1;
      PlaySound(sound_bounce);
}
else if (ball.y < 0)
{
   ball.y += ball.height;
   ball.movey *= -1;
   PlaySound(sound_bounce);
}

//move the paddle
paddle.x += Mouse_X();
if (paddle.x > SCREEN_WIDTH - paddle.width)
     paddle.x = SCREEN_WIDTH - paddle.width;
else if (paddle.x < 0)
     paddle.x = 0;

//check for left arrow
if (Key_Down(DIK_LEFT))
     paddle.x -= 5;

//check for right arrow
if (Key_Down(DIK_RIGHT))
     paddle.x += 5;
```

```
    //see if ball hit the paddle
    if (Collision(paddle, ball))
    {
        ball.y -= ball.movey;
        ball.movey *= -1;
        PlaySound(sound_hit);
    }
}

//start rendering
if (d3ddev->BeginScene())
{
    //erase the entire background
    d3ddev->StretchRect(back, NULL, backbuffer, NULL, D3DTEXF_NONE);

    //start sprite handler
    sprite_handler->Begin(D3DXSPRITE_ALPHABLEND);

    //draw the ball
    position.x = (float)ball.x;
    position.y = (float)ball.y;
    sprite_handler->Draw(
        ball_image,
        NULL,
        NULL,
        &position,
        D3DCOLOR_XRGB(255,255,255));

    //draw the paddle
    position.x = (float)paddle.x;
    position.y = (float)paddle.y;
    sprite_handler->Draw(
        paddle_image,
        NULL,
        NULL,
        &position,
        D3DCOLOR_XRGB(255,255,255));

    //stop drawing
    sprite_handler->End();

    //stop rendering
    d3ddev->EndScene();
}
```

```
    //display the back buffer on the screen
    d3ddev->Present(NULL, NULL, NULL, NULL);

    //check for mouse button (to exit program)
    if (Mouse_Button(0))
        PostMessage(hwnd, WM_DESTROY, 0, 0);

    //check for escape key (to exit program)
    if (Key_Down(DIK_ESCAPE))
        PostMessage(hwnd, WM_DESTROY, 0, 0);
}

//frees memory and cleans up before the game ends
void Game_End(HWND hwnd)
{

    if (ball_image != NULL)
        ball_image->Release();

    if (paddle_image != NULL)
        paddle_image->Release();

    if (back != NULL)
        back->Release();

    if (sprite_handler != NULL)
        sprite_handler->Release();

    if (sound_bounce != NULL)
        delete sound_bounce;

    if (sound_hit != NULL)
        delete sound_hit;

}
```

Paddle Game Explained

Most of the code for this partial game is straightforward and familiar from previous projects. The one difference here is inclusion of a function that detects sprite collisions; it is also used to determine when the paddle and ball collide on the screen. When such a collision takes place, the ball reverses direction.

Windows provides a very convenient function that you can use to check for collisions, called IntersectRect. The function has this syntax:

```
BOOL IntersectRect(
  LPRECT lprcDst,
  CONST RECT *lprcSrc1,
  CONST RECT *lprcSrc2
);
```

The first parameter is not needed, so I just pass a dummy RECT to it. The second and third parameters also expect a RECT, and these are populated with data from two sprites before calling IntersectRect. This function uses the two rectangles to determine if an intersection between them exists, based on the left, top, right, and bottom values in each. If you really care about the intersection rectangle, then you can actually use the RECT filled in with data in the first parameter. The only thing I worry about when using this function is the return value, which is zero on failure or one on success. If it returns one, then you know there was a collision between the two sprites.

Can you think of a good use for this function? One great idea would be to add a bunch of blocks to the game (using an array of RECTs to keep track of their positions), and then use IntersectRect to see if the ball hits any of the blocks. You can then destroy the block and have the ball bounce away just like it does when it hits the paddle. Presto! There you have your very own traditional ball-and-paddle game.

What You Have Learned

This chapter has ventured into the subject of how to handle keyboard and mouse input using DirectInput. Here are the key points:

- You learned how to initialize DirectInput.

- You learned how to create a keyboard handler.

- You learned how to create a mouse handler.

- You added a new DirectInput component to the game framework.

- You wrote a nearly complete game called *Paddle Game.*

- You learned about sprite collision.

Review Questions

The following review questions will challenge your comprehension of the subject material covered in this chapter.

1. What is the name of the primary DirectInput object?

2. What is the function that creates a DirectInput device?

3. What is the name of the struct that contains mouse input data?

4. What function do you call to poll the keyboard or mouse?

5. What is the name of the function that helps check for sprite collisions?

On Your Own

The following exercises will challenge your retention of the information presented in this chapter.

Exercise 1. *Paddle Game* featured a single ball bouncing on the screen with support for collision with the paddle. This is obviously just the start of what could become a great game. Add support for blocks that the ball can strike. When the ball hits a block, the block should disappear and the ball should reverse direction.

Exercise 2. In addition to adding blocks to make this a functional game, add the logic to cause the player to lose when the ball hits the bottom edge of the screen.

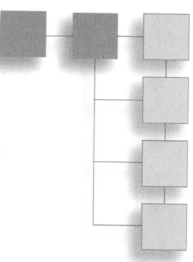

CHAPTER 11

TILE-BASED SCROLLING
BACKGROUNDS

Most action and arcade games use the technique of tile-based scrolling to achieve the moving background you see in such games. Although this technique is now decades old, it is still employed for rendering backgrounds, and this style of 2D game is still used frequently today. Back in the old days, when computer memory was very limited, tile-based scrolling was used because it is very efficient. We take for granted multiple gigabytes of memory today, but that much memory was unbelievable, even in a hard drive, let alone main memory (RAM). The concept of a *virtual screen buffer,* which you will learn about in this chapter, was used with very limited video cards at the time (with 256 to 1024 KB of video memory). Back then, you would be very lucky to have two 320×240 screens (or buffers), let alone enough memory for a large scrolling world. This chapter focuses on creating tile-based backgrounds with scrolling using secondary buffers. As you will discover, this is far easier than trying to wrangle memory out of a video card as programmers were forced to do years ago. A memory buffer will work well with either full-screen or windowed mode.

Here is a breakdown of the major topics in this chapter:

- Introduction to scrolling.

- Creating tile-based backgrounds.

- Using a single large scroll buffer.

- Using dynamically drawn tiles.

Introduction to Scrolling

What is scrolling? In today's gaming world, where 3D is the focus of everyone's attention, it's not surprising to find gamers and programmers who have never heard of scrolling. What a shame! The heritage of modern games is a long and fascinating one that is still relevant today, even if it is not understood or appreciated. The console industry puts great effort and value into scrolling, particularly on handheld systems, such as the Game Boy Advance. Given the extraordinary sales market for the GBA, would you be surprised to learn that more 2D games may be sold in a given day than 3D games? Figure 11.1 illustrates the concept of scrolling.

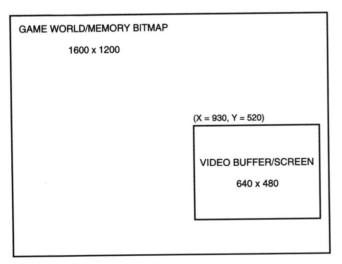

Figure 11.1
The scroll window shows a small part of a larger game world.

Note

Scrolling is the process of displaying a small portion of a large virtual game world in a window on the screen, and moving the view of that window to reflect the changing position within the game world.

You could display one huge bitmap image in the virtual game world, representing the current level of the game, and then copy (blit) a portion of that virtual world onto the screen. This is the simplest form of scrolling. Another method uses tiles to create the game world, which I'll cover shortly. First, you'll write a short program to demonstrate how to use bitmap scrolling.

Introduction to Tile-Based Backgrounds

You have seen what a simple scroller looks like, even though it relied on keyboard input to scroll. A high-speed scrolling arcade game would automatically scroll horizontally or vertically, displaying a ground-, air-, or space-based terrain below the player (usually represented by an airplane or a spaceship). The point of these games is to keep the action moving so fast that the player doesn't have a chance to rest from one wave of enemies to the next. Two upcoming chapters have been dedicated to these very subjects! For the time being, I want to keep things simple to cover the basics of scrolling before you delve into these advanced chapters.

Backgrounds and Scenery

A background is comprised of imagery or terrain in one form or another, upon which the sprites are drawn. The background might be nothing more than a pretty picture behind the action in a game, or it might take an active part, as in a scroller. When you are talking about scrollers, they need not be relegated only to the high-speed arcade games. Role-playing games are usually scrollers too, as are most sports games.

You should design the background around the goals of your game, not the other way around. You should not come up with some cool background and then try to build the game around it. (However, I admit that this is often how games are started.) You never want to rely on a single cool technology as the basis for an entire game, or the game will be forever remembered as a trendy game that tried to cash in on the latest fad. Instead of following and imitating, set your own precedents and make your own standards!

What am I talking about, you might ask? You might have the impression that anything and everything that could possibly have been done with a scrolling game has already been done ten times over. Not true. Not true! Remember when *Doom* first came out? Everyone had been imitating *Wolfenstein 3D* when Carmack and Romero bumped up the notch a few hundred points and raised everyone's expectations so high that shockwaves reverberated throughout the entire game industry—console and PC alike.

Do you really think it has all been done before and there is no more room for innovation, that the game industry is saturated and it's impossible to make a successful "indie" game? That didn't stop Bungie from going for broke on their first game project. *Halo* has made its mark in gaming history by upping everyone's expectations for superior physics and intelligent opponents. Now, a few years hence, what kinds of games are coming out? What is the biggest industry buzzword? Physics. Design a game today without it, and suddenly your game is so 1990s in the gaming press. It's all about physics and AI now, and that started with *Halo*. Rather, it was perfected with *Halo*—I can't personally recall a game with that level of interaction before *Halo* came along. There is absolutely no reason why you can't invent the next innovation or revolution in gaming, even in a 2D game.

Creating Backgrounds from Tiles

The real power of a scrolling background comes from a technique called tiling. Tiling is a process in which there really is no background, just an array of tiles that make up the background as it is displayed. In other words, it is a virtual background and it takes up very little memory compared to a full bitmapped background. Take a look at Figure 11.2 for an example.

Can you count the number of tiles used to construct the background in Figure 11.2? Eighteen tiles make up this image, actually. Imagine that—an entire game screen built using a handful of tiles, and the result is pretty good! Obviously, a real game would have more than just grass, roads, rivers, and bridges; a real game would have sprites moving on top of the background. How about an example? I thought you'd like that idea.

Tile-Based Scrolling

The ScrollTest program, which you will write soon, uses tiles to fill the large background bitmap when the program starts. It loads up the tiles from a bitmap (containing the tiles arranged in rows and columns), and then uses the map data to fill in the virtual scroll surface represented by a large bitmap in memory. Take a look at Figure 11.3.

Figure 11.2
A bitmap image constructed of tiles

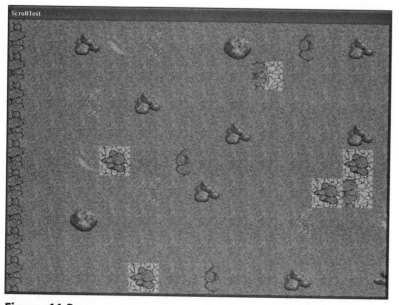

Figure 11.3
The ScrollTest program demonstrates how to perform tile-based background scrolling.

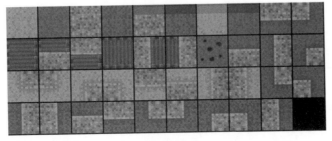

Figure 11.4
The source file containing the tiles used in the ScrollTest program

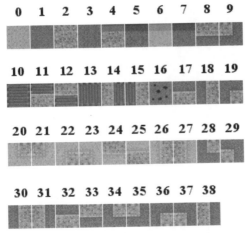

Figure 11.5
A legend of the tiles and their reference numbers used to create a map in the DynamicScroll program

This program creates the tiles that you see in this figure by drawing the tiles onto a large bitmap image created in memory (which is actually a Direct3D surface—and we're using a surface rather than a texture because no transparency is needed). The actual bitmap containing the tiles is shown in Figure 11.4. These tiles were created by Ari Feldman (http://www.flyingyogi.com) as part of his free SpriteLib.

I have prepared a legend of the tiles and the value for each in Figure 11.5. You can use the legend while building your own maps.

ScrollTest Header File

Now, let's write a test program to demonstrate, because theory only gets one so far when trying to build an actual game. I don't know about you, but I learn better by doing rather than by reading. I'm assuming that you're going to follow the same steps from the previous chapter for creating a new project, and adding the necessary library files. For reference, here are the library files again that must be added to the Additional Dependencies field under Project Properties, Linker, Input:

- d3d9.lib

- d3dx9.lib

- dsound.lib

- dinput8.lib

- dxguid.lib

- dxerr9.lib

- winmm.lib

Here's the header file for the ScrollTest program. This is the code that goes in the game.h file.

```
// Beginning Game Programming, Second Edition
// ScrollTest program header file

#ifndef _GAME_H
#define _GAME_H

#include <d3d9.h>
#include <d3dx9.h>
#include <d3dx9math.h>
#include <time.h>
#include <stdio.h>
#include <stdlib.h>
#include "dxgraphics.h"
#include "dxinput.h"

//application title
#define APPTITLE "ScrollTest"

//screen setup
#define FULLSCREEN 0          //0 = windowed, 1 = fullscreen
#define SCREEN_WIDTH 800
#define SCREEN_HEIGHT 600

//data for the scrolling map
#define TILEWIDTH 64
```

```
#define TILEHEIGHT 64
#define MAPWIDTH 25
#define MAPHEIGHT 18
#define GAMEWORLDWIDTH (TILEWIDTH * MAPWIDTH)
#define GAMEWORLDHEIGHT (TILEHEIGHT * MAPHEIGHT)

//macros to read the keyboard asynchronously
#define KEY_DOWN(vk_code) ((GetAsyncKeyState(vk_code) & 0x8000) ? 1 : 0)
#define KEY_UP(vk_code)((GetAsyncKeyState(vk_code) & 0x8000) ? 1 : 0)

//function prototypes
int Game_Init(HWND);
void Game_Run(HWND);
void Game_End(HWND);

//scrolling map support functions
void ScrollScreen();
void BuildGameWorld();
void DrawTile(LPDIRECT3DSURFACE9,int,int,int,int,LPDIRECT3DSURFACE9,int,int);

#endif
```

ScrollTest Source Code

Now let's write the main source code for the ScrollTest program, which is typed into the game.cpp source code file. The map data shown in this code has been compacted in order to save space and to fit on a line without wrapping, but it is hard to read this way. If you prefer, you may type in the map data as shown in Figure 11.6.

```
// Beginning Game Programming, Second Edition
// ScrollTest program

#include "game.h"

int ScrollX, ScrollY;               //current scroll position
int SpeedX, SpeedY;                 //scroll speed
LPDIRECT3DSURFACE9 gameworld;       //scroll buffer
long start;                         //timing variable

int MAPDATA[MAPWIDTH*MAPHEIGHT] = {
    80,81,81,81,81,81,81,81,81,81,81,81,81,81,81,81,81,81,81,81,
    81,81,81,82,90,3,3,3,3,3,3,3,3,3,3,3,3,3,3,92,3,3,3,3,3,92,3,
    92,90,3,13,83,96,3,3,23,3,92,3,13,92,3,3,3,3,3,3,11,3,13,3,3,92,
```

```
90,3,3,3,3,3,3,3,10,3,3,3,3,3,23,3,3,3,3,3,3,3,3,13,3,92,90,3,96,
3,13,3,3,3,3,3,3,3,3,3,3,3,3,96,3,23,3,96,3,3,92,90,3,3,3,3,3,3,
13,3,3,3,13,3,3,11,3,3,3,3,3,3,3,3,13,3,92,90,3,83,11,3,92,3,3,3,
3,3,11,3,3,3,3,3,3,3,83,3,3,3,92,92,90,3,3,3,96,3,13,3,3,3,3,11,
10,3,3,3,3,3,13,3,3,13,3,3,3,92,90,3,23,3,3,3,3,3,3,96,3,3,83,
3,3,3,92,3,3,3,3,3,13,3,92,90,3,3,3,3,3,3,3,3,3,3,3,3,23,3,3,3,
3,3,3,3,3,3,3,3,92,90,3,3,3,11,3,92,3,3,13,3,3,131,3,10,3,3,3,96,
3,92,3,96,3,92,90,3,13,83,3,3,3,3,3,3,3,3,3,3,3,13,3,3,3,3,3,3,3,
3,3,92,90,3,3,3,3,13,3,3,3,3,3,3,11,96,3,3,3,3,3,3,3,13,3,13,3,11,
92,90,92,3,13,3,3,3,3,3,3,92,3,10,3,23,3,3,3,3,3,3,3,3,3,3,92,90,
3,3,3,3,3,96,3,23,3,3,3,3,3,3,3,3,3,83,3,3,13,3,96,3,92,90,3,3,3,
3,92,3,3,3,3,3,3,13,3,3,3,13,3,3,3,3,11,3,3,3,3,3,92,90,3,13,3,3,3,3,
3,3,3,96,3,3,3,3,3,3,3,3,3,92,3,3,92,100,101,101,101,101,101,
101,101,101,101,101,101,101,101,101,101,101,101,101,101,101,101,
101,101,102
};
```

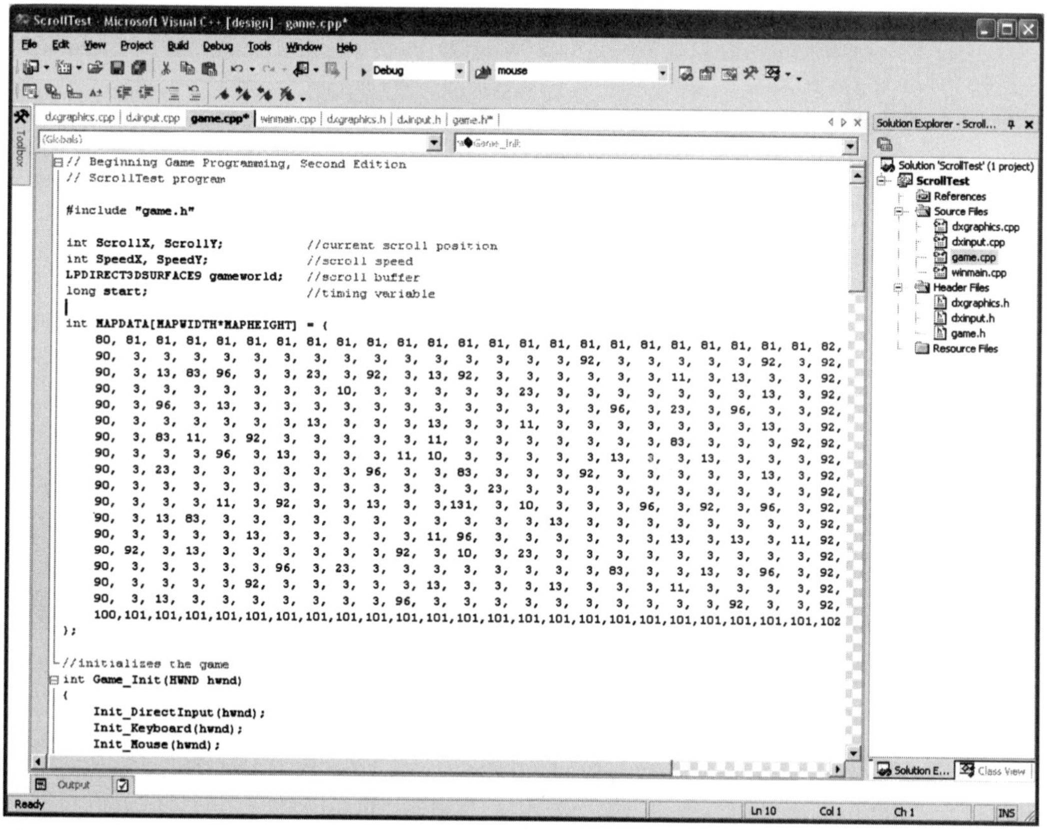

Figure 11.6
The map data in the ScrollTest program

```
//initializes the game
int Game_Init(HWND hwnd)
{
    Init_DirectInput(hwnd);
    Init_Keyboard(hwnd);
    Init_Mouse(hwnd);
    start = GetTickCount();
    BuildGameWorld();
    return 1;
}

//the main game loop
void Game_Run(HWND hwnd)
{
    //make sure the Direct3D device is valid
    if (d3ddev == NULL)
        return;

    //poll DirectInput devices
    Poll_Keyboard();
    Poll_Mouse();

    //check for escape key (to exit program)
    if (Key_Down(DIK_ESCAPE))
        PostMessage(hwnd, WM_DESTROY, 0, 0);

    //scroll based on mouse input
    if (Mouse_X() != 0) ScrollX += Mouse_X();
    if (Mouse_Y() != 0)   ScrollY += Mouse_Y();

    //keep the game running at a steady frame rate
    if (GetTickCount() - start >= 30)
    {
        //reset timing
        start = GetTickCount();

        //start rendering
        if (d3ddev->BeginScene())
        {
            //update the scrolling view
            ScrollScreen();
```

```
            //stop rendering
            d3ddev->EndScene();
        }
    }
    //display the back buffer on the screen
    d3ddev->Present(NULL, NULL, NULL, NULL);
}


//frees memory and cleans up before the game ends
void Game_End(HWND hwnd)
{
    Kill_Keyboard();
    Kill_Mouse();
    dinput->Release();
}


void BuildGameWorld()
{
    HRESULT result;
    int x, y;
    LPDIRECT3DSURFACE9 tiles;

    //load the bitmap image containing all the tiles
    tiles = LoadSurface("groundtiles.bmp", D3DCOLOR_XRGB(0,0,0));

    //create the scrolling game world bitmap
    result = d3ddev->CreateOffscreenPlainSurface(
        GAMEWORLDWIDTH,          //width of the surface
        GAMEWORLDHEIGHT,         //height of the surface
        D3DFMT_X8R8G8B8,
        D3DPOOL_DEFAULT,
        &gameworld,              //pointer to the surface
        NULL);

    if (result != D3D_OK)
    {
        MessageBox(NULL,"Error creating working surface!","Error",0);
        return;
    }

    //fill the gameworld bitmap with tiles
    for (y=0; y < MAPHEIGHT; y++)
```

```
        for (x=0; x < MAPWIDTH; x++)
            DrawTile(tiles, MAPDATA[y * MAPWIDTH + x], 64, 64, 16,
            gameworld, x * 64, y * 64);

        //now the tiles bitmap is no longer needed
        tiles->Release();
}

void DrawTile(LPDIRECT3DSURFACE9 source,        // source surface image
                int tilenum,                    // tile #
                int width,                      // tile width
                int height,                     // tile height
                int columns,                    // columns of tiles
                LPDIRECT3DSURFACE9 dest,        // destination surface
                int destx,                      // destination x
                int desty)                      // destination y
{

        //create a RECT to describe the source image
        RECT r1;
        r1.left = (tilenum % columns) * width;
        r1.top = (tilenum / columns) * height;
        r1.right = r1.left + width;
        r1.bottom = r1.top + height;

        //set destination rect
        RECT r2 = {destx,desty,destx+width,desty+height};

        //draw the tile
        d3ddev->StretchRect(source, &r1, dest, &r2, D3DTEXF_NONE);
}

void ScrollScreen()
{
        //update horizontal scrolling position and speed
        ScrollX += SpeedX;
        if (ScrollX < 0)
        {
            ScrollX = 0;
            SpeedX = 0;
        }
    else if (ScrollX > GAMEWORLDWIDTH - SCREEN_WIDTH)
```

```
    {
       ScrollX = GAMEWORLDWIDTH - SCREEN_WIDTH;
       SpeedX = 0;
    }

    //update vertical scrolling position and speed
    ScrollY += SpeedY;
    if (ScrollY < 0)
    {
        ScrollY = 0;
        SpeedY = 0;
    }
    else if (ScrollY > GAMEWORLDHEIGHT - SCREEN_HEIGHT)
    {
        ScrollY = GAMEWORLDHEIGHT - SCREEN_HEIGHT;
        SpeedY = 0;
    }

    //set dimensions of the source image
    RECT r1 = {ScrollX, ScrollY, ScrollX+SCREEN_WIDTH-1,
        ScrollY+SCREEN_HEIGHT-1};

    //set the destination rect
    RECT r2 = {0, 0, SCREEN_WIDTH-1, SCREEN_HEIGHT-1};

    //draw the current game world view
    d3ddev->StretchRect(gameworld, &r1, backbuffer, &r2,
        D3DTEXF_NONE);
}
```

Dynamically Rendered Tiles

Displaying tiles just to make a proof-of-concept is one thing, but it is not very useful. True, you have some code to create a virtual background, load tiles onto it, and then scroll the game world. In the past, I have generated a realistic-looking game map with source code, using an algorithm that matched terrain curves and straights (such as the road, bridge, and river) so that I created an awesome map from scratch, all by myself. Building an algorithmic landscape is one thing, but constructing it at run time is not a great solution—even if your map-generating routine is very good.

For instance, many games, such as *Warcraft III*, *Age of Mythology*, and *Civilization IV* can generate the game world on the fly. Obviously, the programmers spent a lot of time perfecting the world-generating routines. If your game would benefit by featuring a randomly generated game world, then your work is cut out for you, but the results will be worth it. This is simply one of those design considerations that you must make, given that you have time to develop it.

The Tile Map

Assuming you don't have the means to generate a random map (or simply do not want to go that route), you can simply create one within an array, as we did in the ScrollTest program. But where did this map data actually come from? And, furthermore, where do you start? First of all, you should realize that the tiles are numbered and should be referenced this way in the map array. Each number in the tile map represents a tile image in a bitmap file. Here is what the array looks like, as defined in the DynamicScroll program (which we'll cover here in a minute).

```
int MAPDATA[MAPWIDTH*MAPHEIGHT] = {
1, 2, 3, 4, 5, 6, 7, 8, 9, 10, 11, 12, 13, 14, 15, 16,
17, 18, 19, 20, 21, 22, 23, 24, 25, 26, 27, 28, 29, 30, 31, 32,
33, 34, 35, 36, 37, 38, 39, 40, 41, 42, 43, 44, 45, 46, 47, 48,
49, 50, 51, 52, 53, 54, 55, 56, 57, 58, 59, 60, 61, 62, 63, 64,
65, 66, 67, 68, 69, 70, 71, 72, 73, 74, 75, 76, 77, 78, 79, 80,
81, 82, 83, 84, 85, 86, 87, 88, 89, 90, 91, 92, 93, 94, 95, 96,
97, 98, 99, 100, 101, 102, 103, 104, 105, 106, 107, 108, 109, 110, 111, 112,
113, 114, 115, 116, 117, 118, 119, 120, 121, 122, 123, 124, 125, 126, 127, 128,
129, 130, 131, 132, 133, 134, 135, 136, 137, 138, 139, 140, 141, 142, 143, 144,
145, 146, 147, 148, 149, 150, 151, 152, 153, 154, 155, 156, 157, 158, 159, 160,
161, 162, 163, 164, 165, 166, 167, 168, 169, 170, 171, 172, 173, 174, 175, 176,
177, 178, 179, 180, 181, 182, 183, 184, 185, 186, 187, 188, 189, 190, 191, 192,
1, 2, 3, 4, 5, 6, 7, 8, 9, 10, 11, 12, 13, 14, 15, 16,
17, 18, 19, 20, 21, 22, 23, 24, 25, 26, 27, 28, 29, 30, 31, 32,
33, 34, 35, 36, 37, 38, 39, 40, 41, 42, 43, 44, 45, 46, 47, 48,
49, 50, 51, 52, 53, 54, 55, 56, 57, 58, 59, 60, 61, 62, 63, 64,
65, 66, 67, 68, 69, 70, 71, 72, 73, 74, 75, 76, 77, 78, 79, 80,
81, 82, 83, 84, 85, 86, 87, 88, 89, 90, 91, 92, 93, 94, 95, 96,
97, 98, 99, 100, 101, 102, 103, 104, 105, 106, 107, 108, 109, 110, 111, 112,
113, 114, 115, 116, 117, 118, 119, 120, 121, 122, 123, 124, 125, 126, 127, 128,
129, 130, 131, 132, 133, 134, 135, 136, 137, 138, 139, 140, 141, 142, 143, 144,
145, 146, 147, 148, 149, 150, 151, 152, 153, 154, 155, 156, 157, 158, 159, 160,
161, 162, 163, 164, 165, 166, 167, 168, 169, 170, 171, 172, 173, 174, 175, 176,
177, 178, 179, 180, 181, 182, 183, 184, 185, 186, 187, 188, 189, 190, 191, 192
};
```

Figure 11.7
This starfield image used by the DynamicScroll program was shot by the Hubble Space Telescope (courtesy of NASA).

The trick here is that this is really only a single-dimensional array, but the listing makes it obvious how the map will look because there are 16 numbers in each row—the same number of tiles in each row of the bitmap file, which is shown in Figure 11.7. I did this intentionally so you can use this as a template for creating your own maps. And you can create more than one map if you want. Simply change the name of each map and reference the map you want to draw so that your new map will show up. You are not limited in adding more tiles to each row. One interesting thing you can try is making MAPDATA a two-dimensional array containing many maps, and then changing the map at run time! You could use this simple scrolling code as the basis for any of a hundred different games if you have the creative gumption to do so.

Creating a Tile Map Using Mappy

I'm going to go through the steps with you for creating a very simple tile map using the awesome (and free) tile-editing program, Mappy. This program is available at http://www.tilemap.co.uk, and is provided on the CD-ROM in \software\Mappy. It is my favorite level/map-editing program for tile-based games, and is used by many professional game developers as well (especially those working on handheld and strategy games). I wish we had time for a full tutorial on using Mappy, because it really is jam-packed with an amazing assortment of features (tucked away in its various sub-menus). We'll have to rely on simplistic coverage of Mappy here, just enough to read in a large photograph and convert it to a tile map.

Note

If you enjoy this subject and want to learn more, I recommend you pick up *Game Programming All in One, Third Edition*, which contains five whole chapters on just the subject of scrolling backgrounds, including a complete tutorial chapter on using Mappy! Although that book focuses on the open-source Allegro Game Library, it uses DirectX behind the scenes.

Let's start by firing up Mappy. When it starts running, open the File menu and select New Map. This will bring up the New Map dialog box shown in Figure 11.8. As shown in this figure, type in **64 × 64** for the tile size and **16 × 24** for the map size (which is a count of the number of tiles in the tile map). The new map will be created, but will be void of any tiles as of yet, as you can see in Figure 11.9.

Importing an Existing Bitmap File

Next, we're going to import the space photograph taken by Hubble into Mappy and convert it to a tile map. As shown in Figure 11.10, open the MapTools menu, and select Useful Functions, followed by the option "Create map from big picture". Browse for the space1.bmp file, located in \sources\chapter11\DynamicScroll\map on the CD-ROM. When you select this file, Mappy will import it into the palette of tiles, as shown in Figure 11.11.

As you can see from this figure, there are a *lot* of tiles that made up the image! If you are curious about the number of tiles in this palette, let's take a look! Open

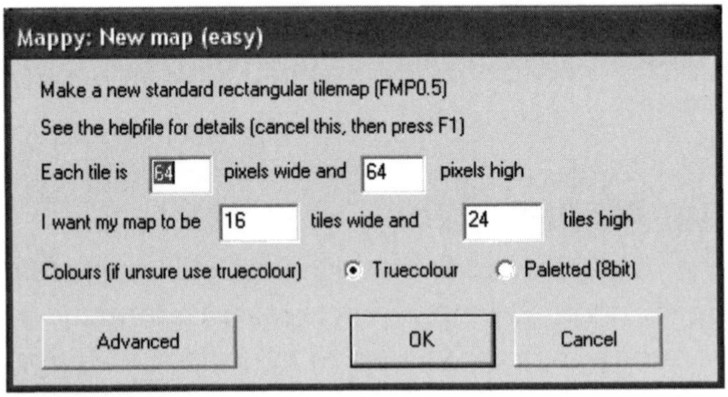

Figure 11.8
Creating a new map using Mappy

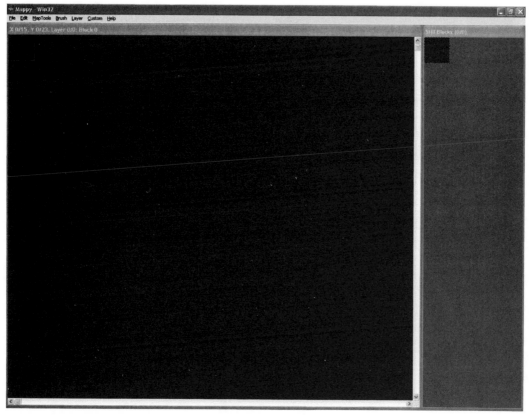

Figure 11.9
The new map that has been created by Mappy, awaiting your custom tiles

up the MapTools menu and select Map Properties. This brings up the Map Properties dialog box, shown in Figure 11.12. Take a look at the text values on the left side of the dialog: Map Array, Block Str, Graphics, and so on. The Map Array text tells you the size of the map in tiles (16×24, just as we specified). Now take a look at the Graphics information. Here we see that there are 193 tiles in this tile map, and they are all 64×64 pixels in size, and have a color depth of 24 bits.

When you import a large bitmap into Mappy, it grabs tiles starting at the upper-left corner of the bitmap, and goes through the image in a grid, from left to right and from top to bottom, until the entire image has been encoded into tiles. It then constructs the tile map using those tile numbers and inserts the tile map into the editor, so that it resembles the original bitmap image. Note that you must create the tile map in the first place so that it is at least as large as the bitmap image (in this case, 1024×768) or larger.

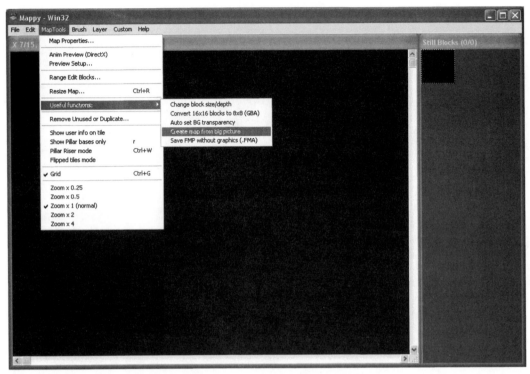

Figure 11.10
Preparing to import a large bitmap file as the source for our tiles

Exporting the Tile Map

First, let's just save the tile map in the native Mappy file format, so it can be edited later. Open the File menu and select Save. I have named this tile map "spacemap". The default extension for a Mappy file is .fmp.

Now, you can go ahead and edit the tile map if you want, but I'm going to just go ahead and export the tile map now and show you how to do that. First, open up the File menu and select the Export option. This brings up the Export dialog, shown in Figure 11.13. Select the options on this dialog as follows:

- Map array as comma values only (?.CSV)

- Graphics Blocks as picture (?.BMP)

- 16 blocks per row

These options will cause Mappy to export a new bitmap file comprised of the tiles in the order that they appear in the palette—which means this bitmap image will

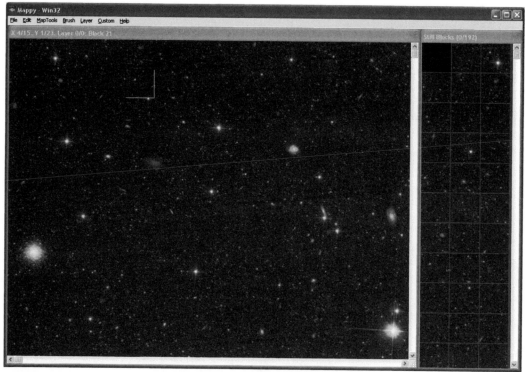

Figure 11.11
The palette of tiles has been imported from the large space photograph.

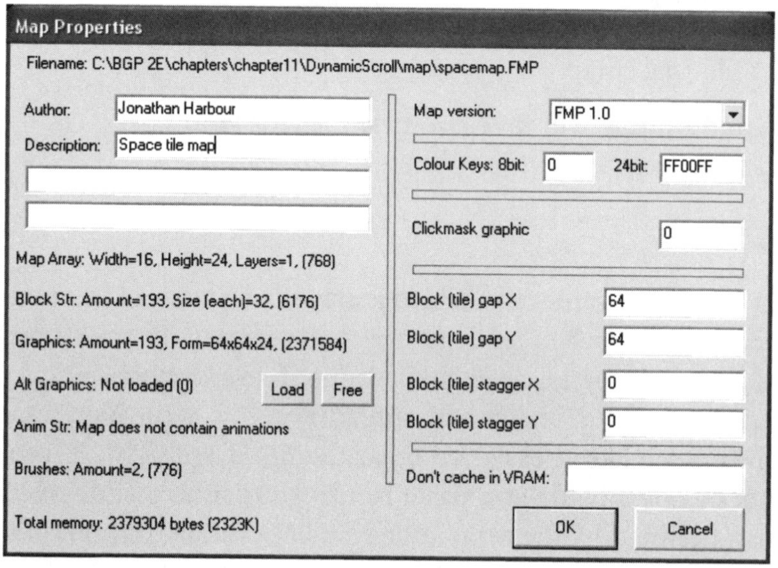

Figure 11.12
The Map Properties dialog box shows the properties of the tile map.

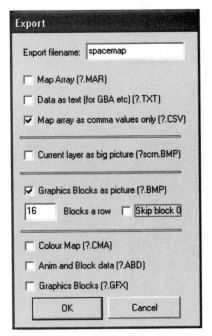

Figure 11.13
The Export dialog box is used to export a tile map to a text file.

then be used to draw the tiles in your game. Note that Mappy automatically inserts a blank tile first in the palette. You want to keep that blank tile in place, because the tile map values begin with that first blank tile (index number zero). I have named the export file spacemap.

Click the Okay button and Mappy will save two new files for your use:

- spacemap.csv

- spacemap.bmp

The .csv file is a comma-separated values file, which is actually just stored in a text format (which can be opened in Notepad or any text editor). If you have Microsoft Excel installed, it will try to open the .csv file if you double-click it, because Excel uses that format for text-based spreadsheets as well. You can rename it to spacemap.txt to make it easier to open the file if you wish. Once open, copy the contents out of this file and paste it into your source code over any pre-existing tile map (defined by the array called MAPDATA in the examples in this chapter).

The DynamicScroll Project

Now let's create a new project. You may just re-use one of the projects from the previous chapter if you want, since it will already be configured with the proper library files and so forth. Or, if you created the ScrollTest program, feel free to reuse that project.

If you are creating a new project file, call it DynamicScroll, since that is the name of this program. This program is similar to ScrollTest, but it draws the tiles directly to the screen without the need for a large bitmap in memory. This program will also use a smaller virtual background to cut down on the size of the map array. Why? Not to save memory, but to make the program more manageable. Because the virtual background was 1600×1200 in the previous program, it would require 50 columns of tiles across and 37 rows of tiles down to fill it! That is no problem at all for a map editor program, but it's too much data to type in manually.

To make it more manageable, the new virtual background will be 1024 pixels across, which also happens to be the width of the screen in this program. That was intentional, because the DynamicScroll program will simulate a vertically scrolling arcade shooter game! The point is to demonstrate how it will work, not to build a game engine, so don't worry about precision at this point. If you want to type in the values to create a bigger map, by all means, go for it! That would be a great learning experience, as a matter of fact. For your purposes here (and with my primary goal of being able to print an entire row of numbers in a single source code line in the book), I'll stick to 16 tiles across and 24 tiles down.

In the example tile map, I have doubled its size by copying the entire tile map of values and pasting them at the end, which effectively doubles the map size; otherwise, you would not be able to scroll it. We're just going to scroll the screen of tiles over and over again in such a game, but in this example, the scrolling will be controlled by the mouse. You can work with a map that is deeper than it is wide, so that will allow you to test scrolling up and down fairly well. Figure 11.14 shows the output from the DynamicScroll program.

DynamicScroll Header File

Here's the DynamicScroll header file, which goes in the game.h header file.

```
// Beginning Game Programming, Second Edition
// DynamicScroll program header
```

Figure 11.14
The DynamicScroll program scrolls a map that was defined in the map array.

```
#ifndef _GAME_H
#define _GAME_H

#include <d3d9.h>
#include <d3dx9.h>
#include <d3dx9math.h>
#include <time.h>
#include <stdio.h>
#include <stdlib.h>
#include "dxgraphics.h"
#include "dxinput.h"
#include "dxaudio.h"


//application title
#define APPTITLE "DynamicScroll"


//screen setup
#define FULLSCREEN 0        //0 = windowed, 1 = fullscreen
#define SCREEN_WIDTH 1024
#define SCREEN_HEIGHT 768
```

```
//data for the scrolling map
#define TILEWIDTH 64
#define TILEHEIGHT 64
#define MAPWIDTH 16
#define MAPHEIGHT 24
#define GAMEWORLDWIDTH (TILEWIDTH * MAPWIDTH)
#define GAMEWORLDHEIGHT (TILEHEIGHT * MAPHEIGHT)
//scrolling window size
#define WINDOWWIDTH (SCREEN_WIDTH / TILEWIDTH) * TILEWIDTH
#define WINDOWHEIGHT (SCREEN_HEIGHT / TILEHEIGHT) * TILEHEIGHT
//scroll buffer size
#define SCROLLBUFFERWIDTH (SCREEN_WIDTH + TILEWIDTH * 2)
#define SCROLLBUFFERHEIGHT (SCREEN_HEIGHT + TILEHEIGHT * 2)

//macros to read the keyboard asynchronously
#define KEY_DOWN(vk_code) ((GetAsyncKeyState(vk_code) & 0x8000) ? 1 : 0)
#define KEY_UP(vk_code)((GetAsyncKeyState(vk_code) & 0x8000) ? 1 : 0)

//function prototypes
int Game_Init(HWND);
void Game_Run(HWND);
void Game_End(HWND);

//scrolling map support functions
void DrawTile(LPDIRECT3DSURFACE9,int,int,int,int,LPDIRECT3DSURFACE9,int,
int);
void DrawScrollWindow();
void DrawTiles();
void UpdateScrollPosition();

#endif
```

DynamicScroll Source Code

Now let's type in the source code for the DynamicScroll program. This code goes in the game.cpp file.

```
// Beginning Game Programming, Second Edition
// DynamicScroll program

#include "game.h"

int ScrollX, ScrollY;        //current scroll position
int SpeedX, SpeedY;          //scroll speed
```

```
LPDIRECT3DSURFACE9 scrollbuffer;    //scroll buffer
LPDIRECT3DSURFACE9 tiles;           //source image containing tiles
long start;                         //timing variable

int MAPDATA[MAPWIDTH*MAPHEIGHT] = {
1,2,3,4,5,6,7,8,9,10,11,12,13,14,15,16,17,18,19,20,21,22,23,24,25,
26,27,28,29,30,31,32,33,34,35,36,37,38,39,40,41,42,43,44,45,46,47,
48,49,50,51,52,53,54,55,56,57,58,59,60,61,62,63,64,65,66,67,68,69,
70,71,72,73,74,75,76,77,78,79,80,81,82,83,84,85,86,87,88,89,90,91,
92,93,94,95,96,97,98,99,100,101,102,103,104,105,106,107,108,109,
110,111,112,113,114,115,116,117,118,119,120,121,122,123,124,125,
126,127,128,129,130,131,132,133,134,135,136,137,138,139,140,141,
142,143,144,145,146,147,148,149,150,151,152,153,154,155,156,157,
158,159,160,161,162,163,164,165,166,167,168,169,170,171,172,173,
174,175,176,177,178,179,180,181,182,183,184,185,186,187,188,189,
190,191,192,1,2,3,4,5,6,7,8,9,10,11,12,13,14,15,16,17,18,19,20,
21,22,23,24,25,26,27,28,29,30,31,32,33,34,35,36,37,38,39,40,41,
42,43,44,45,46,47,48,49,50,51,52,53,54,55,56,57,58,59,60,61,62,
63,64,65,66,67,68,69,70,71,72,73,74,75,76,77,78,79,80,81,82,83,
84,85,86,87,88,89,90,91,92,93,94,95,96,97,98,99,100,101,102,103,
104,105,106,107,108,109,110,111,112,113,114,115,116,117,118,119,
120,121,122,123,124,125,126,127,128,129,130,131,132,133,134,135,
136,137,138,139,140,141,142,143,144,145,146,147,148,149,150,151,
152,153,154,155,156,157,158,159,160,161,162,163,164,165,166,167,
168,169,170,171,172,173,174,175,176,177,178,179,180,181,182,183,
184,185,186,187,188,189,190,191,192
};

//initializes the game
int Game_Init(HWND hwnd)
{
    HRESULT result;

    Init_DirectInput(hwnd);
    Init_Keyboard(hwnd);
    Init_Mouse(hwnd);

    //load the tile images
    tiles = LoadSurface("spacemap.bmp", D3DCOLOR_XRGB(0,0,0));

    //create the scroll buffer surface in memory, slightly bigger
//than the screen
    result = d3ddev->CreateOffscreenPlainSurface(
```

```
               SCROLLBUFFERWIDTH, SCROLLBUFFERHEIGHT,
               D3DFMT_X8R8G8B8, D3DPOOL_DEFAULT,
               &scrollbuffer,
               NULL);

    start = GetTickCount();
    return 1;
}

//the main game loop
void Game_Run(HWND hwnd)
{
    //make sure the Direct3D device is valid
    if (d3ddev == NULL)
        return;

        //poll DirectInput devices
        Poll_Keyboard();
        Poll_Mouse();

    //check for escape key (to exit program)
    if (Key_Down(DIK_ESCAPE))
        PostMessage(hwnd, WM_DESTROY, 0, 0);

    //scroll based on mouse input
    if (Mouse_X() != 0) ScrollX += Mouse_X();
    if (Mouse_Y() != 0)   ScrollY += Mouse_Y();

    //keep the game running at a steady frame rate
    if (GetTickCount() - start >= 30)
    {
        //reset timing
        start = GetTickCount();

            //update the scrolling view
            UpdateScrollPosition();

            //start rendering
            if (d3ddev->BeginScene())
            {

                //draw tiles onto the scroll buffer
                DrawTiles();
```

```
        //draw the scroll window onto the back buffer
        DrawScrollWindow();

        //stop rendering
        d3ddev->EndScene();
    }
  }

  //display the back buffer on the screen
  d3ddev->Present(NULL, NULL, NULL, NULL);
}

//frees memory and cleans up before the game ends
void Game_End(HWND hwnd)
{
    Kill_Keyboard();
    Kill_Mouse();
    dinput->Release();
}

//This function updates the scrolling position and speed
void UpdateScrollPosition()
{
   //update horizontal scrolling position and speed
   ScrollX += SpeedX;

   if (ScrollX < 0)
       {
         ScrollX = 0;
         SpeedX = 0;
       }
   else if (ScrollX > GAMEWORLDWIDTH - WINDOWWIDTH)
      {
         ScrollX = GAMEWORLDWIDTH - WINDOWWIDTH;
         SpeedX = 0;
      }

   //update vertical scrolling position and speed
   ScrollY += SpeedY;
   if (ScrollY < 0)
       {
         ScrollY = 0;
         SpeedY = 0;
       }
```

```
    else if (ScrollY > GAMEWORLDHEIGHT - WINDOWHEIGHT)
    {
      ScrollY = GAMEWORLDHEIGHT - WINDOWHEIGHT;
      SpeedY = 0;
    }
  }
}


//This function does the real work of drawing a single tile from the
//source image onto the tile scroll buffer. Parameters provide much
//flexibility.
void DrawTile(LPDIRECT3DSURFACE9 source,     // source surface image
                    int tilenum,       // tile #
                    int width,         // tile width
                    int height,        // tile height
                    int columns,       // columns of tiles
                    LPDIRECT3DSURFACE9 dest,     // destination surface
                    int destx,         // destination x
                    int desty)         // destination y
{
    //create a RECT to describe the source image
    RECT r1;
    r1.left = (tilenum % columns) * width;
    r1.top = (tilenum / columns) * height;
    r1.right = r1.left + width;
    r1.bottom = r1.top + height;

    //set destination rect
    RECT r2 = {destx,desty,destx+width,desty+height};

    //draw the tile
    d3ddev->StretchRect(source, &r1, dest, &r2, D3DTEXF_NONE);
}


//This function fills the tile buffer with tiles representing
//the current scroll display based on scrollx/scrolly.
void DrawTiles()
{
    int tilex, tiley;
    int columns, rows;
    int x, y;
    int tilenum;

    //calculate starting tile position
```

```
    tilex = ScrollX / TILEWIDTH;
    tiley = ScrollY / TILEHEIGHT;

    //calculate the number of columns and rows
    columns = WINDOWWIDTH / TILEWIDTH;
    rows = WINDOWHEIGHT / TILEHEIGHT;

    //draw tiles onto the scroll buffer surface
    for (y=0; y<=rows; y++)
    {
       for (x=0; x<=columns; x++)
       {
           //retrieve the tile number from this position
           tilenum = MAPDATA[((tiley + y) * MAPWIDTH + (tilex + x))];

           //draw the tile onto the scroll buffer
           DrawTile(tiles,tilenum,TILEWIDTH,TILEHEIGHT,16,scrollbuffer,
             x*TILEWIDTH,y*TILEHEIGHT);
       }
    }
}

//This function draws the portion of the scroll buffer onto the back buffer
//according to the current "partial tile" scroll position.
void DrawScrollWindow()
{
    //calculate the partial sub-tile lines to draw using modulus
    int partialx = ScrollX % TILEWIDTH;
    int partialy = ScrollY % TILEHEIGHT;

    //set dimensions of the source image as a rectangle
    RECT r1 = {partialx,partialy,partialx+WINDOWWIDTH,partialy+WINDOWHEIGHT};

    //set the destination rectangle
    //This line draws the virtual scroll buffer to the screen exactly as is,
    //without scaling the image to fit the screen. If your screen does not
    //divide evenly with the tiles, then you may want to scale the scroll
    //buffer to fill the entire screen. It's better to use a resolution that
    //divides evenly with your tile size.

    //use this line for scaled display
    //RECT r2 = {0, 0, WINDOWWIDTH-1, WINDOWHEIGHT-1};
```

```
//use this line for non-scaled display
RECT r2 = {0, 0, SCREEN_WIDTH-1, SCREEN_HEIGHT-1};

//draw the "partial tile" scroll window onto the back buffer
d3ddev->StretchRect(scrollbuffer, &r1, backbuffer, &r2, D3DTEXF_NONE);
}
```

Figure 11.15 shows the completed project with all the source files showing up in the Solution Explorer, for your reference.

This program was quite a bit to chew on all at once, and we didn't explain every detail very carefully—because we have to move on to 3D and can't spare any more time on 2D graphics at this point! But all of this code is reusable and you can build a scrolling arcade game with it very easily. Just get your scroller moving on its own (without requiring user input), and then add some sprites over the top, and presto—you have a scrolling arcade game!

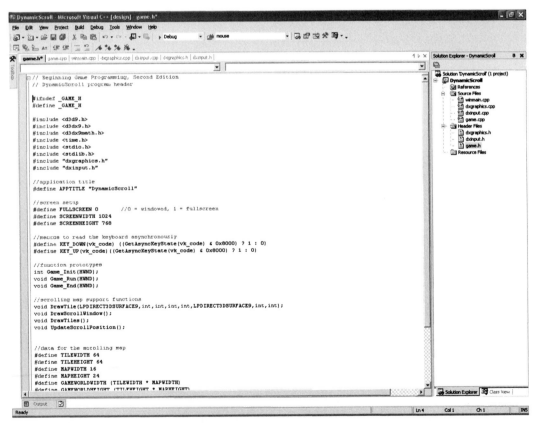

Figure 11.15
The complete DynamicScroll project in Visual C++

What You Have Learned

In this chapter we learned about scrolling backgrounds. You learned how they are created and how to use them in a game. Working with tiles to create a scrolling game world is by no means an easy subject! Here are the key points:

- You learned how to create a virtual scroll buffer.

- You learned how to use Mappy to create a tile map.

- You learned how to dynamically draw tiles onto the screen.

Review Questions

The following review questions will challenge your comprehension of the subject material covered in this chapter.

1. What was the resolution of the virtual scroll buffer used in the ScrollTest program?

2. Likewise, what was the resolution of the buffer used in the DynamicScroll program?

3. What is the difference between the tile drawing code in the two example programs?

4. How would you create a tile map using Mappy with a *gigantic* level with thousands of tiles?

5. What is the effective limit on map size for a game that draws tiles dynamically?

On Your Own

The following exercises will challenge your retention of the information presented in this chapter.

Exercise 1. This DynamicScroll program sure has a lot of potential and we have only scratched the surface here! See if you can get the program to automatically scroll the tile map without user input.

Exercise 2. The DynamicScroll program almost looks like a rudimentary game with automatic scrolling, so let's take it one step further. Load up a sprite and draw it on the screen over the top of the scroller. Then, allow the player to move the space ship left and right using the arrow keys.

PART III

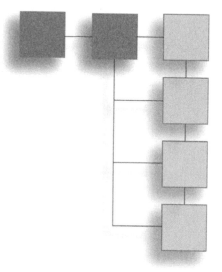

3D PROGRAMMING

Part III is dedicated to the subject of 3D programming.

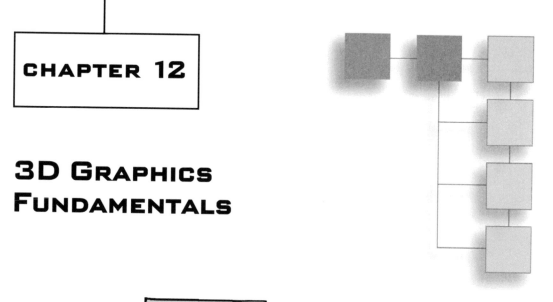

CHAPTER 12

3D GRAPHICS FUNDAMENTALS

This chapter covers the basics of 3D graphics. You will learn the basic concepts so that you are at least aware of the key points in 3D programming. However, this chapter will not go into great detail on 3D mathematics or graphics theory, which are far too advanced for this book. What you will learn instead is the practical implementation of 3D in order to write simple 3D games. You will get just exactly what you need to write a simple 3D game without getting bogged down in theory. If you have questions about how matrix math works and about how 3D rendering is done, you might want to use this chapter as a starting point and then go on and read a book such as *Beginning Direct3D Game Programming*, by Wolfgang Engel (Thomson Course Technology). The goal of this chapter is to provide you with a set of reusable functions that can be used to develop 3D games.

Here is what you will learn in this chapter:

- How to create and use vertices.

- How to manipulate polygons.

- How to create a textured polygon.

- How to create a cube and rotate it.

Introduction to 3D Programming

It's a foregone conclusion today that everyone has a 3D accelerated video card. Even the low-end budget video cards are equipped with a 3D graphics processing unit (GPU) that would be impressive were it not for all the competition in this market pushing out more and more polygons and new features every year. Figure 12.1 shows a typical GeForce 6600 video card.

Figure 12.1
Modern 3D video cards are capable of producing real-time photorealistic graphics.

The Three Steps to 3D Programming

There are three steps involved in 3D graphics programming:

1. **World transformation.** This moves 3D objects around in the "world," which is a term that describes the entire scene. In other words, the world transformation causes things in the scene to move, rotate, scale, and so on.

2. **View transformation.** This is the camera, so to speak, that defines what you see on the screen. The camera can be positioned anywhere in the "world," so if you want to move the camera, you do so with the view transform.

3. **Projection transformation.** This is the final step, in which you take the view transform (what objects are visible to the camera) and draw them on the screen, resulting in a flat 2D image of pixels.

Direct3D provides all the functions and transformations that you need to create, render, and view a scene without using any 3D mathematics—which is good for you, the programmer, because 3D matrix math is not easy.

A transformation occurs when you add, subtract, multiply, or divide one matrix with another matrix, causing a change to occur within the resulting matrix; these changes cause 3D objects to move, rotate, and scale 3D objects. A matrix is a grid or two-dimensional array that is 4×4 (or 16 cells) in size. Direct3D defines all of the standard matrices that you need to do just about everything required for a 3D game.

The 3D Scene

Before you can do anything with the scene, you must first create the 3D objects that will make up the scene. In this chapter, I will show you how to create simple 3D objects from scratch, and will also go over some of the freebie models that Direct3D provides, mainly for testing. There are standard objects, such as a cylinder, pyramid, torus, and even a teapot, that you can use to create a scene.

Of course, you can't create an entire 3D game just with source code because there are too many objects in a typical game. Eventually, you'll need to create your 3D models in a modeling program like 3ds max or the free Anim8or program (included on the CD-ROM). The next two chapters will explain how to load 3D models from a file into a scene. But in this chapter, I'll stick with programmable 3D objects.

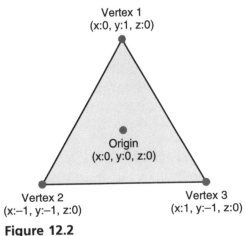

Figure 12.2
A 3D scene is made up entirely of triangles.

Introducing Vertices

The advanced 3D graphics chip that powers your video card sees only vertices. A *vertex* (singular) is a point in 3D space specified with the values of X, Y, and Z. The video card itself really only "sees" the vertices that make up the three angles of each triangle. It is the job of the video card to fill in the empty space that makes up the triangle between the three vertices. See Figure 12.2.

Creating and manipulating the 3D objects in a scene is a job for you, the programmer, so it helps to understand some of the basics of the 3D environment. The entire scene might be thought of as a mathematical grid with three axes. You might be familiar with the Cartesian coordinate system if you have ever studied geometry or trigonometry: The coordinate system is the basis for all geometric and trigonometric math, as there are formulas and functions for manipulating points on the Cartesian grid.

The Cartesian Coordinate System

The "grid" is really made up of two infinite lines that intersect at the origin. These lines are perpendicular. The horizontal line is called the *X axis* and the vertical line is called the *Y axis*. The origin is at position (0,0). The X axis goes up in value toward the right, and it goes down in value to the left. Likewise, the Y axis goes up in the up direction, and goes down in the down direction. See Figure 12.3.

If you have a point at a specified position that is represented on a Cartesian coordinate system, such as at (100, −50), then you can manipulate that point using

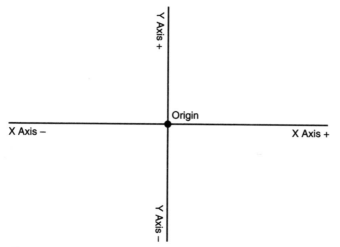

Figure 12.3
The Cartesian coordinate system

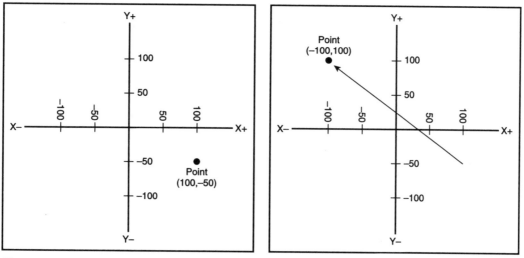

Figure 12.4
A point (100,−50) is translated by a value of (−200,150) resulting in a new position at (−100,100).

mathematical calculations. There are three primary things you can do with a point:

1. **Translation.** This is the process of moving a point to a new location. See Figure 12.4.

2. **Rotation.** This causes a point to move in a circle around the origin at a radius that is based on its current position. See Figure 12.5.

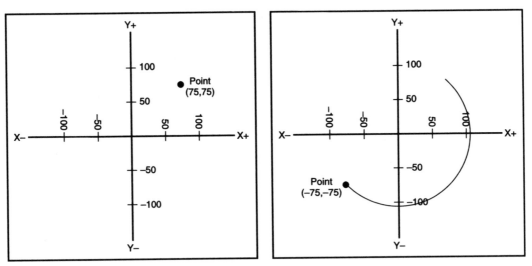

Figure 12.5
A point (75,75) is rotated by 180 degrees, resulting in a new position at (−75,−75).

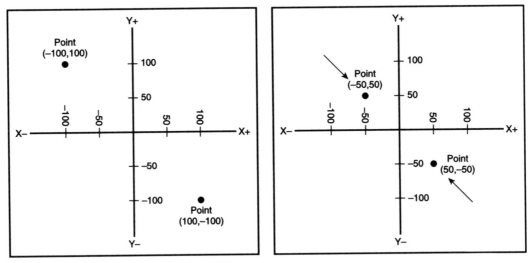

Figure 12.6
A point (75,75) is scaled by −50 percent, resulting in a new position at (−50,50).

3. **Scaling.** You can adjust the point relative to the origin by modifying the entire range of the two axes. See Figure 12.6.

The Origin of Vertices

The one thing you want to remember when working with 3D graphics is that everything works around the origin. So, when you want to rotate a 3D object on the screen, you have to remember that all rotation is based on the origin point. If you translate the object to a new location that is no longer centered at the origin, then rotating the object will cause it to move around the origin in a circle!

So, what's the solution to this problem? This is the biggest sticking point most people run into with 3D programming because it's very hard to get a handle on it unless you have, say, a more senior programmer to explain it to you. In this case, you have an opportunity to learn an important lesson in 3D graphics programming that is all-too-often ignored: The trick is to not really move the 3D objects at all.

What!? No, I'm not kidding. The trick is to leave all of the 3D objects at the origin and not move them at all. Does that mess with your head? Okay, I'll explain myself. You know that a 3D object is made up of vertices (three for every triangle, to be exact). The key is to draw the 3D objects at a specified position, with a specified rotation and scaling value, without moving the "original" object itself. I don't mean that you should make a copy of it; instead, just draw it at the last instant before refreshing the screen. Do you remember how you were able to draw many sprites on the screen with only a single sprite image? It's sort of like that, only you're just drawing a 3D object based on the original "image," so to speak, and the original does not change. By leaving the source objects at the origin, you can rotate them around what is called a *local origin* for each object, which preserves the objects.

So, how do you move a 3D object without moving it? The answer is by using matrices. A *matrix* is a 4×4 grid of numbers that represent a 3D object in "space." Each 3D object in your scene (or game) has its own matrix.

N o t e

> As you might have guessed, matrix mathematics is a subject way, way, way beyond the scope of this book, but I encourage you to look into it if you want to learn what *really* happens in the world of polygons.

The result of using matrices to give each 3D object its own origin is that your 3D world has its own coordinate system—as do all of the objects in the scene—so you can manipulate objects independently of one another. You can even manipulate the entire scene without affecting these independent objects. For example, suppose you are working on a racing game, and you have cars racing around an oval track. You want each car to be as realistic as possible so that each car can rotate and move on its own, regardless of what the other cars are doing.

At some point, of course, you want to add the code that will cause the cars to crash if they collide. You also want the cars to stay "flat" on the pavement of the track, which means calculating the angle of the track and positioning the four corners of the car appropriately.

Imagine taking it even further—think of the possibilities that arise when you can cause individual objects to contain sub-objects, each with their own local origins, that follow along with the "parent" object. You can then position the sub-objects with respect to the origin of the parent object and cause the sub-objects to rotate on their own. Does this help you to visualize how you might program the wheels of a car to roll on their own while the car remains stationary? The wheels "follow along" with the car, meaning they translate/rotate/scale with the parent object, but they also have the ability to roll and turn left or right.

Caution

The most frustrating problem with 3D programming is not seeing anything come up on the screen after you have written what you believe to be clean code that "should work, dang it!" The number one most common mistake in 3D programming is forgetting about the camera and view transform. As you work through this chapter, keep the following points in mind.

The first thing you should set up in the scene is the perspective, camera, and view with a test poly or quad to make sure your scene is set up properly before proceeding. Once you know for sure that the view is good, you can move ahead with the rest of the code for your game. Another frequent problem involves the position of the camera, which might seem okay for your initial test but then may be too close to the object for it to show up, or the object may have moved off "the screen." One good test is to move the camera away from the origin (such as a Z of –100, for instance), and then make sure your target matrix points to the origin (0, 0, 0). That should clear up any viewing problems and allow you to get cracking on the game again.

The second thing you should do to initially set up the scene is check the lighting conditions of your scene. Do you have lighting enabled without any lights? Direct3D is really literal and will not create ambient light for you unless you tell it there will be no light sources!

Moving to the Third Dimension

I hope you are now getting the hang of the Cartesian coordinate system. Although it is crucial to the study of 3D graphics, I will not go into any more detail because the subject requires more theory and explanation than I have room for here. Instead, I'm going to just cover enough material to teach you what you need to know to write a few simple 3D games, after which you can decide which aspect of 3D programming you'd like to study further. It's always more fun to do what works first and work on an actual game rather than try to learn every nook and cranny of a library like Direct3D all at once.

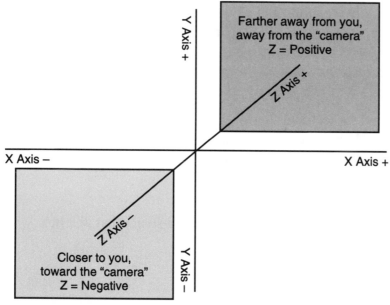

Figure 12.7
The Cartesian coordinate system with a third dimension

Figure 12.7 shows the addition of a third dimension to the Cartesian coordinate system. All of the current rules that you have learned about the 2D coordinate system apply, but each point is now referred to with three values (X,Y,Z) instead of just the two.

Grabbing Hold of the 3D Pipeline

The first thing you need to learn before you can draw a single polygon on the screen is that Direct3D uses a custom vertex format that *you* define. Here is the struct that you'll be using in this chapter:

```
struct VERTEX
{
  float x, y, z;
  float tu, tv;
};
```

The first three member variables are the position of the vertex, and the tu and tv variables are used to describe how a texture is drawn. Now you have an incredible amount of control over how the rendering process takes place. These two variables instruct Direct3D how to draw a texture on a surface, and Direct3D supports wrapping of a texture around the curve of a 3D object. You specify the upper-left corner of the texture with tu = 0.0 and tv = 0.0, and then you specify the bottom-right corner of the texture using tu = 1.0 and tv = 1.0. All the polygons in between these two will usually have zeroes for the texture coordinates, which tells Direct3D to just keep on stretching the texture over them.

Texturing is an advanced subject and there are a thousand options that you will discover as you explore 3D programming in more depth. For now, let's stick to stretching a texture over two triangles in a quad.

Introducing Quads

Using the VERTEX struct as a basis, you can then create a struct that will help with creating and keeping track of quads:

```
struct QUAD
{
    VERTEX vertices[4];
    LPDIRECT3DVERTEXBUFFER9 buffer;
    LPDIRECT3DTEXTURE9 texture;
};
```

The QUAD struct is completely self-contained as far as the data goes. Here you have the four vertices for the four corners of the quad (made up of two triangles); you have the vertex buffer for this single quad (more on that in a minute) and you have the texture that is mapped onto the two triangles. Pretty cool, huh? The only thing missing is the code that actually creates a quad and fills the vertices with real 3D points. First, let's write a function to create a single vertex. That can then be used to create the four vertices of the quad:

```
VERTEX CreateVertex(float x, float y, float z, float tu, float tv)
{
    VERTEX vertex;
    vertex.x = x;
    vertex.y = y;
    vertex.z = z;
    vertex.tu = tu;
    vertex.tv = tv;
    return vertex;
}
```

This function just declares a temporary VERTEX variable, fills it in with the values passed to it via parameters, and then returns it. This is very convenient because there are five member variables in the VERTEX struct. I'll show you how to create and draw a quad in a bit. But first you need to learn about the vertex buffer.

The Vertex Buffer

The vertex buffer is not as scary as it might sound. My first impression of a vertex buffer was that it was some kind of surface onto which the 3D objects are drawn before being sent to the screen, sort of like a double buffer for 3D. I couldn't have been more wrong! A vertex buffer is just a place where you store the points that make up a polygon so that Direct3D can draw it. You *can* technically have many vertex buffers in your program—one for each triangle if you want. However, this is extremely inefficient and will cause a 3D program to run quite slowly.

For the sake of clarity and for illustrative purposes, I will be showing you how to get 3D objects on the screen by giving each object its own vertex buffer. But in general practice, this is a very bad idea. As I'm basing this chapter on the concept of a quad (made up of two triangles arranged in a "strip"), it makes sense to create a vertex buffer for each quad in the scene, to help you understand what's going on, and it really helps when you are just learning this material for the first time. Having a vertex buffer for each quad makes it crystal-clear what's going on when a quad is rendered.

Giving every quad its own vertex buffer is sort of like an airline company transporting a single person in a passenger jumbo jet. Imagine a Boeing 747 with a full complement of pilots and crew just to serve a single customer! But for educational purposes, I suppose this scenario *does* demonstrate how commercial aviation works.

Just be aware that this is a big issue with 3D engines, where the vertex buffer is the subject of much discussion regarding optimization and efficiency. In fact, most 3D engines employ what is called a *vertex buffer cache* that contains *all* of the vertices that will be visible in the camera's view. Powerful 3D engines also use what's called a *texture cache* so that textures are re-used by polygons that share them. In case you are curious as to why this is the case, understand that a 3D card can only "use" one texture at a time. Therefore, it is more efficient to tell Direct3D to *use* a texture only once—and then use that texture throughout the scene on any polygon that needs it before going to the next texture. This is where a texture cache comes in handy, as it will take care of these kinds of issues.

Creating a Vertex Buffer

To get started, you must define a variable for the vertex buffer:

```
LPDIRECT3DVERTEXBUFFER9 buffer;
```

Next, you can create the vertex buffer by using the `CreateVertexBuffer` function. It has this format:

```
HRESULT CreateVertexBuffer(
    UINT Length,
    DWORD Usage,
    DWORD FVF,
    D3DPOOL Pool,
    IDirect3DVertexBuffer9** ppVertexBuffer,
    HANDLE* pSharedHandle
);
```

The first parameter specifies the size of the vertex buffer, which should be big enough to hold all of the vertices for the polygons you want to render. The second parameter specifies the way in which you plan to access the vertex buffer, which is usually write-only. The third parameter specifies the vertex stream type that Direct3D expects to receive. You should pass the values corresponding to the type of vertex struct you have created. Here, we have just the position and texture coordinates in each vertex, so this value will be D3DFVF_XYZ | D3DFVF_TEX1 (note that values are combined with *or*). Here is how I define the vertex format:

```
#define D3DFVF_MYVERTEX (D3DFVF_XYZ | D3DFVF_TEX1)
```

The fifth parameter specifies the vertex buffer pointer, and the last parameter is not needed. How about an example? Here y'go:

```
d3ddev->CreateVertexBuffer(
    4*sizeof(VERTEX),
    D3DUSAGE_WRITEONLY,
    D3DFVF_MYVERTEX,
    D3DPOOL_DEFAULT,
    &buffer,
    NULL);
```

As you can see, the first parameter receives an integer that is `sizeof(VERTEX)` times four (because there are four vertices in a quad). If you are drawing just a single triangle, you would specify 3 * `sizeof(VERTEX)`, and so on for however many vertices are in your 3D object. The only really important parameters, then, are the vertex buffer length and pointer (first and fifth, respectively).

Filling the Vertex Buffer

The last step in creating a vertex buffer is to fill it with the actual vertices of your polygons. This step must follow any code that generates or loads the vertex array, as it will plug the data into the vertex buffer. For reference, here is the definition for the QUAD struct once more (pay particular attention to the VERTEX array):

```
struct QUAD
{
    VERTEX vertices[4];
    LPDIRECT3DVERTEXBUFFER9 buffer;
    LPDIRECT3DTEXTURE9 texture;
};
```

You can use the CreateVertex function, for instance, to set up the default values for a quad:

```
vertices[0] = CreateVertex(-1.0f, 1.0f, 0.0f, 0.0f, 0.0f);
vertices[1] = CreateVertex(1.0f, 1.0f, 0.0f, 1.0f, 0.0f);
vertices[2] = CreateVertex(-1.0f,-1.0f, 0.0f, 0.0f, 1.0f);
vertices[3] = CreateVertex(1.0f,-1.0f, 0.0f, 1.0f, 1.0f);
```

That is just one way to fill the vertices with data. You might define a different type of polygon somewhere in your program or load a 3D shape from a file (more on that in the next chapter!).

After you have your vertex data, you can plug it into the vertex buffer. To do so, you must Lock the vertex buffer, copy your vertices into the vertex buffer, and then Unlock the vertex buffer. Doing so required a temporary pointer. Here is how you set up the vertex buffer with data that Direct3D can use:

```
void *temp = NULL;
buffer->Lock( 0, sizeof(vertices), (void**)&temp, 0 );
memcpy(temp,vertices, sizeof(vertices) );
buffer->Unlock();
```

For reference, here is the Lock definition. The second and third parameters are the important ones; they specify the length of the buffer and a pointer to it.

```
HRESULT Lock(

    UINT OffsetToLock,
    UINT SizeToLock,
    VOID **ppbData,
    DWORD Flags
);
```

Rendering the Vertex Buffer

After initializing the vertex buffer, it will be ready for the Direct3D graphics pipeline and your source vertices will no longer matter. This is called the "setup," and it is one of the features that have been moved out of the Direct3D drivers and into the GPU in recent years. Streaming the vertices and textures from the vertex buffer into the scene is handled much more quickly by a hard-coded chip than it is by software.

In the end, it's all about rendering what's inside the vertex buffer, so let's learn how to do just that. To send the vertex buffer that you're currently working on to the screen, set the stream source for the Direct3D device so that it points to your vertex buffer, and then call the DrawPrimitive function. Before doing this, you must first set the texture to be used. This is one of the most confusing aspects of 3D graphics, especially for a beginner. Direct3D deals with just one texture at a time, so you have to tell it which texture to use each time it changes or Direct3D will just use the last-defined texture for the entire scene! Kind of weird, huh? Well, it makes sense if you think about it. There is no pre-programmed way to tell Direct3D to use "this" texture for one polygon and "that" texture for the next polygon. You just have to write this code yourself each time the texture needs to be changed.

Well, in the case of a quad, we're just dealing with a single texture for each quad, so the concept is easier to grasp. You can create any size vertex buffer you want, but you will find it easier to understand how 3D rendering works by giving each quad its own vertex buffer. This is not the most efficient way to draw 3D objects on the screen, but it works great while you are learning the basics! Each quad can have a vertex buffer as well as a texture, and the source code to render a quad is therefore easy to grasp. As you can imagine, this makes things a lot easier to deal with because you can write a function to draw a quad, with its vertex buffer and texture easily accessible in the QUAD struct.

First, set the texture for this quad:

```
d3ddev->SetTexture(0, texture);
```

Next, set the stream source so that Direct3D knows where the vertices come from and how many need to be rendered:

```
d3ddev->SetStreamSource(0, q.buffer, 0, sizeof(VERTEX));
```

Finally, draw the primitive specified by the stream source, including the rendering method, starting vertex, and number of polys to draw:

```
d3ddev->DrawPrimitive(D3DPT_TRIANGLESTRIP, 0, 2);
```

Obviously, these three functions can be put into a reusable Draw function together (more on that shortly).

Creating a Quad

I don't know if *quad* is an official term, but it doesn't matter, because the term describes what I want to do on two levels. The first aspect of the term *quad* is that it represents four corners of a rectangle, which is the building block of most 3D scenes. You can build almost anything with a bunch of cubes (each of which is made up of six quads). As you might have guessed, those corners are represented as vertices. The second aspect of a quad is that it represents the four vertices of a triangle strip.

Drawing Triangles

There are two ways you can draw objects (all of which are made up of triangles):

- A Triangle List draws every single polygon independently, each with a set of three vertices.

- A Triangle Strip draws many polygons that are connected with shared vertices.

Obviously, the second method is more efficient and, therefore, preferable, and it helps to speed up rendering because fewer vertices must be used. But you can't render the entire scene with triangle strips because most objects are not connected to each other. Now, triangle strips work great for things like ground terrain, buildings, and other large objects. It also works well for smaller objects like the characters in your game. But what helps here is an understanding that Direct3D will render the scene at the same speed regardless of whether all the triangles are in a single vertex buffer or in multiple vertex buffers. Think of it as a series of `for` loops. Tell me which one of these two sections of code is faster. Ignore the num++ part and just assume that "something useful" is happening inside the loop.

```
for (int n=0; n<1000; n++) num++;
```

or

```
(for int n=0; n<250; n++) num++;
(for int n=0; n<250; n++) num++;
(for int n=0; n<250; n++) num++;
(for int n=0; n<250; n++) num++;
```

What do you think? It might seem obvious that the first code is faster because there are fewer calls. Someone who is into optimization might think the second code listing is faster because perhaps it avoids a few `if` statements here and there (it's always faster to unroll a loop and put `if` statements outside of them).

Unrolling a Loop

What do I mean when I say *unrolling a loop*? (This is not directly related to 3D, but helpful nonetheless.) Take a look at the following two groups of code (from a fictional line-drawing function, assume x and y have already been defined):

```
for (x=0; x<639; x++)
    if (x % 2 == 0)
        DrawPixel(x, y, BLUE);
    else
        DrawPixel(x, y, RED);
and
for (x=0; x<639; x+=2)
    DrawPixel(x, y, BLUE);
for (x=1; x<639; x+=2)
    DrawPixel(x, y, RED);
```

The second snippet of code is probably twice as fast as the first one because the loops have been unrolled and the `if` statement has been removed. Try to think about optimization issues like this as you work on a game because loops should be coded carefully. The *for loop* doesn't actually take up any processor time itself; it's the code executed *by* the *for loop* that is important to consider.

A quad is made up of two triangles. The quad requires only four vertices because the triangles will be drawn as a triangle strip. Check out Figure 12.8 to see the difference between the two types of triangle rendering methods.

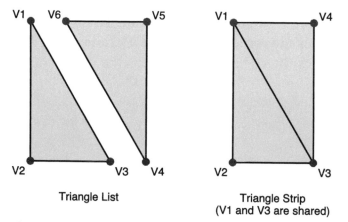

Triangle List

Triangle Strip
(V1 and V3 are shared)

Figure 12.8
Triangle List and Triangle Strip rendering methods compared and contrasted

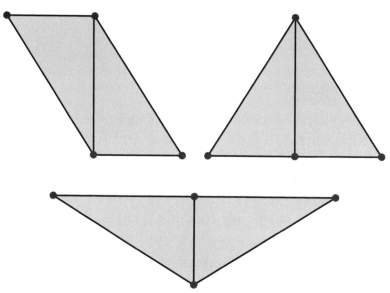

Figure 12.9
A triangle strip can take many forms. Note also that many more than two polygons can be used.

Figure 12.9 shows some other possibilities for triangle strips. You can join any two vertices that share a side.

Creating the Quad

Creating a quad requires even less effort than creating two attached triangles, thanks to the triangle strip rendering process. To draw any polygon, whether it is a triangle, quad, or complete model, there are two basic steps involved.

First, you must copy the vertices into a Direct3D vertex stream. To do this, you first lock the vertex buffer, then copy the vertices to a temporary storage location with a pointer variable, then unlock the vertex buffer.

```
void *temp = NULL;
quad->buffer->Lock(0, sizeof(quad->vertices), (void**)&temp, 0);
memcpy(temp, quad->vertices, sizeof(quad->vertices));
quad->buffer->Unlock();
```

The next step is to set the texture, tell Direct3D where to find the stream source containing vertices, and then call on the DrawPrimitive function to draw the polygons specified in the vertex buffer stream. I like to think of this as a *Star Trek*-esque transporter. The polygons are transported from the vertex buffer into the stream and re-assembled on the screen!

```
d3ddev->SetTexture(0, quad->texture);
d3ddev->SetStreamSource(0, quad->buffer, 0, sizeof(VERTEX));
d3ddev->DrawPrimitive(D3DPT_TRIANGLESTRIP, 0, 2);
```

The Textured Cube Demo

Let's get realistic here. No one cares about drawing shaded and colored triangles, so I'm not going to waste time on the subject. Are you going to create a complete 3D game by programming triangles to assemble themselves into objects and then move them around and do collision checking and so on? Of course not, so why spend time learning about it? Triangles are critical to a 3D system, but not very useful in the singular sense. Only when you combine triangles do things get interesting.

The really interesting thing about modern 3D APIs is that it is easier to create a textured quad than one with shading. I will avoid the subject of dynamic lighting because it is beyond the scope of this book; ambient lighting will absolutely suffice for our purposes here. Did you know that *most* retail games use ambient lighting? Most of the dynamically-lit games are first-person shooters.

Modifying the Framework

What comes next? Well, now that you have all this great code for doing stuff in 3D, let's just plug it into the Direct3D module in the game framework you've been building in the book. And it's about time, right? That "Direct3D" module has been stuck in 2D land for several chapters now!

There is a lot of information here, and I don't want to overwhelm you if this is your first experience with Direct3D or in 3D graphics programming in general. Anything that you do not fully grasp (or that I skim over) in this chapter will be covered again in a little more detail in the next chapter, in accordance with my "learn by repetition" concept.

The unfortunate fact of the situation at this point is that the framework is getting pretty big. There are now all of the following components in the framework that has been developed in this book:

- dxgraphics.h

- dxgraphics.cpp

- dxaudio.h

- dxaudio.cpp

- dxinput.h

- dxinput.cpp

- winmain.cpp

- game.h

- game.cpp

In addition, the DirectX components need the following support files, which are distributed with the DirectX SDK:

- dsutil.h

- dsutil.cpp

- dxutil.h

- dxutil.cpp

My goal is not to create some big game-engine type of library; it is just to group reusable code in a way that makes it more convenient to write DirectX programs. The problem is that many changes must be made to both the header and source file for each struct, function, and variable. So what I'm going to do at this point is just show you what code I'm adding to the framework, explain to you where it goes, and then just encourage you to open the project from the CD-ROM. The "open file and insert this code..." method is just too confusing, don't you agree? Due to the way compilers work, it's just not a simple copy-and-paste operation because variables need to be defined in the header (using extern) before they are "declared" in the actual source file. It's an unwieldy process to say the least.

That said, I encourage you to open up the cube_demo project from \sources\ chapter12 on the CD-ROM, which you should have copied to your hard drive already.

dxgraphics.h

First, let's add the definitions for the VERTEX and QUAD structures and the camera to the dxgraphics.h file:

```
#define D3DFVF_MYVERTEX (D3DFVF_XYZ | D3DFVF_TEX1)
struct VERTEX
{
    float x, y, z;
    float tu, tv;
};
struct QUAD
{
    VERTEX vertices[4];
    LPDIRECT3DVERTEXBUFFER9 buffer;
    LPDIRECT3DTEXTURE9 texture;
};

extern D3DXVECTOR3 cameraSource;
extern D3DXVECTOR3 cameraTarget;
```

Next, let's add the following sections of code to dxgraphics.h. First, the function prototypes:

```
void SetPosition(QUAD*,int,float,float,float);
void SetVertex(QUAD*,int,float,float,float,float,float);
VERTEX CreateVertex(float,float,float,float,float);
QUAD* CreateQuad(char*);
void DeleteQuad(QUAD*);
void DrawQuad(QUAD*);
void SetIdentity();
void SetCamera(float,float,float,float,float,float);
void SetPerspective(float,float,float,float);
void ClearScene(D3DXCOLOR);
```

I have not covered camera movement yet, but it is essential, and is not something I intend to just ignore. I will explain how the camera works below in the section on writing the actual cube_demo program.

dxgraphics.cpp

Now, opening up the dxgraphics.cpp source file, let's first add the variable declarations for cameraSource and cameraTarget, which were previously defined in the header file.

```
D3DXVECTOR3 cameraSource;
D3DXVECTOR3 cameraTarget;
```

Okay, how about some really great reusable functions for 3D programming? I have gone over most of the basic code for these functions already. The rest are really just support functions that are self-explanatory. For instance, SetPosition just sets the position of a vertex inside a particular quad (without affecting the texture coordinates). The SetVertex function actually sets the position *and* the texture coordinates. These are very helpful support functions that will greatly simplify the 3D code in the main program (coming up!).

```
void SetPosition(QUAD *quad, int ivert, float x, float y, float z)
{
   quad->vertices[ivert].x = x;
   quad->vertices[ivert].y = y;
   quad->vertices[ivert].z = z;
}

void SetVertex(QUAD *quad, int ivert, float x, float y, float z, float tu, float tv)
{
   SetPosition(quad, ivert, x, y, z);
   quad->vertices[ivert].tu = tu;
   quad->vertices[ivert].tv = tv;
}

VERTEX CreateVertex(float x, float y, float z, float tu, float tv)
{
   VERTEX vertex;
   vertex.x = x;
   vertex.y = y;
   vertex.z = z;
   vertex.tu = tu;
```

```
      vertex.tv = tv;
      return vertex;
}


QUAD *CreateQuad(char *textureFilename)
{
   QUAD *quad = (QUAD*)malloc(sizeof(QUAD));

   //load the texture
   D3DXCreateTextureFromFile(d3ddev, textureFilename, &quad->texture);

   //create the vertex buffer for this quad
     d3ddev->CreateVertexBuffer(
     4*sizeof(VERTEX),
     0,
     D3DFVF_MYVERTEX, D3DPOOL_DEFAULT,
     &quad->buffer,
     NULL);

   //create the four corners of this dual triangle strip
   //each vertex is X,Y,Z and the texture coordinates U,V
   quad->vertices[0] = CreateVertex(-1.0f, 1.0f, 0.0f, 0.0f, 0.0f);
   quad->vertices[1] = CreateVertex( 1.0f, 1.0f, 0.0f, 1.0f, 0.0f);
   quad->vertices[2] = CreateVertex(-1.0f,-1.0f, 0.0f, 0.0f, 1.0f);
   quad->vertices[3] = CreateVertex( 1.0f,-1.0f, 0.0f, 1.0f, 1.0f);

   return quad;
}


void DeleteQuad(QUAD *quad)
{
   if (quad == NULL)
      return;

   //free the vertex buffer
   if (quad->buffer != NULL)
      quad->buffer->Release();

   //free the texture
   if (quad->texture != NULL)
      quad->texture->Release();
   //free the quad
```

```
      free(quad);
}

void DrawQuad(QUAD *quad)
{
   //fill vertex buffer with this quad's vertices
   void *temp = NULL;
   quad->buffer->Lock(0, sizeof(quad->vertices), (void**)&temp, 0);
   memcpy(temp, quad->vertices, sizeof(quad->vertices));
   quad->buffer->Unlock();

   //draw the textured dual triangle strip
   d3ddev->SetTexture(0, quad->texture);
   d3ddev->SetStreamSource(0, quad->buffer, 0, sizeof(VERTEX));
      d3ddev->DrawPrimitive(D3DPT_TRIANGLESTRIP, 0, 2);
}

void SetIdentity()
{
   //set default position, scale, and rotation
   D3DXMATRIX matWorld;
   D3DXMatrixTranslation(&matWorld, 0.0f, 0.0f, 0.0f);
   d3ddev->SetTransform(D3DTS_WORLD, &matWorld);
}

void ClearScene(D3DXCOLOR color)
{
   d3ddev->Clear(0, NULL, D3DCLEAR_TARGET | D3DCLEAR_ZBUFFER, color, 1.0f, 0 );
}

void SetCamera(float x, float y, float z, float lookx, float looky, float lookz)
{
   D3DXMATRIX matView;
   D3DXVECTOR3 updir(0.0f,1.0f,0.0f);

   //move the camera
   cameraSource.x = x;
   cameraSource.y = y;
   cameraSource.z = z;

   //point the camera
   cameraTarget.x = lookx;
   cameraTarget.y = looky;
```

```
    cameraTarget.z = lookz;

    //set up the camera view matrix
    D3DXMatrixLookAtLH(&matView, &cameraSource, &cameraTarget, &updir);
    d3ddev->SetTransform(D3DTS_VIEW, &matView);
}

void SetPerspective(float fieldOfView, float aspectRatio, float nearRange,
float farRange)
{
    //set the perspective so things in the distance will look smaller
    D3DXMATRIX matProj;
    D3DXMatrixPerspectiveFovLH(&matProj, fieldOfView, aspectRatio, nearRange,
farRange);
    d3ddev->SetTransform(D3DTS_PROJECTION, &matProj);
}
```

The Cube_Demo Program

The next step is the main code, which uses all of these reusable functions you just
added to the dxgraphics module of the framework. The Cube_Demo program
(shown in Figure 12.10) draws a textured cube on the screen and rotates it in the
x and z axes.

Figure 12.10
The Cube_Demo program demonstrates everything covered in this chapter about 3D programming.

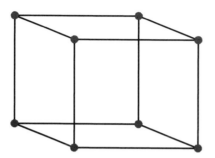

Figure 12.11
A cube might have only eight corners, but is comprised of many vertices.

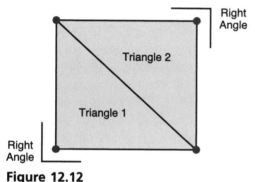

Figure 12.12
A rectangle is made up of two right triangles.

While it might seem like there are only eight vertices in a cube (refer to Figure 12.11), there are actually many more, because each triangle must have its own set of three vertices. But as you learned recently, a triangle strip works well to produce a quad with only four vertices.

As you have just worked with triangles and quads up to this point, a short introduction to cubes is in order. A cube is considered one of the simplest 3D objects you can create, and is a good shape to use as an example because it has six equal sides. As all objects in a 3D environment must be made up of triangles, it follows that a cube must also be made up of triangles. In fact, each side of a cube (which is a rectangle) is really two right triangles positioned side by side with the two right angles at opposing corners. See Figure 12.12.

Note

A right triangle is a triangle that has one 90-degree angle.

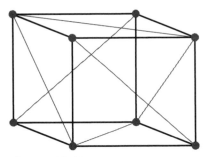

Figure 12.13
A cube is made up of six sides, with twelve triangles in all.

After you have put together a cube using triangles, you end up with something like Figure 12.13. This figure shows the cube sub-divided into triangles.

game.cpp

Well, now it's time to go over the main source code for the Cube_Demo program. I encourage you to load the project off the CD-ROM (which should be copied to your hard drive for convenience—and don't forget to turn off the read-only attribute so you can make changes to the files).

Nothing has changed in game.h since the last project, so you can just use one of your recent copies of game.h for this project or follow along with the Cube_ Demo project itself. So much information has been covered that I elected to skip over setting up the project and so on.

If you think it's strange to create a 3D model using code as shown below, you would be right on the mark. This is indeed very strange, but it is helpful at this point to illustrate how vertices are used to build polygons, which then make up models (also called meshes). It would be very difficult to create any type of complex 3D model using code like this, so it's only really useful in our simple cube example. Soon we'll learn how to load a mesh file into memory and render models directly from a file.

```
#include "game.h"

#define BLACK D3DCOLOR_ARGB(0,0,0,0)

VERTEX cube[] = {
    {-1.0f, 1.0f,-1.0f, 0.0f,0.0f},    //side 1
    { 1.0f, 1.0f,-1.0f, 1.0f,0.0f },
```

```
    {-1.0f,-1.0f,-1.0f, 0.0f,1.0f },
    { 1.0f,-1.0f,-1.0f, 1.0f,1.0f },

    {-1.0f, 1.0f, 1.0f, 1.0f,0.0f },    //side 2
    {-1.0f,-1.0f, 1.0f, 1.0f,1.0f },
    { 1.0f, 1.0f, 1.0f, 0.0f,0.0f },
    { 1.0f,-1.0f, 1.0f, 0.0f,1.0f },

    {-1.0f, 1.0f, 1.0f, 0.0f,0.0f },    //side 3
    { 1.0f, 1.0f, 1.0f, 1.0f,0.0f },
    {-1.0f, 1.0f,-1.0f, 0.0f,1.0f },
    { 1.0f, 1.0f,-1.0f, 1.0f,1.0f },

    {-1.0f,-1.0f, 1.0f, 0.0f,0.0f },    //side 4
    {-1.0f,-1.0f,-1.0f, 1.0f,0.0f },
    { 1.0f,-1.0f, 1.0f, 0.0f,1.0f },
    { 1.0f,-1.0f,-1.0f, 1.0f,1.0f },

    { 1.0f, 1.0f,-1.0f, 0.0f,0.0f },    //side 5
    { 1.0f, 1.0f, 1.0f, 1.0f,0.0f },
    { 1.0f,-1.0f,-1.0f, 0.0f,1.0f },
    { 1.0f,-1.0f, 1.0f, 1.0f,1.0f },

    {-1.0f, 1.0f,-1.0f, 1.0f,0.0f },    //side 6
    {-1.0f,-1.0f,-1.0f, 1.0f,1.0f },
    {-1.0f, 1.0f, 1.0f, 0.0f,0.0f },
    {-1.0f,-1.0f, 1.0f, 0.0f,1.0f }
};

QUAD *quads[6];

void init_cube()
{
    for (int q=0; q<6; q++)
    {
        int i = q*4;   //little shortcut into cube array
        quads[q] = CreateQuad("cube.bmp");
        for (int v=0; v<4; v++)
        {
            quads[q]->vertices[v] = CreateVertex(
                cube[i].x, cube[i].y, cube[i].z,   //position
                cube[i].tu, cube[i].tv);           //texture coords
            i++;   //next vertex
```

```
        }
    }
}

//initializes the game
int Game_Init(HWND hwnd)
{

    //initialize keyboard
    if (!Init_Keyboard(hwnd))
    {
        MessageBox(hwnd, "Error initializing the keyboard", "Error", MB_OK);
        return 0;
    }

    //position the camera
    SetCamera(0.0f, 2.0f, -3.0f, 0, 0, 0);

    float ratio = (float)SCREEN_WIDTH / (float)SCREEN_HEIGHT;
    SetPerspective(45.0f, ratio, 0.1f, 10000.0f);

    //turn dynamic lighting off, z-buffering on
    d3ddev->SetRenderState(D3DRS_LIGHTING, FALSE);
    d3ddev->SetRenderState(D3DRS_ZENABLE, TRUE);

    //set the Direct3D stream to use the custom vertex
    d3ddev->SetFVF(D3DFVF_MYVERTEX);

    //convert the cube values into quads
    init_cube();

    //return okay
    return 1;
}

void rotate_cube()
{
    static float xrot = 0.0f;
    static float yrot = 0.0f;
    static float zrot = 0.0f;

    //rotate the x and Y axes
    xrot += 0.05f;
    yrot += 0.05f;
```

```
    //create the matrices
    D3DXMATRIX matWorld;
    D3DXMATRIX matTrans;
    D3DXMATRIX matRot;

    //get an identity matrix
    D3DXMatrixTranslation(&matTrans, 0.0f, 0.0f, 0.0f);

    //rotate the cube
      D3DXMatrixRotationYawPitchRoll(&matRot,
                                     D3DXToRadian(xrot),
                                     D3DXToRadian(yrot),
                                     D3DXToRadian(zrot));
    matWorld = matRot * matTrans;

      //complete the operation
      d3ddev->SetTransform(D3DTS_WORLD, &matWorld);
}

//the main game loop
void Game_Run(HWND hwnd)
{
    ClearScene(BLACK);

    rotate_cube();

    if (d3ddev->BeginScene())
    {
      for (int n=0; n<6; n++)
          DrawQuad(quads[n]);

      d3ddev->EndScene();
    }

  d3ddev->Present(NULL, NULL, NULL, NULL);

  Poll_Keyboard();
  if (Key_Down(DIK_ESCAPE))
      PostMessage(hwnd, WM_DESTROY, 0, 0);
}
```

```
void Game_End(HWND hwnd)
{
   for (int q=0; q<6; q++)
       DeleteQuad(quads[q]);
}
```

What's Next?

That's a lot of information to digest in a single chapter, and I wouldn't be surprised if you needed to go over the information here again to really get a grasp of it. 3D programming is no easy chore, and mastery of the subject can take *years*. Don't be discouraged, though, because there are a *lot* of great things you can do *before* you have mastered it! For instance, this chapter has just scratched the surface of what you can do with even a novice understanding of Direct3D.

Figure 12.14 shows an image of a car that I created with Anim8or, a free 3D modeling program that is included on this book's CD-ROM. This powerful 3D modeling tool supports the 3D Studio Max file format (.3DS). The next two chapters will teach you how to create your own 3D models and how to load those models from a file into your Direct3D program.

Figure 12.14
You will learn how to create and use your own 3D models in the next two chapters!

What You Have Learned

This chapter has given you an overview of 3D graphics programming. You have learned a lot about Direct3D, and have seen a textured cube demo. Here are the key points:

- You learned what vertices are and how they make up a triangle.

- You learned how to create a vertex structure.

- You learned about triangle strips and triangle lists.

- You learned how to create a vertex buffer and fill it with vertices.

- You learned about quads and how to create them.

- You learned about texture mapping.

- You learned how to create a spinning cube.

Review Questions

The following questions will help to reinforce the information you have learned in this chapter.

1. What is a vertex?

2. What is the vertex buffer used for?

3. How many vertices are there in a quad?

4. How many triangles make up a quad?

5. What is the name of the Direct3D function that draws polygons?

On Your Own

The following exercises will help to challenge your retention of the information in this chapter.

Exercise 1. The Cube_Demo program creates a rotating cube that is textured. Modify the program so that the cube spins faster or slower based on keyboard input.

Exercise 2. Modify the Cube_Demo program so that each of the six sides of the cube has a different texture. Hint: You may need to copy the code from `DrawQuad` into your main source code file in order to use different textures.

CHAPTER 13

CREATING YOUR OWN 3D MODELS WITH ANIM8OR

This chapter will teach you how to create your own 3D models using a freeware modeling program called Anim8or. This program is powerful and full-featured and easy to learn and use. The interface is a study in interaction design (pioneered by Alan Cooper, see http://www.cooper.com), as the most commonly used features are readily available, and below this layer are more complex features (such as animation). This chapter will introduce you to Anim8or and go over the basic features of the program, and then it will teach you how to create a simple model of a car.

Here is what you will learn in this chapter:

- How to use Anim8or to create 3D models, meshes, and objects.

- How to manipulate a mesh into a desired shape.

- How to apply a material to the face of a mesh.

- How to create the components of a car and build it.

Introducing Anim8or

Anim8or is an advanced, modern, full-featured, absolutely free 3D modeling program that you can use to use to create 3D models for just about anything you want, including games. The current version of Anim8or at the time of this writing is 0.85, with 0.9 just around the corner. The author of this program, R. Steven Glanville, considers Anim8or to be still in beta stage, although it is fully functional at this point and loaded with great features. As a software engineer for NVIDIA—the company responsible for the mystical GeForce chips and responsible for bringing "GPU" and "T&L" into consumer awareness, Steven knows a thing or two about graphics. The primary goal of Anim8or is to make it easy to create 3D animations. While it's a great program for creating static models for games, it also includes extensive support for key-frame animation of models. Anim8or allows you to easily create, edit, and animate models with its intuitive interface. See Figure 13.1.

Note

As this is just a quick overview of Anim8or and not a full reference of the program, I encourage you to bookmark the following URL where the latest edition of the Anim8or manual may be found: http://www.anim8or.com/manual.

Getting into 3D Modeling

First of all, I need to insert a disclaimer of sorts here: I am a programmer, not an artist. Therefore, what you can expect is a very primitive tutorial in 3D modeling that a modeler might find amusing. I make no apology for being a programmer; I am simply not a modeler. However, as with programming, modeling is a skill that *can* improve over time.

Why, then, should I include a chapter about 3D modeling if I'm an amateur at the subject myself? Because coming up with artwork and models is one of the most frustrating aspects of game programming on your own, but whatever you

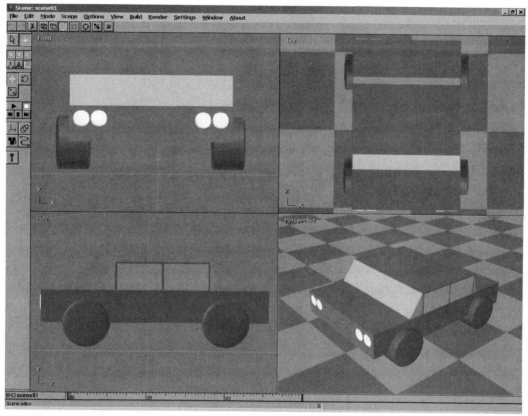

Figure 13.1
Anim8or is a full-featured 3D modeling and animation program.

can learn to do on your own is extremely valuable and timesaving. And even a simple overview of a modeling tool and tutorial on how to create a model will help you tremendously.

That being said, I want to encourage you to study the subject further if it interests you. I have found that books on 3ds max 4 are particularly helpful because that interface is *sort of* similar to Anim8or. By *sort of* I mean that the basic concepts are similar enough that you can figure out what to do in Anim8or by reading a book on 3ds max 4. Newer versions of 3ds max have been loaded with new features that I find daunting. I know exactly where to direct you for the absolute best tutorial for a beginner, though, and I don't hesitate for a moment because I have found this book to be outstanding. It is called *Modeling a Character in 3DS Max,* by Paul Steed. Paul worked for id Software as a modeler on *Quake III,* so he knows what he's talking about. Paul will teach you step-by-step how to create a female character the likes of which you might find in any modern game. There are other references available to you, too, and I strongly encourage you to look them up because even a basic familiarity with 3D modeling will help wonderfully as you hone your 3D programming skills.

If you do pick up a few books on 3D modeling but you don't own a copy of 3ds max, there are two immediate options that you can try. First, Discreet has provided a free modeling tool called GMAX. This is a scaled-down version of 3ds max that does not include any capability for creating animations or scenes with cameras and so on. All you can do with GMAX is edit 3D models. That aspect of the program is identical to 3ds max, and I particularly like it because the interface resembles 3ds max 4, which is better for learning than the newer versions because it is simpler.

It is also very nice to be able to create your own models. It is a pain to try to locate free models on the Web, mainly because almost none of the free models you are likely to find will be suitable for your game. However, there is a lot of good stock available for scenery and miscellaneous objects, for which I direct you to 3D Cafe (located at http://www.3dcafe.com), where you can download free models and purchase licenses for model sets that can be used in your games.

Another excellent source of models on the Web is 3D Modelworks, located at http://www.3dmodelworks.com. I particularly like this site because it includes a Web-based model browser so that you can actually see the models on the screen, rotate, and zoom in and out, before purchasing the model. The browser also animates those models on the screen that are animated.

Features

There are four modes in Anim8or, three for editing and one for putting objects into a scene. Anim8or lets you zoom in and out of the workspace to rotate, move, and scale individual polygons as well as entire models; to group objects together; and to edit the vertices of an object.

The Object Editor

The Object Editor is where you create and edit models. Anim8or can import the following types of files into the Object Editor:

- 3D Studio (.3ds)
- LightWave (.lwo)
- Wavefront (.obj)
- Anim8or (.an8)

The Figure Editor

The Figure Editor is used to animate characters using bone animation techniques. First, you define the structure of a character using jointed bones with various properties (such as direction and limits of movement), and then add polygons to the bones to construct a character that can be easily animated.

The Sequence Editor

The Sequence Editor lets you define segments of motion by manipulating a model for each step; then these segments can be assembled into a sequence using the Scene Editor.

The Scene Editor

The Scene Editor is where you construct animated or static scenes using objects, figures, and sequences you have created in the other program modes. The scene is where you can add cameras and create a movie that can be saved as an AVI file.

The Interface

Your mouse is the primary editing device in Anim8or. You move the mouse in a left/right motion to manipulate the X axis, an up/down motion to manipulate the Y axis, and the right mouse button along with up/down motion to manipulate the Z axis. I'll assume that you can navigate the Anim8or menus (after a little practice) and can load and save files. Manipulating objects and using the four modes are what really require some explanation.

Take a look at Figure 13.2, which shows the Object Editor as it appears when Anim8or first starts up.

If you open the Mode menu (shown in Figure 13.3), you will find the four primary parts of Anim8or: Object, Figure, Sequence, and Scene. The Browser is a feature that allows you to browse all of the objects, figures, or sequences currently loaded into Anim8or (meaning that yes, you can have many of each item in the scene). I will go over each of the four modes in the following sections of this chapter.

Installing Anim8or

Anim8or does not need to be installed at all, and you will be surprised to know that it comes as a single 1,200KB executable file, Anim8or.exe, without any setup file, documentation files, or the like. You just copy the Anim8or.exe file to a convenient place (such as your Windows Desktop) and run it; it's as simple as

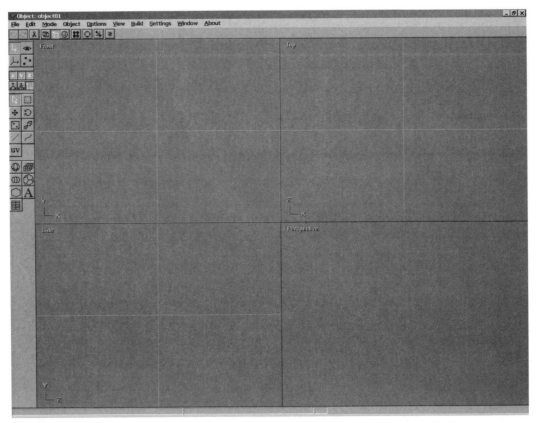

Figure 13.2
Anim8or's Object Editor is ready for some polygons.

that. Anim8or uses OpenGL to render 3D graphics, so you will need a video card with an OpenGL driver (I suspect you knew that already).

To install Anim8or, just copy the Anim8or.exe file from the CD-ROM; the file is located in \Anim8or. Although 0.9 is the version covered in this chapter, I encourage you to visit the main Anim8or home page, at http://www.anim8or.com, in order to download a newer version of the program that may be available.

Using Anim8or

I am going to give you a step-by-step tutorial now on how to create a model with Anim8or's Object Editor. You should be able to get the hang of Anim8or by following along in this tutorial enough to be able to create your own models. If Anim8or is not already in Object mode, then switch to it with the Mode menu. You are presented with a blank object-editing screen, as shown in Figure 13.4.

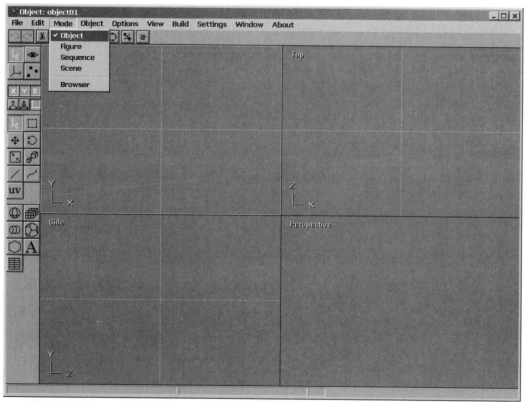

Figure 13.3
The Mode menu is where you can change the editing mode of Anim8or.

Stock Primitives

It's easy to get stuck in a modeling program when you don't know how to change the views on the screen, so let's go over that now. First, let's add a stock primitive to the Edit window so that there's something to view. Figure 13.5 shows the toolbar on the left side of the screen.

Look down toward the bottom of the toolbar for a few icons, as shown in Figure 13.6. Select the Add Sphere icon. You are now in Insert mode and will be able to add a sphere to the scene by dragging the mouse in one of the four view windows.

Adding a Sphere

Drag the mouse in one of the four views to add a sphere to the scene, as shown in Figure 13.7. Note that the sphere will be centered where your mouse starts, so you may want to start at the center.

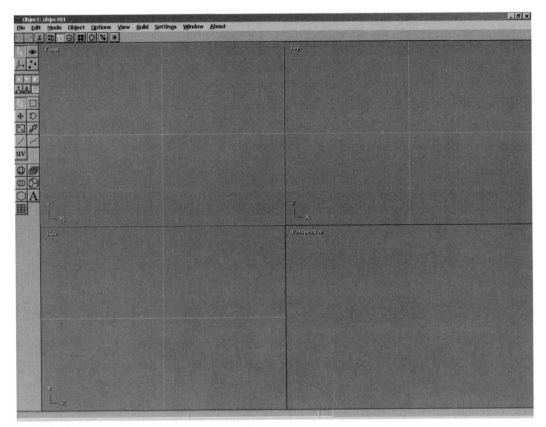

Figure 13.4
The Object Editor is waiting for you to begin crafting a model.

Figure 13.5
The toolbar in Anim8or

Figure 13.6
Stock primitives available for import into your model

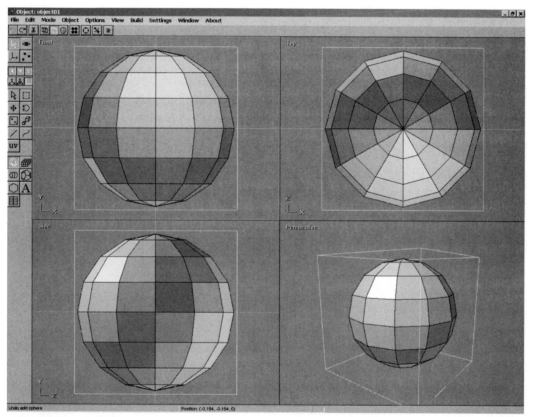

Figure 13.7
Adding a sphere to the scene

That was pretty neat, huh? I'm amazed at how easy it is to add primitives to the scene. Primitives are what a scene is made up of, and you'll be doing it a lot. Right now, the sphere object is selected. If it's not, just click on it once.

You can double-click an object to edit its properties. Double-click the sphere now, and you will see the Sphere Editor dialog, shown in Figure 13.8. You may change the sphere's name here if you think doing so will help you when editing—you will be selecting objects by name after the scene becomes filled with objects (and it becomes difficult to select them with the mouse).

Figure 13.8
Editing the sphere's properties

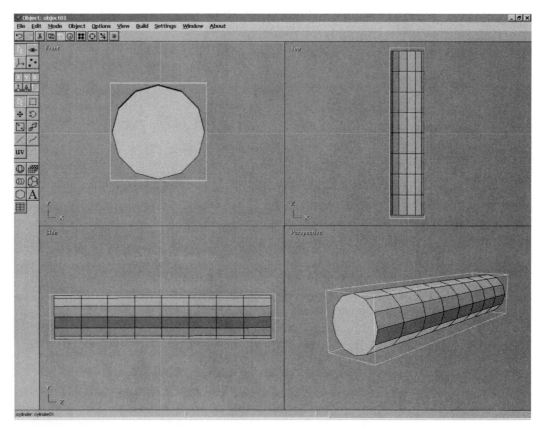

Figure 13.9
Adding a cylinder to the scene

Adding a Cylinder

Next, let's see what a cylinder looks like. Select the sphere with the mouse and press the Delete key to delete it. You can also cut the object by pressing Alt + X, or by using the Edit menu to select Delete Object. Once your scene is clear again, you can add a cylinder.

The cylinder is different from the sphere in that it is not centered at the point where you start dragging. Instead, the cylinder is created beginning at the click-drag point and ending in the spot where you release the mouse button. Try it now. Select the Cylinder icon (below the Sphere icon) and click-drag in one of the view windows. The cylinder will be added to the scene, as in Figure 13.9.

Adding a Cube

You can add a cube to the scene in a similar fashion. The Cube icon is located just to the right of the Sphere icon. The result is shown in Figure 13.10.

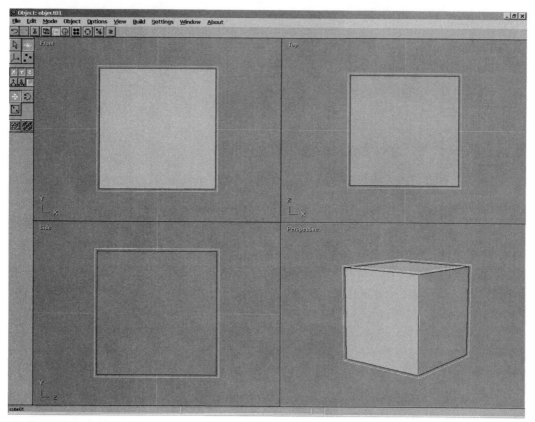

Figure 13.10
Adding a cube to the scene

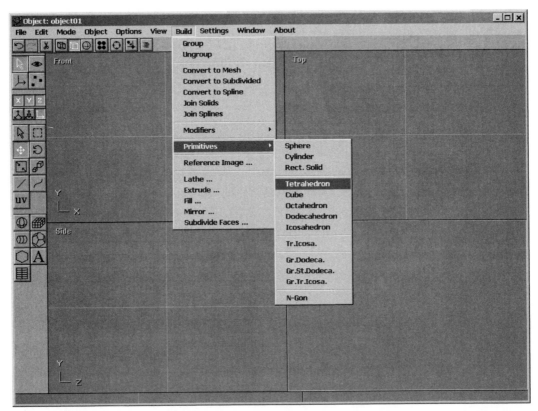

Figure 13.11
Viewing the available stock primitives

Adding Other Stock Primitives

There are many more stock primitives that you can add to your scene that are not included on the toolbar. Take a look at the Build menu—scroll down to the Primitives menu item to see a list, as shown in Figure 13.11.

Manipulating Objects

Add a whole bunch of stock primitives to the scene, as I have done in Figure 13.12, so that I can show you how to move objects and change the view.

Click on the Select icon on the toolbar to enter Selection mode. In this mode, you can click on objects in the scene to select them. Select one of the objects in your scene as I have done in Figure 13.13, in which I selected a sphere.

Tip

The shortcut key for Select mode is A.

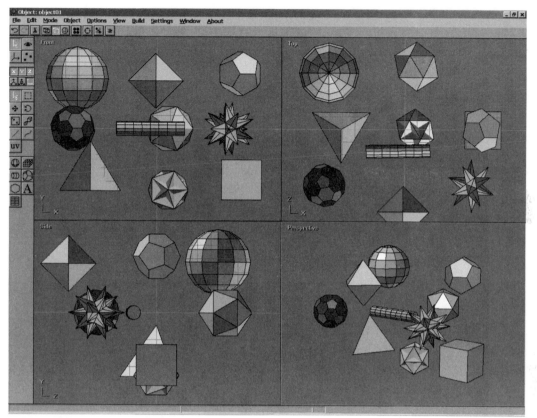

Figure 13.12
Adding a bunch of stock primitives to the scene

Moving Objects

Now, look at the toolbar and find the Move icon. I have selected it in Figure 13.14.

Now that you have depressed the Move icon, Anim8or is in Move Object mode. You can move the selected object in any of the views by dragging it with the mouse. Here is where changing the viewport comes in handy; by doing so, you can zoom in and do more up-close work. You can make any of the four viewports fill the screen by clicking the name of the viewport to bring up a pop-up menu and selecting 1-View, as shown in Figure 13.15.

Tip

The shortcut key for Move mode is M.

The 1-View option will cause that selected view to fill the screen, as shown in Figure 13.16.

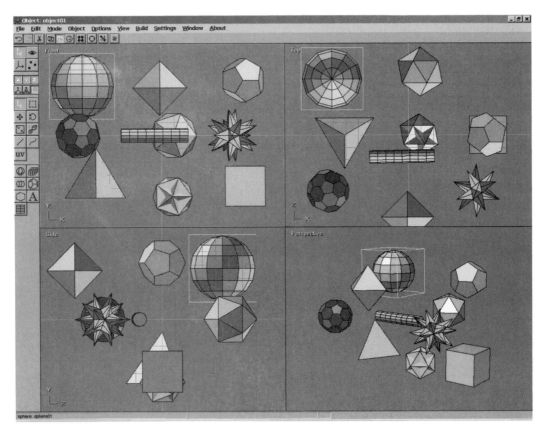

Figure 13.13
Selecting an object in the scene

Figure 13.14
Selecting the Move icon on the toolbar at the left side of the screen

You can click the viewport name again and select All to return to the four-way view. Using this pop-up menu, you can change any viewport to one of the following choices:

■ Front

■ Side

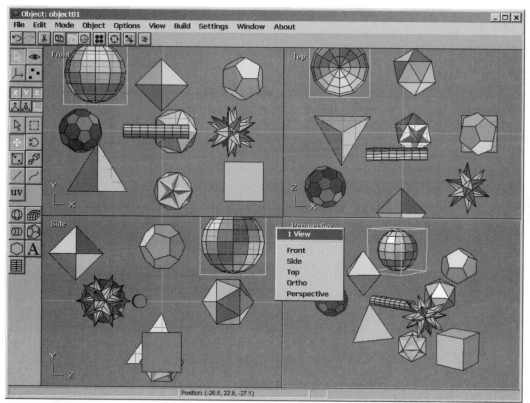

Figure 13.15
Changing the Perspective view to fill the screen

- Top

- Ortho

- Perspective

Try going into 1-View mode and then change the viewport to one of these to see the effect.

Tip

> A quick shortcut to return a view to its standard facing is the F key. This is particularly handy when you have zoomed in or out of the viewport.

Rotating Objects

In addition to moving (translating) objects, you can also rotate and scale them. The Rotate and Scale icons are on the toolbar, but you can also use the R and S

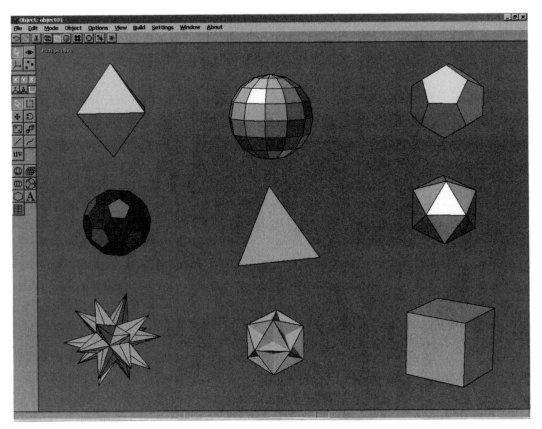

Figure 13.16
The Perspective view now occupies the entire viewport for the scene.

keys to quickly switch to those modes. So, to quickly select an object and enter Rotate mode, press A, click an object, and then press R. Once in Rotate mode, just drag the mouse over the object to rotate it, as shown in Figure 13.17.

Scaling Objects

To scale an object, simply select an object by pressing A, then clicking the mouse, and then pressing S (or using the Scale icon on the toolbar). Dragging the mouse inside the viewport changes the scale of the object, as shown in Figure 13.18.

Manipulating the Entire Scene

You can manipulate the entire scene using tools similar to those used to manipulate individual objects. The scene is usually referred to as the *world* in modeling lingo, but I prefer to call it a *scene* when manipulating a single object

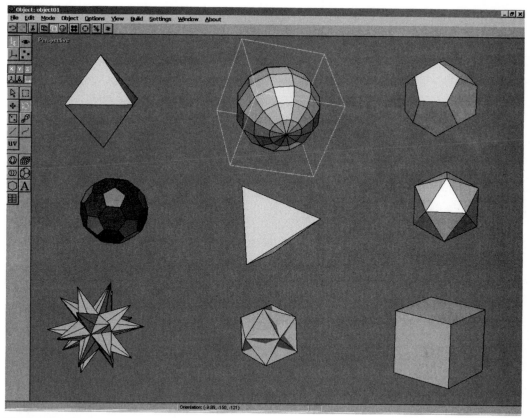

Figure 13.17
Rotating objects independently of one another

(while in the Object Editor). The term *world* may be found elsewhere in Anim8or—in the Scene Editor, to be exact (more on that later).

If you look at the toolbar at the left edge of the Anim8or screen, you'll see an icon that looks like an eyeball. That is the Object/Viewpoint icon, which places Anim8or in a mode that allows you to adjust the scene (or the viewport, through which you "see" the scene).

Moving the Viewport

When you select the Object/Viewpoint icon, Anim8or goes into Viewpoint mode, in which you can move, rotate, and scale the entire scene (that is, all of the objects together). First, select the Move icon (or press the M key), and then drag the mouse inside the viewport. All of the objects in the scene will move together along with the origin. What this essentially means is that you are changing the

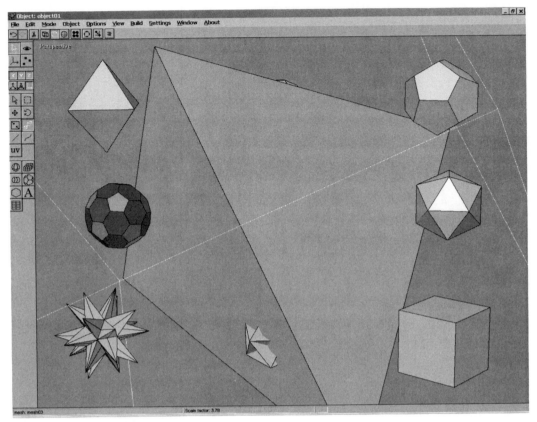

Figure 13.18
Changing the scale of an object

viewport's simulated "camera" but not actually moving the scene. Put another way: you are moving the "camera," not the scene itself. See Figure 13.19.

Rotating the Viewport

You can rotate the scene only with the Perspective viewport because the other viewport modes are fixed. Make sure the Perspective viewport is currently the active viewport (or switch it to 1-View), and make sure you are in Object/ Viewport mode rather than Object/Edit mode. You can then rotate the viewport by dragging the mouse. See Figure 13.20.

Scaling the Viewport

Fortunately, you can change the scaling of any viewport. To change the scale, make sure you are in Object/Viewport mode, select the Zoom View icon, and then drag the mouse in the viewport to zoom in and out. See Figure 13.21.

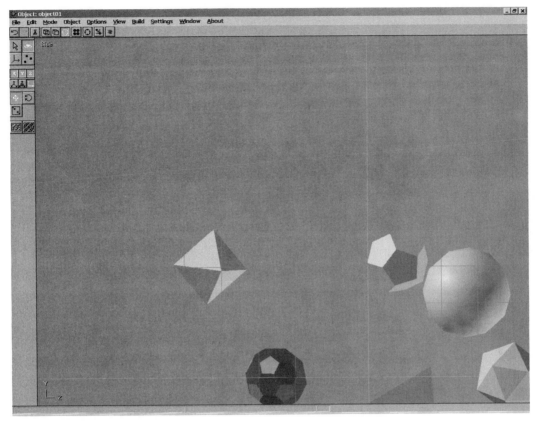

Figure 13.19
Moving the viewport

Tip

The shortcut key for Viewport Zoom mode is N.

Changing the Shading Mode

You can change the shading mode at any time, but it makes sense to cover the subject here, while we're talking about the entire scene. In addition to the left toolbar there is a top toolbar that is right below the program menus (see Figure 13.22).

Aside from a few convenient icons for Undo, Redo, and Cut, this is where you change the shading mode of the scene. The default shading mode is Flat Shaded. Here are the options available:

- Wireframe

- Flat Shaded

- Smooth Shaded

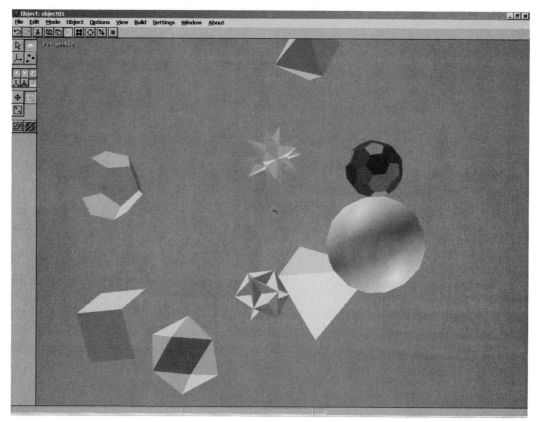

Figure 13.20
Rotating the viewport

The wireframe display is shown in Figure 13.23. Why would you want to use Wireframe mode when a better shading mode is available? For one thing, you can edit individual polygons and vertices in Wireframe mode, in which you can see the individual parts that make up an object. There may also be times when you want to see parts of an object that are hidden in a shaded mode.

Figure 13.24 shows the scene with Smooth Shaded enabled. It makes quite a difference in the appearance of the objects in the scene, especially curved surfaces like a sphere.

Creating the Car Model

You should now have a pretty good idea how to get around in Anim8or, so the next step is to learn how to create a complete model from scratch. The trick to creating really attractive meshes is to start with a primitive and subdivide it, thus

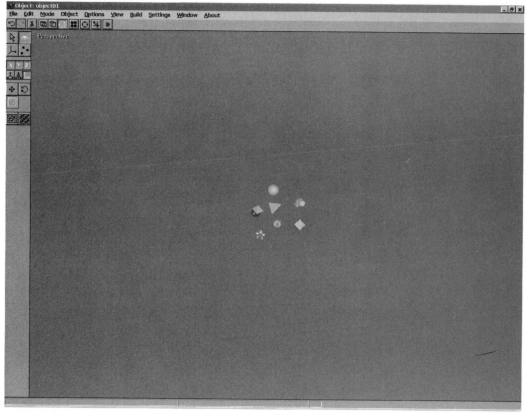

Figure 13.21
Scaling the viewport

Figure 13.22
The top toolbar in Anim8or

tweaking it into shape. This is not too dissimilar to a blacksmith pounding metal into a certain shape. In fact, the more subdividing and custom manipulation you do with a mesh, the better it will look. You will take a basic cylinder and turn it into a wheel by subdividing and tweaking it. Figure 13.25 shows a wireframe model of the completed car that you will create from scratch. Are you ready?

The Wheels

The wheels of the car will be surprisingly easy; you watch. First, we'll start with a tiny cylinder, and then we'll scale it up to a manageable size before subdividing it. The same wheel mesh will be used for all four wheels of the car.

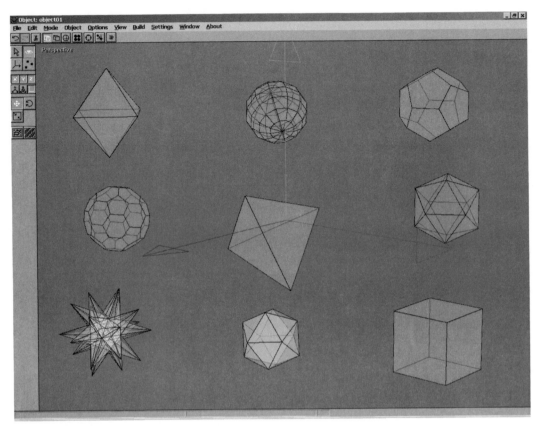

Figure 13.23
Changing the shading mode to Wireframe

Starting with a Cylinder

If Anim8or is not in Object Edit mode, select it from the Mode menu. Next, open the Object menu and select New to create a new, empty object workspace.

Select the Cylinder icon from the left toolbar. Highlight the Front viewport, and then drag only a tiny amount to create a cylinder (a cylinder fragment, really). You might have to do this several times to get just the right width for the wheel because you can't clearly see the cylinder as you are drag-creating it. You will need to drag the mouse only a few pixels. To see what the initial wheel looks like, hit S to enter Scale mode, and then drag the mouse over the viewport to zoom into the cylinder fragment.

You want the cylinder to be taller than it is wide—and don't make it too narrow, either! If the cylinder is too narrow in width, then subdividing the wheel to bend it into shape will result in a thin, funky-looking wheel. If the cylinder is too long, it won't work as a wheel. Figure 13.26 shows a cylinder that is more suited for the barrel of a steamroller than for a car wheel. Try again!

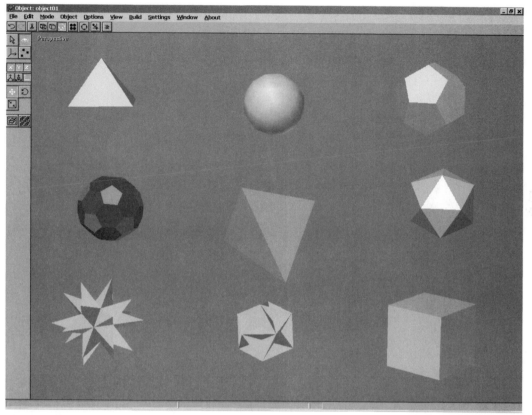

Figure 13.24
Changing the shading mode to Smooth Shaded

Repeat until you have a cylinder that looks like a wheel, something like in Figure 13.27.

The next thing you need to do is adjust the wheel's position, orientation, and scale factor until the wheel is centered on the origin and facing in the correct direction. The end result should look similar to Figure 13.28.

Tip

> If you have a hard time re-orienting the wheel in the proper position, try this: Select the wheel, then open the Edit menu. Scroll down to the Locate menu item, then select Center About Origin.

Converting the Cylinder to a Mesh

The wheel looks pretty good already, doesn't it? If you were creating a car for a city view, this wheel would work fine. But we need more detail in this wheel, especially if the final car will be used in a game.

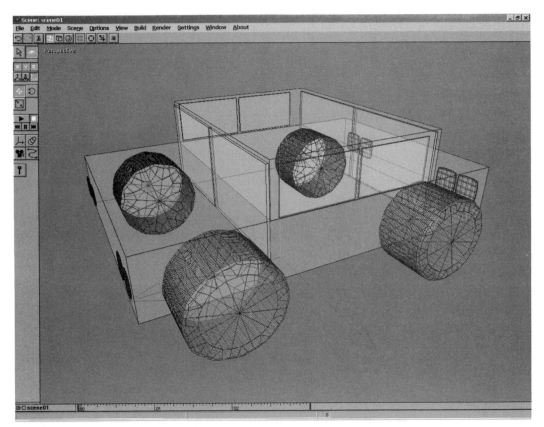

Figure 13.25
Wireframe view of the Hummer

If you are looking for a certain cartoonish look, try this quick method of turning the wheel into sort of a cartoon doughnut: Open the Build menu and select Convert to Subdivided. Presto! There is your doughnut. If you apply a black-shaded or textured material to the wheel, it would work fine for some purposes. But that is not the direction I'm taking with this car (no pun intended).

Open Build and select Convert to Mesh. The wheel is now a mesh, which is an editable object.

Tip

If you make any mistakes while editing a mesh, simply press Ctrl + Z for Undo. You can also use the Edit menu to Undo or Redo. You will use Undo frequently while working with meshes in order to get the result you're looking for. You should save your work often.

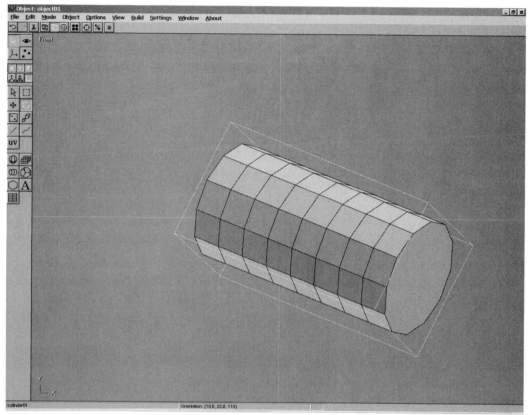

Figure 13.26
This cylinder is way too oddly shaped to become a wheel.

Subdividing the Mesh to Increase Detail

Now it's time to subdivide the cylinder to add more detail to it. Open Build and select Subdivide Faces to bring up the Smooth Parameters dialog, shown in Figure 13.29.

This is where you input the tension that should be applied to the mesh. Type **1** for the tension and click OK. The result is shown in Figure 13.30.

Okay, let's subdivide the wheel once more. The first attempt left a lot of blockiness, so we'll divide the wheel down one more time to add more polygons and, in turn, improve the roundness of the wheel. Open the Smooth Parameters dialog again by selecting Build, Subdivide Faces.

This time, type in **0.1** in the Tension field and click OK. The result is shown in Figure 13.31.

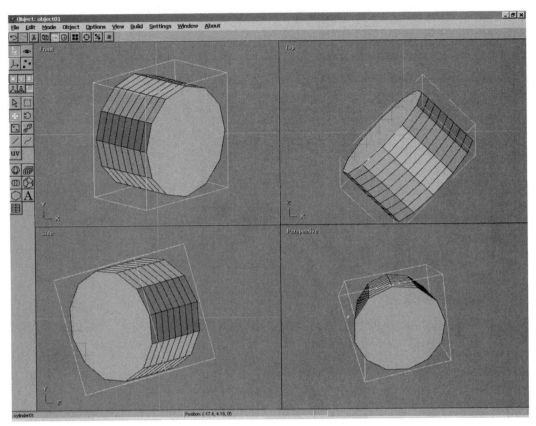

Figure 13.27
This cylinder is just right for a wheel.

Applying Materials

You now have a very nice-looking wheel, but it is in plain, drab gray, which means it has no materials. You can apply complex combinations of colors and textures to the polygons (also called *faces*) in a mesh. The last chapter explained how to programmatically apply texture to a cube, but a real mesh created in a modeling program may have hundreds of different materials applied to it. Now I'll show you how to make the wheel look like, well, a wheel. It needs two materials: one for the tire, another for the rim.

Bring up the Materials toolbar if it is not visible. You can do so from the top toolbar or by selecting Options, Materials from the menu. Double-click the first empty material to bring up the Material Editor dialog.

Tip

You can create custom materials for individual faces in a mesh by double-clicking a face or a mesh in the viewport.

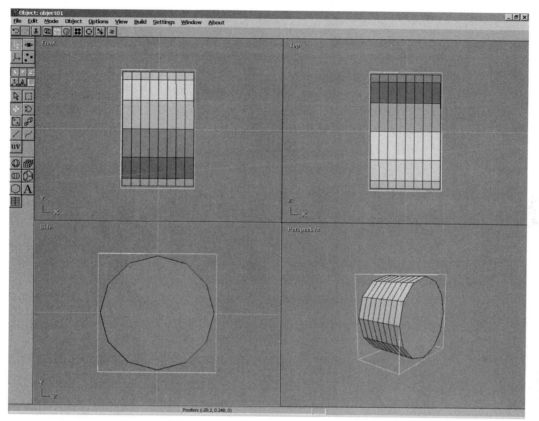

Figure 13.28
Re-orienting the wheel to center it at the origin

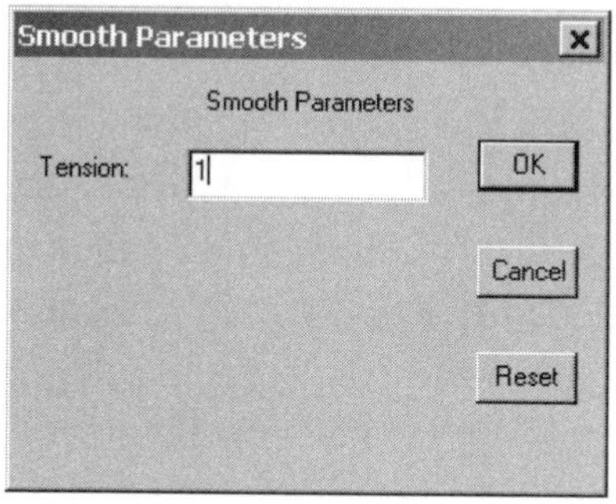

Figure 13.29
The Smooth Parameters dialog is used to subdivide a mesh.

Click the Ambient color selector and choose a dark gray color for the tire material. You can also type **TIRE** in the name field to give this material a name if you want. The result is shown in Figure 13.32. Click OK and the new material will be added to the materials list.

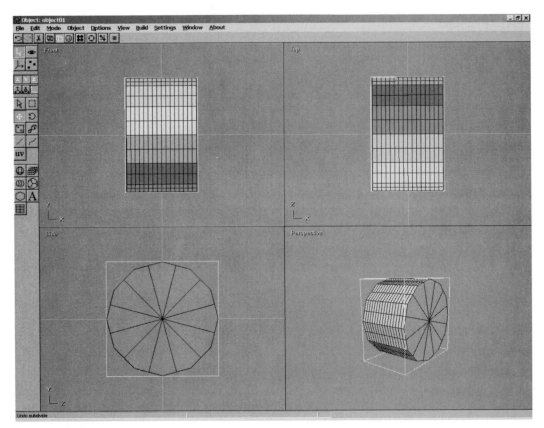

Figure 13.30
The wheel mesh has been subdivided and is now more detailed.

Now, double-click the next "new" material to bring up the Material Editor dialog again. Change the name to **CHROME**. This material will be a little more complex because it needs to shine like chrome. You are going to have to do what you think is best here—it is more important for you to experiment with the Materials Editor than for me to give you precise values; after all, my opinion of chrome might differ from yours. I have set Specular to 0.7 and Emissive to 0.2, and selected a dull gray color for the Ambient and Diffuse properties (without touching their values). Figure 13.33 shows the properties for this material.

The great thing about the materials in Anim8or is that you can use the same material for all similar objects in your model, and then, if you want to tweak the material, it will be applied to every face to which you applied the material!

Editing Faces, Lines, and Vertices

In order to apply the chrome material to the rims of the wheel, you'll need to go in using the Object/Point Edit mode. The Object/Point icon is located below the

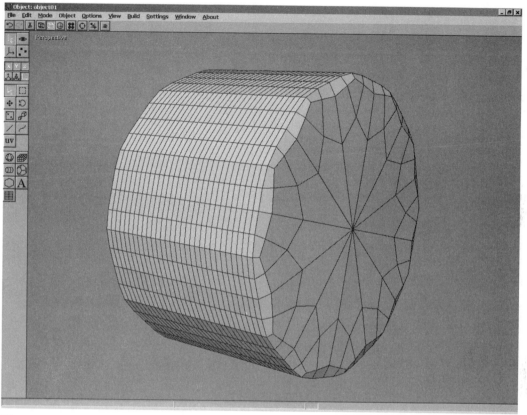

Figure 13.31
The wheel is now smooth with a very round surface.

Object/Viewpoint icon (which looks like an eye). When you select this icon, the toolbar changes and the viewport goes into Wireframe mode. You now have access to the individual vertices, lines, and faces that make up the mesh. Very powerful fine-tuning capabilities here, indeed! If there's anything you don't like about your mesh, you can tweak it in Object/Point Edit mode.

Figure 13.34 shows the toolbar for Object/Point Edit mode. Take a look at the three options below the X/Y/Z Axis Enable icons. One is called Point Select, one is called Edge Select, and the last is called Face Select.

Click the Face Select icon to enable Face Select Edit mode. You can do a lot of interesting things with these tools, but I'm just going to show you how to use them to apply materials to individual faces so that you can give the wheel some chrome rims.

After you have turned on the Face Select mode, choose the Drag Select icon so that you can drag the selection rectangle around a group of faces to edit. If you have a hard time with this, select each individual face (press A) and then apply

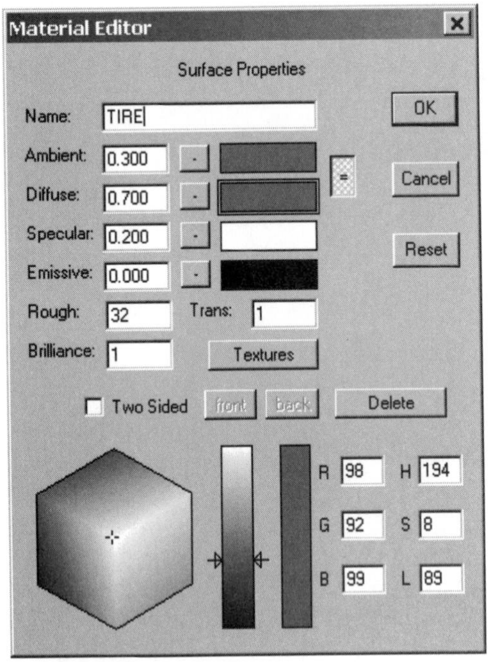

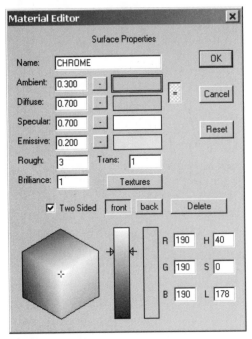

Figure 13.32
The Material Editor dialog

Figure 13.33
Creating the CHROME material

Figure 13.34
The Object/Point toolbar

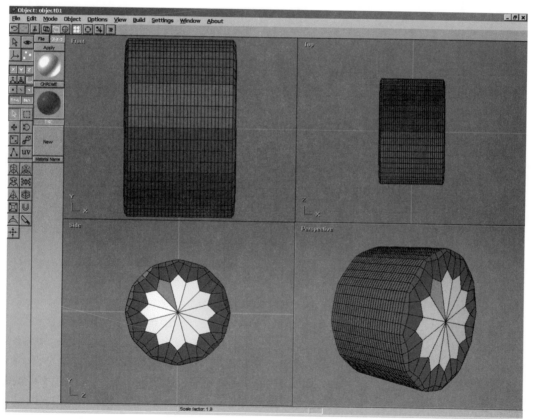

Figure 13.35
Selecting the rim part of the wheel and applying the chrome material to it.

the material to each one. There aren't very many faces that need to be chromed, so you can select each one and chrome it. You can see the results right away by switching to Flat Shaded mode; Wireframe mode is only helpful when you are changing vertices or lines.

Select each of the faces at the center of the outer side of the wheel and apply the chrome material to it, as shown in Figure 13.35.

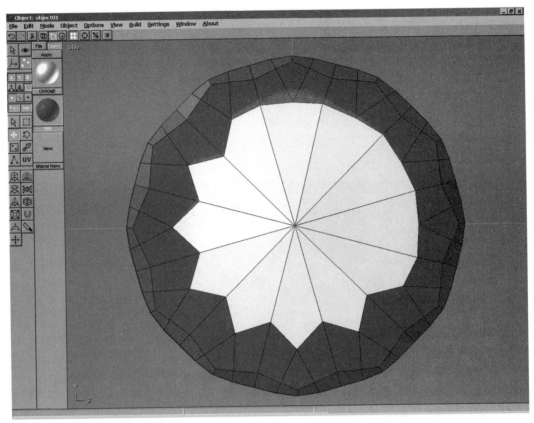

Figure 13.36
Fine-tuning the geometry of the rim part of the wheel

I consider the wheel complete, but I suppose the "star" pattern on the wheel might cause some in the perfectionist crowd to pause. Never fear: it's a simple matter to switch back to Wireframe mode and nudge the vertices up to beat the rim of the wheel into a semi-circular shape. You can manipulate vertices and lines directly in Flat Shaded mode; often this is quite difficult, but I think this wheel is simple enough that you can mange it. Just remember to hit A each time you want to select a vertex, then hit M to move it, then drag it to a new location, and then hit A again to select the next one. Working in 1-View mode is easier. (See Figure 13.36.)

While I'm at it, I think I'll fine-tune the tire as well, as there are some weird jagged edges there. You can do this if you want or you can just move on. . . .

The Frame

Well, after the experience of creating the wheel, the rest of the car will seem like child's play. As you can see from the tutorial on creating the wheel, it's easy to keep adding more and more detail to a 3D model. However, if you have the time and willingness, the results are always better when you add more details to each mesh. Now let's work on the frame, which will be simplistic in comparison. Go ahead and add a new object for the car frame.

Tip

When you need to add a new object in Anim8or, open the Object menu and select New.

The important thing to remember when working on meshes is that they can be scaled in the scene, so don't worry about making everything to scale right now (in other words, don't worry about comparing the car frame to the wheel mesh).

Creating the Main Car Frame

First, add a rectangular solid to the scene and then convert it to a mesh using the Build menu. The actual shape is not all that important right away because you can use the Object/Point Edit mode to grab a side of the mesh and drag it to the dimensions you want. Try to make the car frame look like the one in Figure 13.37.

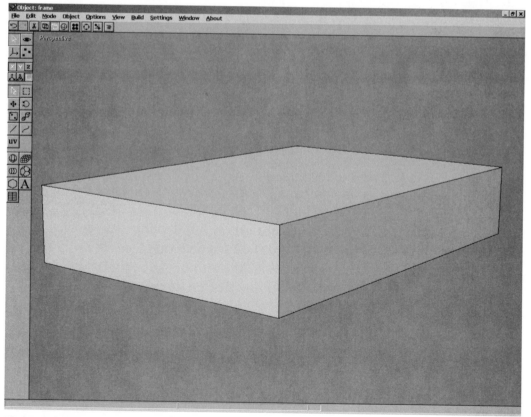

Figure 13.37
The main car frame is basically just a rectangular solid.

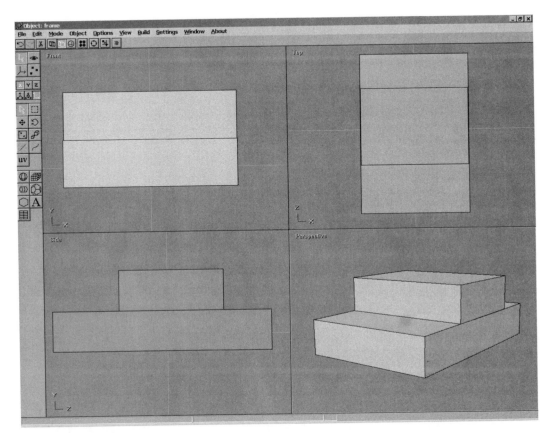

Figure 13.38
The cabin/roof mesh has been added on top of the car frame.

Tip

Whenever you manipulate the vertices, lines, or faces of a mesh to resize it, you can use the Build, Join Solids menu option to redefine the mesh at the new size.

Add a second cube (or rectangular solid from the Build menu) and convert it to a mesh. Resize the mesh using the Object/Point Edit mode—select the lines of a face and move them out so that the mesh sits on top of the car frame. The mesh should be about half the length of the frame, as this is the cab or roof of the car. See Figure 13.38.

Once you have completed the car's body, click the Drag Select icon and drag a selection box around both mesh objects to select both of them. Open the Build menu and select Group. The car body will now be treated as a single mesh.

Now open up the Materials toolbar (Options, Materials) and double-click the first empty material. Change the ambient color to an attractive car-paint color.

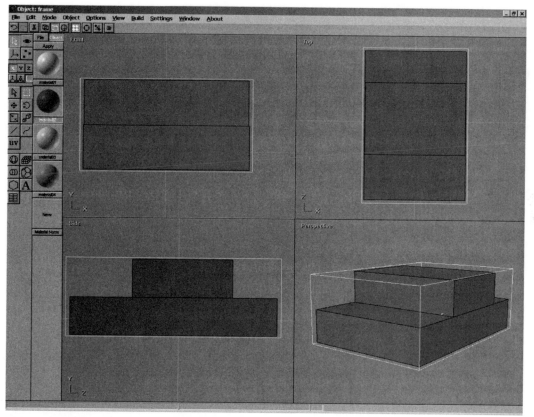

Figure 13.39
The car body has been grouped and a colorful material applied.

Add a few more materials in like manner using several different colors. You will be able to change the car's color by applying any one of these materials to the car body. Choose a material that you like and apply it to the two car body pieces. See Figure 13.39.

Tip

If you haven't done so yet, save your work now!

The Windows

The windows are the same for both the front and rear of the car, while a second set of windows is used for the two sides of the car. Figure 13.40 shows the windows used for the front and rear. We won't be modeling doors now, but that would be a great project to try after the basic car is done. The windshield has a light gray-colored material applied to it, and is made up of just a simple rectangular

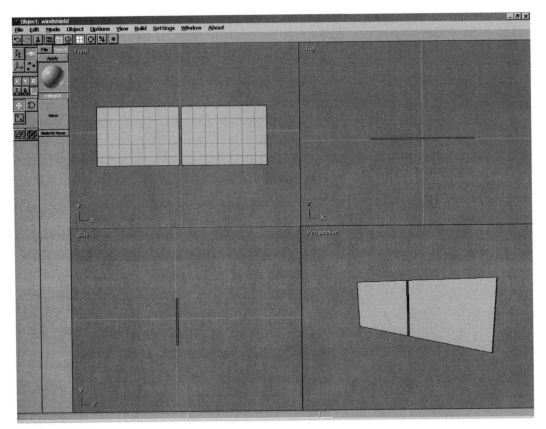

Figure 13.40
The front and rear windows share a mesh and are ready to be installed.

solid that has been stretched into a thin rectangle. It will take some tweaking of the windows to get them to fit in the body of the car during scene-building time, at which point you can return to the windows and edit them. Switching back and forth between objects and scenes is something you will do frequently.

The side windows are similar to, but not quite as large as, the front and rear windows. You can copy the front window, create a new object, and paste it into the new object space, then resize as needed during scene time. Figure 13.41 shows the side windows.

The Headlights and Taillights

All that remains to be done at this point are the headlights and taillights. Of course, you could add a lot more detail to this car. I will leave that up to you (though I may add some new objects to this car and use it in a game at some point in the near future, because I've become quite fond of it!).

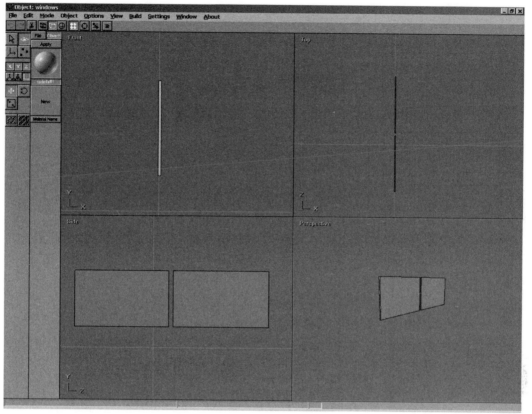

Figure 13.41
The side windows also share a mesh.

The Headlight

Add a new object to the works and then create a new rectangular solid (or a cube) that is rather thin but otherwise square in width and height. Open the Build menu and select Convert to Mesh. Go back into the Build menu and select Subdivide Faces to bring up the Smooth Parameters dialog. Type in **0.25** for the tension value and click OK.

Repeat this step again to subdivide the headlight again by 0.25. You can try to subdivide it again if you want even more smoothness to try to get that headlight bulb shape. See Figure 13.42.

Now the headlight needs a slightly glowing material so that it will look like a real headlight. It won't shoot out a beam of light, but it will at least appear to glow (using the Emissive property), which is a pretty good effect. Figure 13.43 shows the material properties for the headlight.

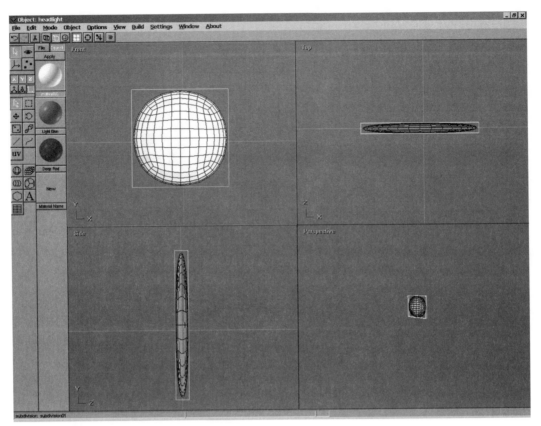

Figure 13.42
The headlight is created by subdividing a simple rectangular solid.

The Taillight

Now for the taillights. The process will be similar to that of the headlights, except that the taillight needs to be square rather than round. Add a new object and add a rectangular solid or a cube that is very thin but equally wide and high, like you did for the headlight.

Next, select the object and convert it to a mesh using the Build menu. Open the Build menu again and select Subdivide Faces to bring up the Smooth Parameters dialog.

First, subdivide the taillight by 1.0. That will turn it into four solids but will retain the basic shape. Next, subdivide it again by 0.25. This will give it a basically square shape, but with rounded corners.

Create a material that is a deep red with an emissive value of 0.4; this way, it will have a faint glow to it. Figure 13.44 shows the material properties for the

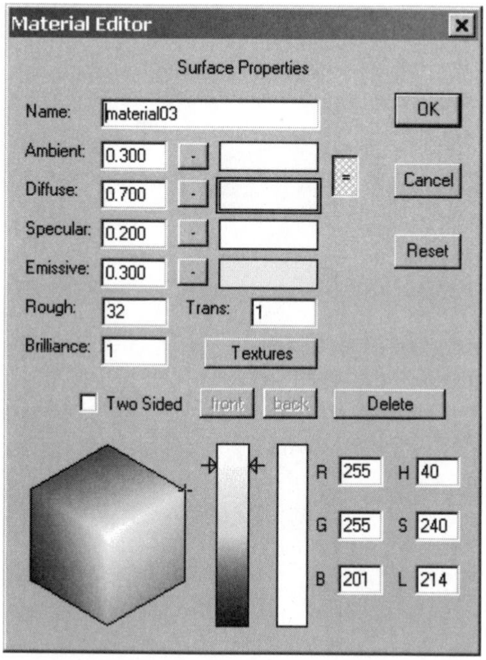

Figure 13.43
The headlight material is white with a faintly illuminated yellow color.

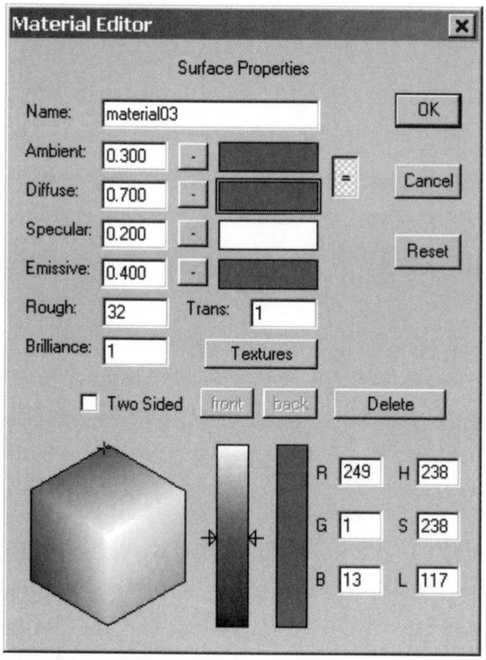

Figure 13.44
The taillight material is a faintly illuminated red color.

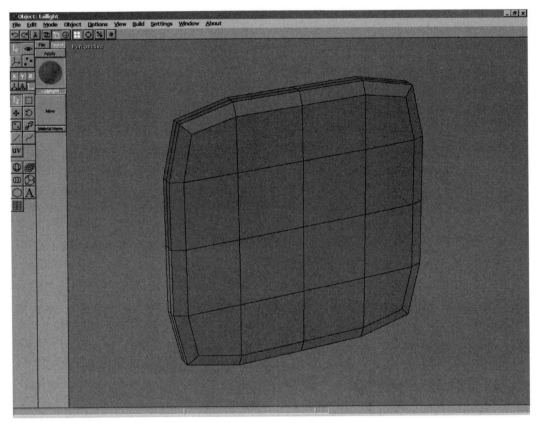

Figure 13.45
The complete taillight mesh with an illuminated red color.

taillight. (Of course, you won't see the actual colors in the black-and-white screenshots.)

Figure 13.45 shows the finished taillight with the material applied to it.

Creating a Scene

Generally, you will want to create an entire model as a single object rather than assembling a model from component parts created as individual meshes in Anim8or's Object Edit mode. However, it is very convenient to be able to edit the meshes on their own without other parts of the model getting in the way, and it is a simple matter to copy and paste meshes from one object into another. If you were going to create a complex scene with more than just the single car, you would want to combine it all into a single object so that it would be possible to control the car as a whole. As a learning experience, though, I think it was easier

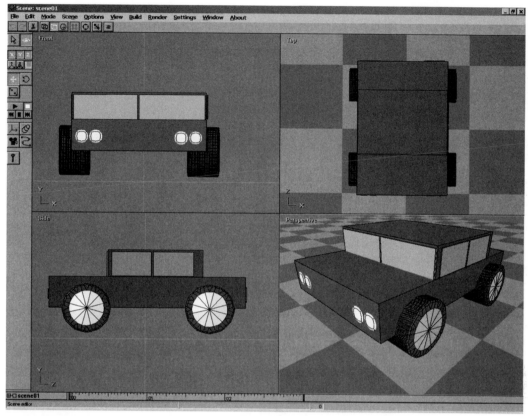

Figure 13.46
The completed Hummer is ready for a test drive.

to construct the car using the Scene Editor. You can export the car to a 3ds max (.3ds) file from the Scene Editor, so this works well for creating models to be used in a game.

Figure 13.46 shows the completed Hummer in the Scene Editor. The most surprising thing about this model is that no textures were used; only materials were used to give the car texture and color! What I'm going to do at this point is show you how to add one of the objects to the scene and then leave it up to you to assemble the car, factory style! Just remember the things you have learned in the chapter so far: how to select, rotate, move, and scale objects. If scaling is a big problem and all of your pieces are way out of kilter, I recommend you switch to the Object Editor and change the scale of the objects at the source rather than inside the Scene Editor. Not only is this much easier, but it ensures that your car model will be uniform and consistent.

First, open the Mode menu and select Scene. This puts you in Scene Edit mode. Next, open the Build menu and select Add Object. You can select an object from the Object Selector dialog. If the objects are all unnamed, you may want to switch back to Object Edit mode and give each part of the car an identifying name. You can do this while in Object Edit mode by opening the Settings dialog and choosing Object, which will bring up a dialog that will allow you to name the object. This is especially helpful when you are working on a complex scene with dozens or even hundreds of objects!

Caution

If you get completely stuck while trying to build the car in this chapter, you can always load the Anim8or file off the CD-ROM. Just be sure to clear the read-only property of the car.an8 file. It is located in \sources\chapter13.

What You Have Learned

This chapter provided a tutorial on how to use Anim8or to create your own 3D models. Here are the key points:

- You learned that Anim8or is a free 3D modeling program.

- You learned where to find Anim8or on the Web.

- You learned how to use viewports to change the view of a scene.

- You learned how to create stock primitive objects.

- You learned how to manipulate points, lines, and faces in a mesh.

- You learned how to create objects and insert them into a scene.

- You learned enough information to create a 3D car from scratch.

Review Questions

The following questions will help you to determine whether you have retained the information presented in this chapter.

1. What is a mesh?

2. How many editing modes are there in Anim8or?

3. How do you convert a stock primitive into a mesh?

4. How to you go into Object/Point Edit mode to manipulate a mesh?

5. How do you bring up the Materials toolbar?

On Your Own

The following exercises will help you to think outside the box and push your limits, helping you to retain the information you've been shown.

Exercise 1. The Hummer model is still very primitive, but it was a good example of what you can do. See if you can improve the model by adding more detail to the car body itself. Add front and rear bumpers, a hood that rises toward the windshield (rather than being flat), and passenger doors.

Exercise 2. This model would really benefit from the use of textures rather than just simple materials. Try to locate the texture for a wheel on the Web and apply it to the Hummer's wheels. If you can't find a wheel texture, then consider creating one yourself using a graphic editor like The Gimp, which is available for free from http://www.gimp.org. Textures can be applied from the Material Editor dialog.

CHAPTER 14

WORKING WITH 3D MODEL FILES

This chapter is a natural follow-up to Chapter 13, in which you learned how to create a 3D model from scratch using Anim8or. This chapter takes it a step further, teaching you how to convert that model into a format that can be loaded into your own Direct3D programs. You will learn how to convert, load, and render the Hummer car model that was created in Chapter 13.

Here is what you will learn in this chapter:

- How to convert a 3DS file to .X.

- How to optimize a model file.

- How to load a model file into memory.

- How to manipulate and draw a model on the screen.

Converting 3D Files

The most difficult part of getting a model into your game is converting it to the Direct3D format, which has an extension of .X. Without some guidance, you face the hit-or-miss task of searching the Web for 3D file converters, and you never know how reliable or up-to-date these programs are. Although Direct3D can read the .X file format, it does not set up the materials and textures for you; this is something that you will have to learn to do yourself. Fortunately, it is possible to read the material and texture counts from the mesh object after an .X file has been loaded, which can then be used to iterate through the materials and textures and then render the .X model. I'll go over this relatively painless code shortly. First, let's talk about converting files.

Converting 3DS to .X

There is a program called conv3ds.exe that was once included in the DirectX SDK up through version 8.1, but was dropped in version 9.0. It *is* true that Discreet no longer supports the 3DS format, and that the MAX format is now the standard, but most software products still work with 3DS files, including Anim8or. The conv3ds.exe tool is very convenient for Anim8or users because Anim8or exports to the 3DS format, so I have included it on the CD-ROM.

Tip
_____

The conv3ds.exe program is included on the book's CD-ROM in \software\conv3ds.
_____

Using the conv3ds Utility

I recommend you copy conv3ds.exe to your \Windows or \WINNT folder on your primary drive partition so it will be available to any command prompt. Or you can just add it to the system path by opening Control Panel, System, then clicking the Advanced tab, and then clicking the Environment Variables button. Here you can edit the path to add any folder you want.

Type **conv3ds.exe** to see the list of options. The most common usage is this:

```
conv3ds -m file.3ds
```

This converts a 3ds file to .X and combines all meshes into a single mesh, which optimizes the file. If the conversion succeeds, nothing is displayed on the screen.

If you want to see some details about the conversion as it takes place, you can add the following verbose option:

```
conv3ds -m -v1 file.3ds
```

The -v1 option will display the meshes that are being converted over and saved in the new .X file. The Hummer model is quite huge compared to the cube in Chapter 11, for instance, so in order to use the same basic rendering options in the code you are used to, it is helpful to reduce the scale of the car model. This isn't totally necessary; you could just zoom out with the camera to an appropriate distance so that the car model will show up, but it's more convenient to rescale the model as it is converted.

So, let's convert over the car.3ds file that was exported from Anim8or. The option to alter the scale of the model is -s, and you give it a scale value:

```
conv3ds -m -v1 -s0.05 car.3ds
```

Tip

You can export an entire scene in Anim8or using the Scene, Export option. To export a single mesh (in Object/Edit mode), use the Object, Export option.

That command will produce a Hummer model that is only five percent of the original size, without losing any details. The scaling problem is just due to the size of the model that I created in Anim8or. When you create your own 3D models, you'll want to load them into your game to see how they scale compared to the rest of the game. It's better to adjust scale of the original model in your modeling program, but in this example, I wanted to also show you an option for changing the scale when the file is converted.

Using the MeshView Utility

After you have converted a 3ds max file to a Direct3D file, you can load it in your program. But first, it's a good idea to use the MeshView program (included with the DirectX SDK). The MeshView program is located in \DX90SDK\Utilities. You can also run it from the Start menu. Go to Programs, Microsoft DirectX 9.0 SDK, DirectX Utilities, Mesh Viewer. Figure 14.1 shows the Mesh Viewer with our Hummer from Chapter 13 loaded.

Mesh Viewer includes a lot of advanced options that will help identify problems with a mesh, such as incorrect texture coordinates, materials, or normals (used for lighting). Take a look at the status bar on the bottom-right of the Mesh

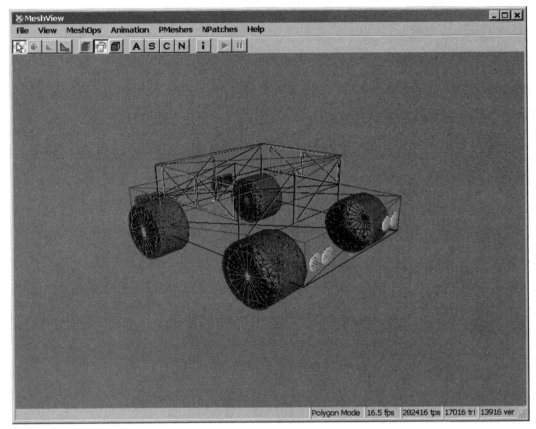

Figure 14.1
The Hummer created in the last chapter has been converted to .X and loaded into Mesh Viewer.

Viewer window and you'll see some information about your .X file. The two values on the right side show the total number of triangles (faces) and vertices, respectively. Remember that a mesh created with triangle strips will share vertices, which is why this model has many more faces than vertices. According to Mesh Viewer, our Hummer model has 17,016 polygons. Not bad for your first attempt at 3D modeling!

Optimizing the Model

What we're really interested in is the optimization features of Mesh Viewer. If you think about it, this Hummer model has been through quite a bit and is not necessarily the most efficient model in the world. First, it was exported from Anim8or's Scene Editor into a .3ds file. Then it was converted to a .X file using the conv3ds utility.

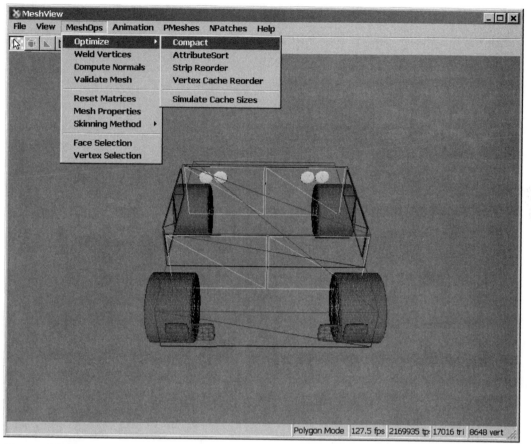

Figure 14.2
Optimizing the mesh can reduce the number of vertices and fix any problems with the faces.

Try optimizing the model using some of the features in Mesh Viewer. Figure 14.2 shows one good option that will try to reduce the polygon count of the model. Go into the MeshOps menu, select Optimize, Compact. Before you do this, take a look at the vertex count at the bottom-right corner of the window. The Hummer model that was converted to .X has 13,916 vertices. Pay attention to that number as you perform various optimizations; it will go down to reflect a model that has been cleaned up.

Triangle Removal Optimization

Another good optimization is in MeshOps, Weld Vertices (see Figure 14.3). This will combine vertices and rebuild the triangle strip for every two polygons (faces) that share two vertices. If you'll recall, this car model was constructed from many

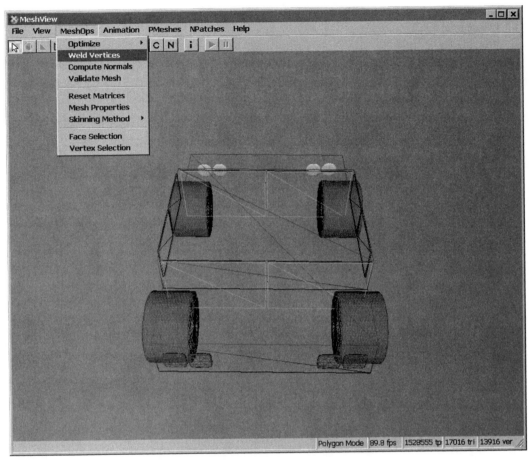

Figure 14.3
Welding the vertices will rebuild the triangle strip and improve the mesh.

individual parts, so most of it is comprised of adjacent polygons that are not joined. Welding the vertices in this way helps to clean up the model quite a bit.

I recommend selecting the first three options and leaving the rest alone, unless you are a 3D guru (in which case, why are you reading this book?). Figure 14.4 shows the Weld Vertices dialog box.

Here are the options I selected:

■ **Remove Back To Back Triangles.** This will eliminate duplicate triangles that are not needed.

■ **Regenerate Adjacency.** This will rebuild the triangle strip structure after the vertices have been welded (or shared).

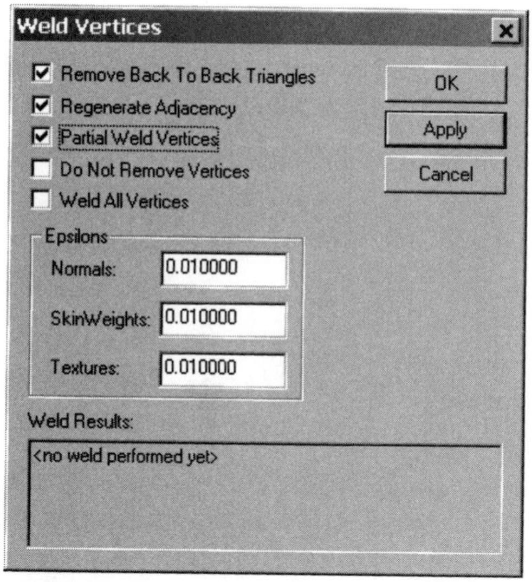

Figure 14.4
The Weld Vertices dialog box

- **Partial Weld Vertices.** This will generate additional polygons, if necessary, to share common vertices not at the line ends.

When you click Apply or OK, the vertex optimization will begin. Whoa—take a look at Figure 14.5. Ten percent of the vertices have been eliminated by this single optimization, from 13,916 vertices down to 11,308!

Weld Vertices Optimization

If your model is fairly simple and does not need to be manipulated at run time, then you can try the next optimization. Go back into MeshOps and select Weld Vertices again. This time, check just the Weld All Vertices option. Click Apply to see the result. Very complex models probably should not have this optimization done to them; then again, it's worth a try to see if the model still looks correct in your game. According to Figure 14.6, this results in 25 percent *more* vertices removed from the model. Altogether, about 35 percent of the vertices have been combined without any apparent change in the model.

Saving the File

Be sure to save the file before you close the Mesh Viewer utility! Go to File, Save Mesh As to bring up the Save As dialog box (see Figure 14.7). You can type in the filename and also the file type, which will be one of the following:

- Text

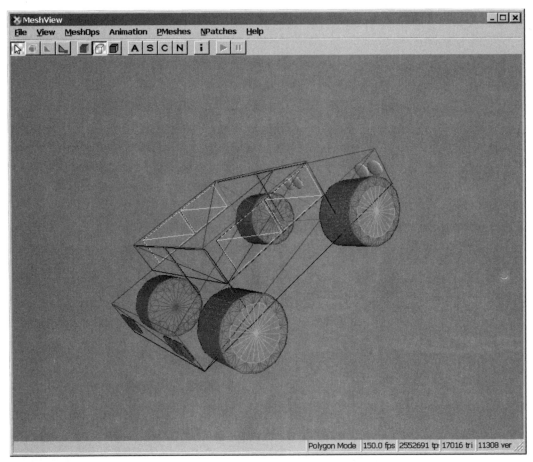

Figure 14.5
The Weld Vertices optimization has eliminated 10 percent of the vertices.

- Binary

- Binary Compressed

This is interesting because you can at least prevent someone from opening your model files in a text editor by saving them in the binary compressed format—it's not much protection, but it does prevent players from modifying your model files without a binary .X reader. Binary compressed .X files are about one-tenth the file size of the text format (on average), so your game installation will be much smaller. Just be sure to keep your source models in the standard 3ds or .X format.

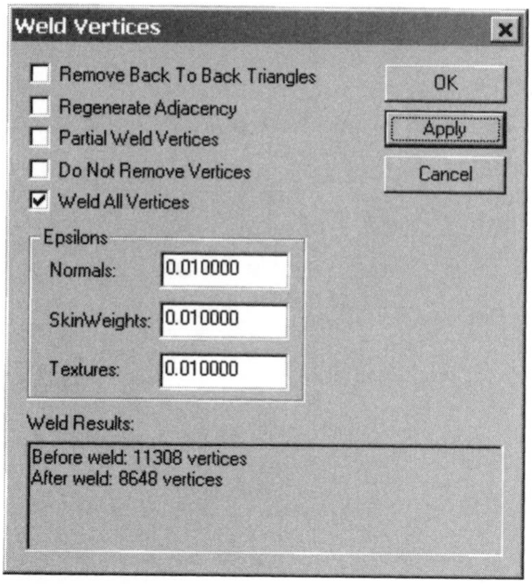

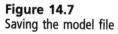

Weld Vertices

☐ Remove Back To Back Triangles
☐ Regenerate Adjacency
☐ Partial Weld Vertices
☐ Do Not Remove Vertices
☑ Weld All Vertices

OK
Apply
Cancel

Epsilons

Normals: 0.010000
SkinWeights: 0.010000
Textures: 0.010000

Weld Results:

Before weld: 11308 vertices
After weld: 8648 vertices

Figure 14.6
Weld All Vertices optimization eliminates 25 percent more vertices.

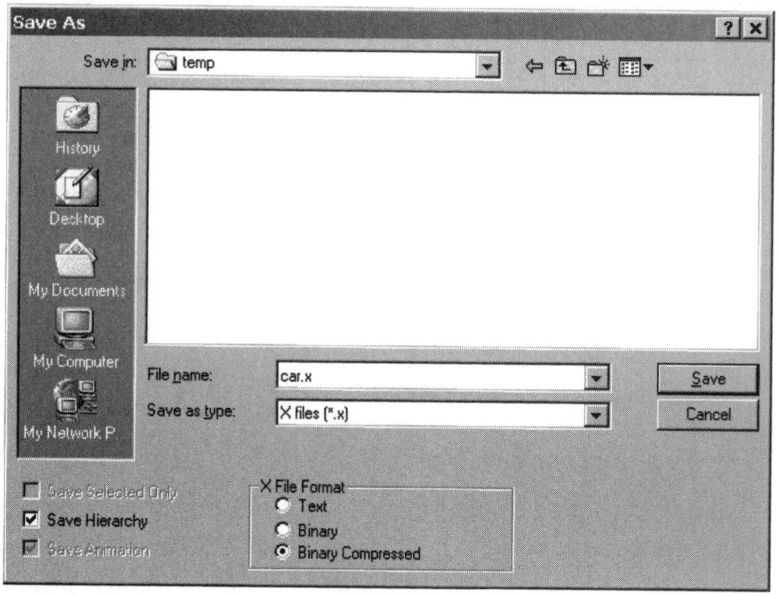

Save As

Save in: temp

History
Desktop
My Documents
My Computer
My Network P...

File name: car.x   Save
Save as type: X files (*.x)   Cancel

☐ Save Selected Only
☑ Save Hierarchy
☑ Save Animation

X File Format
  ○ Text
  ○ Binary
  ● Binary Compressed

Figure 14.7
Saving the model file

Loading and Rendering a Model File

The only thing left to do is learn how to load a model from an .X file into your Direct3D program and render it on the screen! Are you ready? I said, *are you ready!*? Let's get to it, then.

Loading an .X File

Direct3D provides a function to create a mesh out of an .X file that is loaded, and that makes it very simple to read in any model file into your own games (because you now have the ability to convert a 3DS file to .X).

Let's learn how to load a model. Instead of starting off with 100 percent theory, I'm going to show you complete, working code so you'll be able to understand it better when you get to the project I'll give you later in the chapter.

Defining the MODEL Structure

First, we need a new struct to deal with model files that are to be loaded from disk:

```
struct MODEL
{
    LPD3DXMESH mesh;
    D3DMATERIAL9* materials;
    LPDIRECT3DTEXTURE9* textures;
    DWORD material_count;
};
```

Some programmers and modelers prefer to call them "mesh files," but I submit that "mesh" does not properly describe the contents of a typical 3D model file (such as car.X). These files contain meshes, materials, and a lot of data types and animation instructions. So to call it just a mesh file is incorrect. I much prefer "model," hence the name of the struct above.

The MODEL struct contains the primary objects needed to load and render a model file. First, you have the mesh. If your original model file contained many meshes/objects, then it should have been condensed down to a single mesh by the conv3ds utility. Otherwise, the mesh here might represent multiple meshes (which the .X file format supports).

Next, there is a D3DMATERIAL9 pointer variable that will be loaded with an array of materials defined in the model file. LPDIRECT3DTEXTURE9 should already be familiar to you after working with sprites, so no surprises here, except that a model may contain multiple textures. These textures are not stored in the model file itself, but in separate bitmap files, and the texture filenames are stored in the model file.

Finally, there is a member variable that holds the number of materials in the model, which is used during rendering. There may be many materials in a model, but not every one is required to have a texture. However, a texture *must* be defined within a material. Hence, we have a `material_count` variable, but there is no need to keep track of the number of textures.

Loading the Mesh

The key to loading a model file resides in the `D3DXLoadMeshFromX` function:

```
HRESULT WINAPI D3DXLoadMeshFromX(
    LPCTSTR pFilename,
    DWORD Options,
    LPDIRECT3DDEVICE9 pDevice,
    LPD3DXBUFFER *ppAdjacency,
    LPD3DXBUFFER *ppMaterials,
    LPD3DXBUFFER *ppEffectInstances,
    DWORD *pNumMaterials,
    LPD3DXMESH *ppMesh
);
```

The parameters for this function are filled with either defaults (in one form or another) or NULLs, with key parameters being the filename, Direct3D device, material buffer, material count, and mesh object. First, you need a material buffer to load the materials into:

```
LPD3DXBUFFER matbuffer;
```

Let's also assume that a pointer to the `MODEL` struct has already been created:

```
MODEL *model = (MODEL*)malloc(sizeof(MODEL));
```

The model struct is allocated in memory and returned by the `LoadModel` function (which I'll cover in a moment). Then you can read the model file and load the materials and meshes at the same time. Here is sample code that calls this function:

```
result = D3DXLoadMeshFromX(
    filename,                  //filename
    D3DXMESH_SYSTEMMEM,        //mesh options
    d3ddev,                    //Direct3D device
    NULL,                      //adjacency buffer
    &matbuffer,                //material buffer
    NULL,                      //special effects
    &model->material_count,    //number of materials
    &model->mesh);             //resulting mesh
```

Loading the Materials/Textures

The materials are stored in the material buffer, but they need to be converted into Direct3D materials and textures before the model can be rendered. You are familiar with the texture object, but the material object, LPD3DXMATERIAL, is new.

Here is how you copy the materials and textures out of the material buffer and into individual material and texture arrays. First, let's create the arrays:

```
D3DXMATERIAL* d3dxMaterials = (LPD3DXMATERIAL)matbuffer->GetBufferPointer();
model->materials = new D3DMATERIAL9[model->material_count];
model->textures  = new LPDIRECT3DTEXTURE9[model->material_count];
```

The next step is to iterate through the materials and grab them out of the material buffer. For each material, the ambient color is set and the texture is loaded into the texture object. As these are dynamically allocated arrays, a model is limited only by available memory and the ability of your video card to render it. You could have a model with millions of faces, each with a different material.

```
for(i=0; i<model->material_count; i++)
{
    //grab the material
    model->materials[i] = d3dxMaterials[i].MatD3D;

    //set ambient color for material
    model->materials[i].Ambient = model->materials[i].Diffuse;

    model->textures[i] = NULL;
    if( d3dxMaterials[i].pTextureFilename != NULL &&
        lstrlen(d3dxMaterials[i].pTextureFilename) > 0 )
    {
        //load texture file specified in .X file
        result = D3DXCreateTextureFromFile(d3ddev,
            d3dxMaterials[i].pTextureFilename,
            &model->textures[i]);
    }
}
```

Rendering a Complete Model

Drawing the model is a piece of cake after it has been loaded. I'll admit, the code to load a model is not exactly easy to understand until you've walked through it line by line a few times. The rendering code is much easier, and should be quite understandable, because you have used the DrawPrimitive function already.

Remember the Cube_Demo? That was just a simple example of what you must do now to render an entire 3D model.

First, you set the material, the texture, and then call DrawPrimitive to display that polygon (face). The biggest difference is that now you must iterate through the model and render each face individually using the material_count. Here is how it works:

```
for(i=0; i<model->material_count; i++)
{
    d3ddev->SetMaterial(&model->materials[i]);
    d3ddev->SetTexture(0, model->textures[i]);
    model->mesh->DrawSubset(i);
}
```

See, I told you it wasn't difficult. What's next? How about we write the complete program to load our Hummer and render it? After all that work modeling it, I'm eager to see the model actually loaded into a Direct3D program.

The Load_Mesh Program

I have written a complete program to load the Hummer model and render it fully shaded on the screen, and I will now go over the source code for this program with you. Figure 14.8 shows the Load_Mesh program running. Pretty cool, isn't it?

Figure 14.8
The Load_Mesh program loads the Hummer model created in the last chapter.

The ability to create your own model from scratch, optimize it, and then load it into your own game—there's so much potential there for what you can do now that it boggles the mind. The sky's the limit, really! Whatever kind of 3D game you can imagine—you now have the power to make it happen. There are, obviously, a lot of details to fill in along the way, but this is a terrific start.

As usual, you'll need a completely built project with all the usual suspects in order to compile this program. You can load the completed project from the CD-ROM in \sources\chapter14\Load_Mesh, or you can open the Cube_Demo program from Chapter 11 and replace the game.cpp file here.

```
#include "game.h"

#define WHITE D3DCOLOR_ARGB(0,255,255,255)
#define BLACK D3DCOLOR_ARGB(0,0,0,0)

#define CAMERA_X 0.0f
#define CAMERA_Y 4.0f
#define CAMERA_Z 7.0f

//define the MODEL struct
struct MODEL
{
    LPD3DXMESH mesh;
    D3DMATERIAL9* materials;
    LPDIRECT3DTEXTURE9* textures;
    DWORD material_count;
};

MODEL *car;

MODEL *LoadModel(char *filename)
{
    MODEL *model = (MODEL*)malloc(sizeof(MODEL));
    LPD3DXBUFFER matbuffer;
    HRESULT result;
```

```
  //load mesh from the specified file
  result = D3DXLoadMeshFromX(
     filename,                  //filename
     D3DXMESH_SYSTEMMEM,        //mesh options
     d3ddev,                    //Direct3D device
     NULL,                      //adjacency buffer
     &matbuffer,                //material buffer
     NULL,                      //special effects
     &model->material_count,    //number of materials
     &model->mesh);             //resulting mesh

  if (result != D3D_OK)
  {
     MessageBox(NULL, "Error loading model file", "Error", MB_OK);
     return NULL;
  }


//extract material properties and texture names from material buffer
D3DXMATERIAL* d3dxMaterials = (D3DXMATERIAL*)matbuffer->GetBufferPointer();
model->materials = new D3DMATERIAL9[model->material_count];
model->textures  = new LPDIRECT3DTEXTURE9[model->material_count];

//create the materials and textures
for( DWORD i=0; i<model->material_count; i++ )
{
    //grab the material
    model->materials[i] = d3dxMaterials[i].MatD3D;

    //set ambient color for material
    model->materials[i].Ambient = model->materials[i].Diffuse;

    model->textures[i] = NULL;
    if( d3dxMaterials[i].pTextureFilename != NULL &&
        lstrlen(d3dxMaterials[i].pTextureFilename) > 0 )
    {
        //load texture file specified in .X file
        result = D3DXCreateTextureFromFile(d3ddev,
            d3dxMaterials[i].pTextureFilename,
            &model->textures[i]);

        if (result != D3D_OK)
```

```
            {
                MessageBox(NULL, "Could not find texture file", "Error", MB_OK);
                return NULL;
            }
        }
    }

    //done using material buffer
    matbuffer->Release();

    return model;
}

VOID DeleteModel(MODEL *model)
{
    //remove materials from memory
    if( model->materials != NULL )
        delete[] model->materials;

    //remove textures from memory
    if (model->textures != NULL)
    {
        for( DWORD i = 0; i < model->material_count; i++)
        {
            if (model->textures[i] != NULL)
                model->textures[i]->Release();
        }
        delete[] model->textures;
    }

    //remove mesh from memory
    if (model->mesh != NULL)
        model->mesh->Release();

    //remove model struct from memory
    if (model != NULL)
        free(model);

}

void DrawModel(MODEL *model)
```

```
{
    //draw each of the mesh subsets
    for (DWORD i=0; i<model->material_count; i++)
    {
        //set the material and texture for this subset
        d3ddev->SetMaterial(&model->materials[i]);
        d3ddev->SetTexture(0, model->textures[i]);

        //draw the mesh subset
        model->mesh->DrawSubset(i);
    }
}

//initializes the game
int Game_Init(HWND hwnd)
{
    //initialize keyboard
    if (!Init_Keyboard(hwnd))
    {
        MessageBox(hwnd, "Error initializing the keyboard", "Error", MB_OK);
        return 0;
    }

    //set the camera and perspective
    SetCamera(CAMERA_X, CAMERA_Y, CAMERA_Z, 0, 0, 0);
    float ratio = (float)SCREEN_WIDTH / (float)SCREEN_HEIGHT;
    SetPerspective(45.0f, ratio, 0.1f, 10000.0f);

    //use ambient lighting and z-buffering
    d3ddev->SetRenderState(D3DRS_ZENABLE, TRUE);
    d3ddev->SetRenderState(D3DRS_AMBIENT, WHITE);

    car = LoadModel("car.X");
    if (car == NULL)
    {
        MessageBox(hwnd, "Error loading car.X", "Error", MB_OK);
        return 0;
    }

    //return okay
    return 1;
}
```

```
//the main game loop
void Game_Run(HWND hwnd)
{
   ClearScene(BLACK);

   if (d3ddev->BeginScene())
   {
      //rotate the view
      D3DXMATRIXA16 matWorld;
      D3DXMatrixRotationY(&matWorld, timeGetTime()/1000.0f);
      d3ddev->SetTransform(D3DTS_WORLD, &matWorld);

      //draw the car model
      DrawModel(car);

      d3ddev->EndScene();
   }

   d3ddev->Present(NULL, NULL, NULL, NULL);

   Poll_Keyboard();
   if (Key_Down(DIK_ESCAPE))
      PostMessage(hwnd, WM_DESTROY, 0, 0);
}

void Game_End(HWND hwnd)
{
   DeleteModel(car);
}
```

What's Next?

Whoa—this new functionality really adds a whole new dimension to the game framework you've been building in this book. Anyway, the reusable 3D model loading/drawing code from this chapter should be moved into the dxgraphics.cpp file and the function prototypes added to dxgraphics.h. I have done this already, in a project called Framework. This is a good place to grab the project and copy it to a new folder for your own games because it's all configured and ready to go for both 2D and 3D games, with all the code up to this point plugged into the framework. I have left the Game_Run function intentionally empty, for the most part, so it's just sitting there waiting for you to do some magic with it! If you run it, the window will just be blank. For reference, here are the files in the Framework:

- dxgraphics.h
- dxgraphics.cpp
- dxaudio.h
- dsaudio.cpp
- dxinput.h
- dxinput.cpp
- dsutil.h
- dsutil.cpp
- dxutil.h
- winmain.cpp
- game.h
- game.cpp

And also for your reference, here are the libs that are needed by your future Visual C++ projects:

- d3d9.lib
- d3dx9.lib
- dsound.lib
- dinput8.lib
- dxguid.lib
- dxerr9.lib
- winmm.lib

I don't know about you, but I'm absolutely *itching* to put all this code to work in a real game project, which is exactly what we're going to do in the next chapter. When you're ready, we'll build a complete game to finish off the book!

What You Have Learned

This chapter has given you the information you need to load a model file into memory and render it with Direct3D! Here are the key points:

- You learned how to export an Anim8or model to the 3DS format.

- You learned how to convert a 3DS file to an .X file using conv3ds.

- You learned how to optimize an .X file using Mesh Viewer.

- You learned how to load an .X file into your program.

- You learned how to manipulate and render the model.

- You are eager to write a complete game!

Review Questions

The following review questions will help you to determine if you grasped all of the information in this chapter.

1. What is the name of the program that converts 3DS files to the .X format?

2. What program can you use to optimize meshes in an .X file?

3. What is the name of the function you can use to load an .X file into a Direct3D mesh?

4. What function would you use to draw each of the polygons in a model?

5. What does the Weld Vertices optimization accomplish?

On Your Own

The following exercises will help you to learn even more about the information in this chapter.

Exercise 1. This chapter explained how to convert the Hummer model into the Direct3D .X format and then load and render it. Try to create your own model from scratch and repeat the process using your own model.

Exercise 2. The Load_Mesh program demonstrates how to load an .X file and render it on the screen. Modify the program so that it uses the keyboard or mouse to rotate the model rather than just watching it rotate on its own.

CHAPTER 15

COMPLETE 3D GAME

In this chapter, you will learn how to create a complete game using C and DirectX. That is no small feat by any standard, as the language and the libraries are quite difficult to master (as you have learned thus far in the book). The fact that the source code for this game is so short is a testament to the game framework that we've been building in the book. It really does take all of the most difficult parts out of the equation and allows you to focus on just the gameplay—which was the primary goal, as you'll recall, in the beginning. The game is called *Bash,* and it is a 3D version of a ball-and-paddle game.

Here is what you will learn in this chapter:

- How to write a complete 3D game called *Bash*.

- How to detect when 3D objects have collided.

- How to print text using a bitmapped font.

- How to program objects to move on their own.

- How to create custom 3D models for the game.

- How to enhance a game with event-based sound effects.

Bash

The game featured in this chapter uses a stereotypical game design that is not terribly creative. To be honest, though, it is one of the best types of game to use as an example when teaching game programming. You have all the basics here in this complete game:

- Multiple models and sprites on the screen.

- A contained game world that is easy to manage.

- Simple design that the player can immediately get into.

- Direct control of the paddle to help the beginning programmer see cause-effect.

- Multiple sound effects for various events in the game.

- A bitmapped font for displaying information on the screen.

- Score keeping.

- 3D collision detection between the ball and the paddle/blocks.

- Using game state to enhance gameplay.

These aspects of the *Bash* game will help you to pull together all the information you have gleaned in the book and assemble it into an actual game. The game is complete but is purposefully limited in features in order to give you the opportunity to improve it. Thus, the source code for Bash is short and simple, to make it easy to modify. I wanted to put so much more into this game myself, but I realized that it would not do to add all the bells and whistles for you right at the start. For starters, this game seriously needs some powerups, such as firepower (allowing you to shoot at the blocks), paddle resizing, bonus points, and extra lives.

The game plays out until you have destroyed all the blocks, then it displays "GAME OVER" and the game is paused. There is no facility built into the game at present to load levels; that would be a really great feature, though. Instead, after you have cleared all the blocks, the game is over. You can try to play, but the game will just stop, because there are no blocks. That should be remedied so that the player can continue playing the next level after clearing the blocks. There are countless features that you could add to the game, so I'll let you have some fun doing just that!

It will be fun to modify the game to suit your own tastes. Don't like the paddle? Change it! Don't like how the ball bounces off the blocks? Change it! Don't care for the wall texture? Change it! *Bash* is like the game framework itself: a complete, ready-to-use, pre-packaged "kit" that you can use to create your own games.

Figure 15.1 shows what the game looks like.

Figure 15.1
The complete game featured in this chapter is a ball-and-paddle game called *Bash*.

Playing the Game

Let's take a quick tour of *Bash* to see how the game is played before getting into how it was programmed.

Game States

There are three game states in *Bash*:

1. PAUSE

2. RUNNING

3. GAMEOVER

These three states determine how the game behaves. When the game is in PAUSE state (Figure 15.2), the ball will track along with the paddle so that the player can launch it at will. This occurs at the start of the game or after the player misses the ball.

The normal RUNNING state, shown in Figure 15.3, causes the game to play out normally, with collision checking and the whole works. This is the most common game state that is in effect for most of the duration of the game.

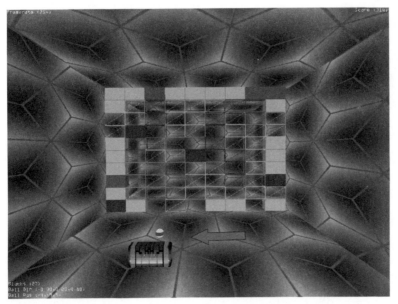

Figure 15.2
The game is in PAUSE state, waiting for the player to launch the ball.

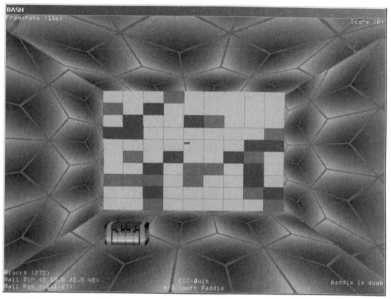

Figure 15.3
The normal game state is RUNNING.

The third state is the GAMEOVER state (see Figure 15.4) that is set when the ball has destroyed all of the blocks. A good enhancement to the game would be to add "lives" that the player loses upon missing the ball. This will allow you to use the GAMEOVER state for cases in which the player runs out of lives as well as for when all the blocks are destroyed. This enhancement is one of the first things I would do to improve the game because without the chance for failure, there is little incentive to play the game. I would also recommend adding a high score!

Collision

When the ball hits a block, a very brief "COLLISION" message is displayed in the lower-right corner, as shown in Figure 15.5.

Keeping Score

The game keeps track of the score by adding one point to the score for every block that is destroyed. See Figure 15.6.

Stats

On the lower-left corner of the screen are printed three status messages (see Figure 15.7). These messages display the number of blocks remaining, the ball's

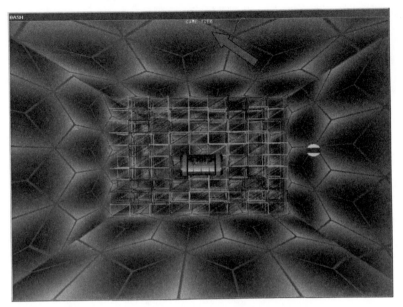

Figure 15.4
When the game is over, all you can do is hit Escape to quit.

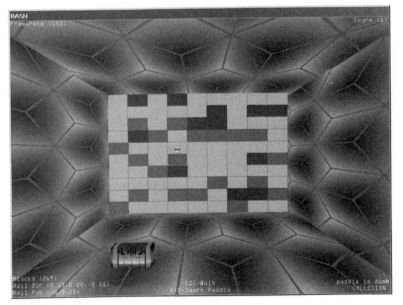

Figure 15.5
Breaking the blocks allows you to see the blocks behind.

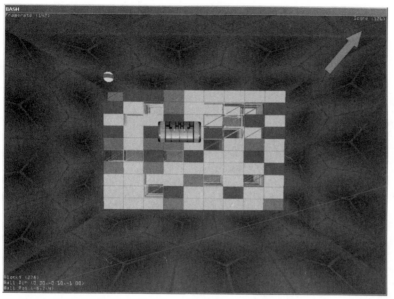

Figure 15.6
The score (displayed in the upper-right corner) is tallied for each block destroyed.

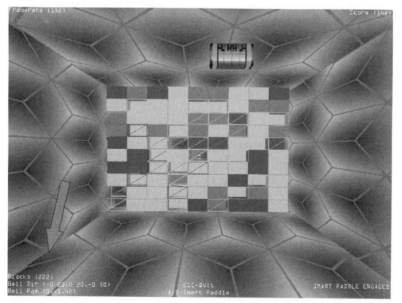

Figure 15.7
The ball position and direction, and a block count, are displayed in the lower-left.

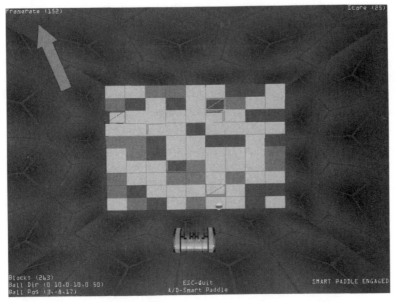

Figure 15.8
The frame rate is displayed in the upper-left corner of the screen.

3D direction, and the ball's 3D position. This is the sort of information you would want displayed while you are developing a game, but not necessarily in a release version.

Frame Rate

The frame rate is displayed in the upper-left corner of the screen (see Figure 15.8). The game calculates the frame rate by incrementing a counter every time Game_Run is called, and the frame count is displayed on the screen once every second.

Smart Paddle

While developing this game, I found that it really helps to have a "smart paddle" or autopilot to test collision detection, particularly in a challenging game like this. It is *really* difficult to judge depth in the game because of the limited colors being used; really, the only depth is provided by the perspective settings, because there is no dynamic lighting. It would be cool to make the ball itself become a light source, but that would require some theory on how to create dynamic lights in Direct3D—very possible, but beyond the goals of this small book. Figure 15.9 shows the game with smart paddle enabled.

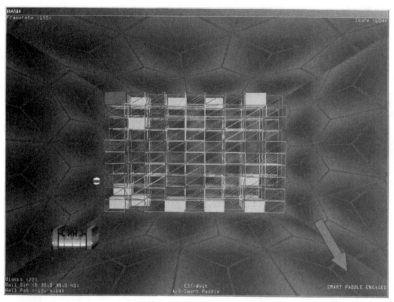

Figure 15.9
Smart Paddle mode causes the paddle to move automatically.

Creating the Models

I won't go into detail on how I created the models and artwork for *Bash* because you already got a very good tutorial on using Anim8or and the utilities required to create a Direct3D-compatible .X model file. I will give you a brief glimpse of each model and texture used in the game so that you will know what to expect if you attempt to modify them. When you are making modifications to the models used in *Bash,* just remember to export using the Object menu in Anim8or, save as a 3DS file, then open a command prompt and run "conv3ds filename.3ds" to convert the model to the Direct3D .X format (the conv3ds options aren't absolutely necessary). I recommend just copying conv3ds.exe to the folder of your project for convenience.

The Ball

The ball is a simple sphere that was created using Anim8or's sphere primitive tool. See Figure 15.10.

The Paddle

Figure 15.11 shows the paddle in Anim8or. As you can see, it is a textured model that uses the bitmap from the paddle game in Chapter 10. How cool is that? This

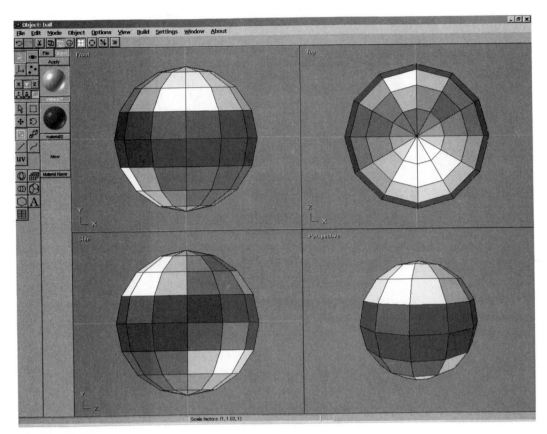

Figure 15.10
The ball is a simple sphere, created with Anim8or's sphere primitive tool.

paddle has been upgraded to 3D. What I did here was first create a rectangular solid (or rather, a cube—the reason I keep using that term is because a "cube" has equal sides). I then converted it to a mesh using the Build menu and subdivided it four times. The first three times, I just used a value of 1 to subdivide the shape into smaller polygons. Then, I subdivided by the value 0 to round off the edges and produce a cool paddle-like shape. The paddle.bmp texture was then applied using the Material Editor in Anim8or. I selected a white color for *both* ambient and diffuse colors, and applied the paddle texture to *both* of them. If you apply the texture to just ambient, it won't show up, so be sure to apply it to both.

The Blocks

There are three types of blocks in the game: green, red, and blue. As a programmer, I find these colors pleasant, but of course they are really obnoxious to

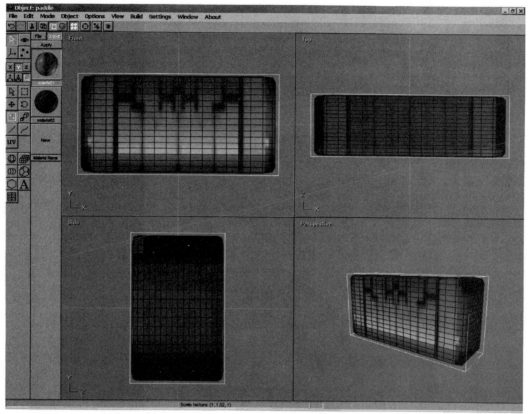

Figure 15.11
The paddle is a subdivided rectangular solid that was "smithed" into the desired shape.

the casual player. One of my first recommendations as you modify the game is to create a lot of different colored blocks. Just use Copy/Paste to copy a block, add a new object in Anim8or, and paste the block there. Remember to press the F key to get the full view. Then you can customize the blocks by entering Object/Point Edit mode, selecting a face, and applying a new material to it; the material might be a different color or even a texture! How about adding your own digital photos to texture the blocks? Now that would be *really* funny! (See Figure 15.12.)

Note

I do not recommend subdividing the blocks to make them look better. Rely on creative materials instead. If you want to subdivide a block, I recommend doing it just *once*, to create four quads per side, to which you can then apply custom materials. Any more than four per side and the game will come to a clunking stop with a frame rate you won't be able to tolerate. Just remember that there are 300 blocks—if each block has *hundreds* of faces (like the paddle and ball), then the game will run too slowly.

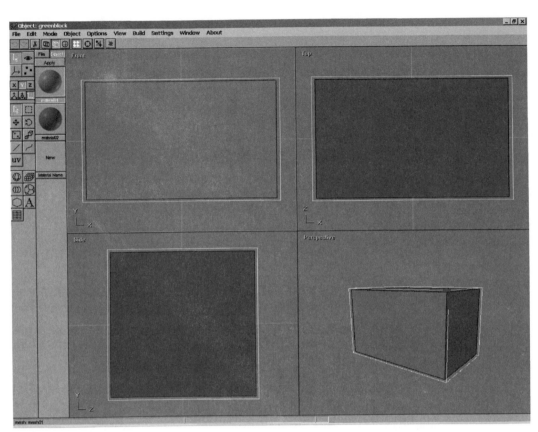

Figure 15.12
The red, green, and blue blocks are all the same size but have different materials applied.

The Walls

The walls in the game are created using quads (which you may recall from Chapter 12), each using the same texture (shown in Figure 15.13). I decided it would be easier to manipulate the walls in the game in code rather than trying to create a model with Anim8or and then rotate/translate it into position. This would have been possible, but I just thought the brute-force method of creating a quad for each of the five walls used in the game was more straightforward. Never ignore the brute force method when it gets the job done swiftly and efficiently (if inelegantly).

Printing Text Using a Bitmapped Font

It goes without saying that the newest feature I will show you how to program in this chapter is the ability to print text on the screen using a bitmapped font. I

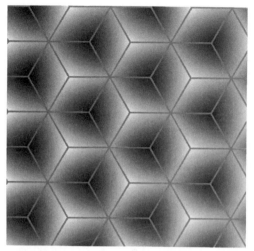

Figure 15.13
The wall texture was created using Paint Shop Pro.

Figure 15.14
The bitmapped font used in the game

would have used this feature several chapters ago, but there was no real need to do so until now, when it became impossible to write a complete game without displaying some text! Well, you know the old saying, "Necessity is the mother of invention."

The bitmapped font is shown in Figure 15.14. You can create your own font if you wish, as long as you make sure that each character has exactly the same dimensions. The characters in this bitmapped font are each 8 × 12 pixels; you may use any dimensions you want for each character, as long as they are all the same.

I wrote two functions to print text on the screen. The functions assume nothing, so they require you to specify everything as parameters. Now, I could have simplified the functions if I had just used global variables for the font details, but by passing font data to the function directly, you can support multiple fonts in your game. If you want to write a generic Print-type function, by all means do so. You may even write a custom function, such as `Print_Small_Font`, for each type of font you want to use in your game. I prefer to just pass the font itself as a parameter because it is just a pointer to a `DIRECT3DTEXTURE9`.

Below are the important parts of the `DrawText` function that you will find in the complete source code listing for the game. Note how a vector is created for the position of the text? What's happening here is that each character of the text message is copied to the screen using the sprite handler's `Draw` function, which you learned about way back in Chapter 8 (look at the trans_sprite program again for reference).

The actual index into the bitmapped font is then calculated as the character code minus 32. That is because this font starts with the space character (32), and then includes 96 characters in the ASCII code, from space (32) to dash (-), with all the usual alphanumeric characters you are likely to need included. A rectangle is then created, pointing to the correct index for that particular character. You learned about this technique back in Chapter 7 (refer to the anim_sprite program). Finally, the `Draw` function of `D3DXSPRITE` is called to actually draw the character (transparently).

```
//create vector to update sprite position
D3DXVECTOR3 position((float)x, (float)y, 0.0f);

//ASCII code of ocrfont.bmp starts with 32 (space)
int index = c - 32;

//configure the rect
RECT srcRect;
srcRect.left = (index % cols) * width;
srcRect.top = (index / cols) * height;
srcRect.right = srcRect.left + width;
    srcRect.bottom = srcRect.top + height;

//draw the sprite
sprite_handler->Draw(
    lpfont,
    &srcRect,
    NULL,
    &position,
    D3DCOLOR_XRGB(255,255,255));
```

Simple 3D Collision Detection

3D collision detection is the next most significant feature in this game that you have not learned about yet. There are some very advanced ways to perform 3D collision detection that are quite beyond the scope of this book; what you'll find in *Bash* is a very simple method of detecting a collision between two 3D objects, using a fixed bounding cube. Thus, you might call this "point-cubic collision detection."

I use the term *point-cubic* because that is exactly what this method does—it checks to see whether a point is located inside a cubic region of 3D space. If the point is found to be within the cube, then the collision test returns true; otherwise, it returns false.

Two D3DXVECTOR3 parameters are passed to the Collision function, followed by a single int parameter specifying the size of the cube. The first vector is the center point of the first object; the second vector is the center point of the second object; the third parameter, size, will specify how far from the second point the collision test will encompass. If the first point is within that boundary, then the collision is true.

```
left = second.x - size;
right = second.x + size;
bottom = second.y - size;
top = second.y + size;
front = second.z - size;
back = second.z + size;

if (first.x > left && first.x < right &&
    first.y > bottom && first.y < top &&
    first.z > front && first.z < back)
{
    //collision detected!
}
```

There are flaws with this simplistic collision detection algorithm, of course. First of all, you have to manually specify the size of the second 3D object because the collision routine doesn't try to figure this out on its own. To do so would require delving into the inner depths of a Direct3D Mesh object, which, unfortunately, is way beyond the scope of this book. But we don't need that kind of precision for a game like *Bash*, which mainly uses rectangular-shaped objects. All you must do manually is run the game and tweak the size until you get a good result. The key is to use the same scale for all of your objects in Anim8or. As long as you try to keep all of the models the same basic size, then you can use the same size value for all of them. The exception might be a model like the ball, which is necessarily smaller than the paddle or blocks. In the case of the ball, 50 percent of the size used by the other models should suffice.

Bash Source Code

The source code for this game is quite short as far as games written in C and DirectX go. Naturally, there are a lot of places where readability and comprehension were more important than shortening the code. But in the end, this is a very manageable code listing for a complete game. You should have no trouble working through it as you try to modify the game to suit your own needs.

This game is not at all efficient, as far as simplicity goes. For instance, the code that fills the playing area with blocks actually loads each block from disk! This is a very bad way to write a game in general, but the focus here is on keeping the code as simple as possible so you will be able to focus on how the game works.

On the CD, you'll find the code for the game.cpp file for the *Bash* game, and I'm assuming you'll use the framework developed in the previous chapter to build this project. The game.h file remains as it is, save for the following line change:

```
//application title
#define APPTITLE "BASH"
```

Note

To conserve space, the entire code listing for *Bash* has been provided on the CD-ROM rather than listed in this chapter. Please load the *Bash* project off the CD-ROM to peruse the source code for the game (which is about 20 pages long).

What's Next?

There are a lot of fun things that you can do with the *Bash* game, and I encourage you to spend some time with the source code to solidify everything you have learned in this book because *Bash* covers all of it in a nutshell.

What You Have Learned

This chapter explained how to create a complete game from scratch to test the game framework that you have been learning about and creating in this book. Here are the specifics:

- You learned how quick and easy it is to create new game models in Anim8or.

- You learned about a simple form of 3D collision detection.

- You learned how to print text using a bitmapped font.

- You learned how to use sound effects to enhance game events.

- You used the keyboard and mouse effortlessly in a real game.

- You put the game framework to the final test!

Review Questions

The following questions will help you to determine how well you have learned the subjects discussed in this chapter.

1. Briefly, how does the simple 3D collision detection in *Bash* work?

2. What type of basic geometric shape is used to test for collisions?

3. What type of struct do you use to print each letter in a bitmapped font?

4. What type of object stores the bitmapped font image in memory?

5. How many milliseconds are used to calculate frame rate for one second?

On Your Own

Rather than provide two exercises in this last chapter, I have decided to just list some of the new features that you might add to the game. You might consider trying these exercises, but don't limit yourself to just these ideas.

- Add the ability to toggle the wireframe view for destroyed blocks on or off.

- Add new levels with some creative geometric block formations.

- Add "lives" so that there is a penalty for missing too many balls.

- Add powerups to enhance gameplay (firepower, multiple balls, and so on).

- Add ball position indicators to the screen edges to help the player with depth.

INDEX

License Agreement/Notice of Limited Warranty